Parental Monitoring of Adolescents

Parental Monitoring of Adolescents

Current Perspectives for Researchers and Practitioners

EDITED BY

VINCENT GUILAMO-RAMOS
JAMES JACCARD

AND

PATRICIA DITTUS

Columbia University Press   *New York*

Columbia University Press
Publishers Since 1893
New York   Chichester, West Sussex
Copyright © 2010 Columbia University Press
All rights reserved

Library of Congress Cataloging-in-Publication Data

Parental monitoring of adolescents : current perspectives for researchers and practitioners /
edited by Vincent Guilamo-Ramos, James Jaccard, and Patricia Dittus.
     p. cm.
   Includes bibliographical references and index.
   ISBN 978-0-231-14080-5 (cloth : alk. paper)—ISBN 978-0-231-14081-2 (pbk. : alk.
paper)—ISBN 978-0-231-52011-9 (ebook)
   1. Parent and teenager.   2. Vigilance (Psychology)   3. Behavior disorders in
adolescence—Prevention.   4. Adolescent psychology.   I. Guilamo-Ramos, Vincent.
II. Jaccard, James.   III. Dittus, Patricia.

HQ799.15.P343   2010
306.874—dc22
                                                                      2010023732

Columbia University Press books are printed on permanent and durable acid-free paper.
This book is printed on paper with recycled content.
Printed in the United States of America

c 10 9 8 7 6 5 4 3 2 1
p 10 9 8 7 6 5 4 3 2 1

References to Internet Web sites (URLs) were accurate at the time of writing.
Neither the author nor Columbia University Press is responsible for URLs that may
have expired or changed since the manuscript was prepared.

To my mother, Silvia Ramos
Vincent Guilamo-Ramos

For Sarita and Liliana
James Jaccard

To my son, Aaron Lee Flores
Patricia Dittus

Contents

Contents

Preface

In 2004 the Centers for Disease Control and Prevention (CDC) sponsored a two-day meeting on parental monitoring of adolescents. The CDC's Division of Adolescent and School Health invited the leading researchers in the field to meet and discuss current knowledge about parental monitoring, what we still need to learn about parental monitoring, and how what we know can best be practically applied in public health intervention efforts. Although public health scientists have long recognized the powerful impact parental monitoring efforts can have on adolescent risk behavior, the public health approach to studying parental monitoring, with some exceptions, has been atheoretical and unsophisticated in nature. We hoped the discussion and exchange of ideas at the meeting would help us to move the public health field forward by identifying common definitions for parental monitoring, improving our understanding of the antecedents and outcomes associated with parental monitoring efforts, and by developing specific ways to help parents become more effective monitors of their children and adolescents.

The meeting sparked such lively discussion and brainstorming of ideas that we decided a book was needed in order to reach a broader audience. We anticipate that audience will include public health researchers and practitioners as well as other applied researchers in the fields of social work, psychology, and sociology. However, we also hope to reach a large non-scientific audience—professionals working in school settings, in community and faith-based organizations, in health care settings, and other settings in which there is frequent contact with parents and adolescents.

The first part of the book presents current research and theorizing about parental monitoring by some of the world's leading experts in this area. The second part of the book is somewhat unorthodox in that it contains a Question and Answer section in which the volume's contributors have each addressed a series of questions concerning research on parental monitoring. Our overall goals are to spark further discussion of parental monitoring, both in terms of research, program, and practice, and to provide useful information for improving parental monitoring practices.

Acknowledgments

We would like to thank the Centers for Disease Control and Prevention's Division of Adolescent and School Health for sponsoring the parental monitoring meeting that led to the creation of this book. We also would like to thank our contributing authors, many of whom attended that two-day meeting years ago, and all of whom have been incredibly patient with us throughout the lengthy process of writing and publishing this book. Finally, we would like to thank our colleagues for providing insightful feedback on portions of the book.

The findings and conclusions in the book are those of the authors and do not necessarily represent the views of the Centers for Disease Control and Prevention.

Introduction

VINCENT GUILAMO-RAMOS, JAMES JACCARD,
and PATRICIA DITTUS

In recent years, interest in the role of parental monitoring has grown considerably. Parental monitoring traditionally has been defined as the acquisition of knowledge about the activities, whereabouts, and companions of
one's son or daughter. Understanding the causes, correlates, and consequences of parental monitoring and adolescents' willingness to be monitored is of keen interest to developmental scientists and applied professionals. There is a large body of literature in the health, social, and psychological
sciences on the nature, extent, antecedents, and consequences of parental
monitoring during childhood, adolescence, and the transition into adulthood. From this body of literature, we know that a lack of parental monitoring is linked to a wide range of adolescent risk behaviors, including drug
use, risky sexual behaviors, alcohol use, and cigarette smoking, to name a
few. At the same time, recent innovations in parental monitoring research
have shown that there is still much work to be done to refine our understanding of parental monitoring.

A 2004 CDC workshop on parental monitoring was a primary catalyst
for this volume, but the decision to edit a book on parental monitoring stems
from a shared belief that empirical research in this domain offers an important opportunity to improve a range of health and psychosocial outcomes
in childhood, adolescence, and early adulthood. In editing a book on parental

monitoring, our goals were to (a) provide a current perspective on what we know about parental monitoring, (b) identify areas where research still needs to be pursued, (c) provide a sense of the types of research programs being conducted by leading experts in the field, (d) highlight the theories and methods used in parental monitoring research, and (e) address the applied implications of research on parental monitoring.

The book has been designed to make contributions at the conceptual, methodological, and practical levels and is divided into two parts. Part I addresses existing gaps in the monitoring literature from each contributor's area of expertise within the field of parental monitoring. Part II presents contributors' responses to a set of six questions that were posed to each team of authors, as well as a synthesis of these responses. A common theme across the chapters is the need to refine the study of parental monitoring. Whereas past research has conceptualized parental monitoring primarily as parental knowledge about children's activities, whereabouts, and companions, the chapters here view monitoring in the broader context of the parent-adolescent relationship and the social realities that families contend with as part of their daily lives. In doing so, the authors address a number of issues fundamental to a contextual study of parental monitoring, including how best to define and measure parental monitoring, how parental monitoring works in the dynamics of the parent-adolescent relationship, how parental monitoring varies across childhood, adolescence, and the transition to adulthood, how parental monitoring manifests in diverse families throughout the world, and how parental monitoring can best be targeted in parent-based interventions designed to keep children, adolescents, and young adults safe from harm.

In our own work as scholars of parental monitoring, we have considered the state of parental monitoring research and have attempted to address these fundamental issues via the introduction of a conceptual framework of parental monitoring (chapter 7). In addition to addressing fundamental issues in the monitoring literature, this chapter also seeks to contextualize many of the issues raised in chapters 1–6 by introducing a framework of parental monitoring that can not only be applied to diverse populations across time but also has implications for the development of applied monitoring interventions. Specifically, three core processes of parental monitoring are discussed: (a) *parental behavioral expectations* (i.e., how a parent expects the child to behave and the clarity with which these expectations are conveyed to adolescents), (b) *parental behavioral monitoring* (i.e., how a parent determines whether a child is behaving in accord with those expectations, also encompassing the notion of how accurate parents are in their behavioral attributions), and (c) *parental behavioral inducement and enforcement* (i.e., how a parent deals with behavioral transgressions from expectations and how parents encourage adolescent compliance). The framework differs from traditional frameworks on parental monitoring in two key ways. First, it focuses on behavior-specific monitoring constructs rather than global monitoring constructs. Second, the framework places parental monitoring in a broader theoretical framework that gives parental monitoring more meaning.

In chapters 1 through 6, the contributors not only address theoretical aspects of parental monitoring, but they also address the applied implications for developing parental monitoring interventions for diverse groups of parents and adolescents. In chapter 1, Håkan Stattin, Margaret Kerr, and Lauree Tilton-Weaver focus on the relationship between parental monitoring knowledge, how parents acquire monitoring knowledge (e.g., through controlling efforts or through spontaneous adolescent disclosures and adolescent adjustment), and adolescent adjustment. A central question addressed in their work is *why* is parental knowledge linked to better adolescent adjustment? In response to this question, the authors describe the results of several studies of adolescents and parents that have been undertaken in Sweden. Their findings call for a reinterpretation of parental monitoring effects that readers should find both informative and provocative. In addition, their work lends support for differentiating between the different types of parental processes that contribute to parental monitoring, including the communication of behavioral expectations, the elicitation of information from adolescents that contribute to parents' monitoring efforts, and the ways in which parents enforce and induce compliance with their behavioral expectations.

In chapter 2 the importance of examining parental monitoring in a broader system of parental influence is addressed by Robert Laird, Matthew Marrero, and Jennifer Sherwood. Laird and colleagues build upon Stattin and Kerr's (2000) call to distinguish between monitoring processes, such as knowledge, and behavior by presenting and applying a conceptual model of developmental and interactional antecedents of monitoring knowledge. Drawing upon data from the Baton Rouge Families and Teens Project, the authors examine how attributes of the parent-adolescent relationship (such as communication, acceptance, conflict, and trust), the monitoring processes of parental solicitation, adolescent disclosure, and the frequency of monitoring related conversations, and parental monitoring knowledge all influence early adolescent involvement in delinquent behavior. In addition, Laird, Marrero, and Sherwood also examine developmental and interactional processes that can explain *why* and *how* some parents become and remain knowledgeable about adolescents' whereabouts and activities while other parents do not. Readers interested in knowing more about the factors that promote parents to monitor their children and the variability in monitoring trajectories over time in the context of the parent-adolescent relationship will be especially interested in their findings.

In addition to occurring in a broader system of parental influences, parental monitoring also takes place in a larger social and environmental milieu. To date, relatively little is known about how broader social factors may facilitate or hinder parents' monitoring efforts. In chapter 3, Deborah Belle and Brenda Phillips present the results of a qualitative study that seeks to identify barriers to parental monitoring among a cohort of working parents. Drawing upon interviews conducted over a four-year period with working parents and their adolescent children, the authors provide a rich description of parental monitoring in action. In doing so, Belle and Phillips provide a valuable contribution to researchers interested in identifying the factors that can help or hinder parents' efforts to monitor their children, especially in the after-school hours when parents are at work and parental monitoring takes on different forms.

In chapter 4 a fundamental question about the cultural equivalence of parental monitoring is examined by Sonia Venkatraman, Thomas Dishion, Jeff Kiesner, and François Poulin. Their effort to determine if parental monitoring has the same meaning and outcomes in different cultural contexts addresses fundamental issues on the measurement of parental monitoring and is a welcome addition to the literature. The work of Venkatraman and colleagues asks us to consider if the meaning and dynamics of parental monitoring are the same in different cultures. Venkatraman and colleagues provide insight into this question by studying the relationship between parental monitoring and adolescent problem behavior in India, Italy, and Canada. Their findings remind us of the importance of examining monitoring *in context* and attending to potential cultural differences in our research and practice.

Whereas chapters 1 through 4 deal with theoretical and conceptual issues of parental monitoring, chapters 5 and 6 discuss the development and evaluation of parental monitoring interventions for diverse groups of young people. To date, there have been a handful of parent-based interventions expressly focused on the construct of parental monitoring. Each developed for distinct adolescent populations and behaviors; these interventions are well described and contextualized in chapters 5 and 6. All readers concerned about understanding how best to develop parental monitoring interventions will be keenly interested in this information.

To date, almost no monitoring interventions have targeted college-aged youth. In part, this is because prevailing wisdom assumes that parental influence wanes as adolescents graduate from high school and transition to college. However, a focus on parental monitoring for this population is especially important because college students are vulnerable to a number of health risk behaviors, including alcohol use and abuse. Despite this, almost all college-drinking interventions fail to involve parents and are delivered to students when they are already on campus. In chapter 5, Rob Turrisi, Anne Ray, and Caitlin Abar further the field of parental monitoring by presenting the results of a parental monitoring intervention for college freshmen. Using a strong theory grounded in empirical literature on social psychological theories of decision making and parent-teen relationships, Turrisi and colleagues examine the relationship between parental monitoring and drinking tendencies during the transition from high school to college, the mediational processes through which parental monitoring affects drinking outcomes, and a set of variables implicated in the alcohol literature that may serve to moderate the effect of parental monitoring on drinking outcomes. Their results suggest that a well-designed parental monitoring intervention for college students can have a beneficial effect on reducing high-risk drinking and preventing harm even at this stage of late adolescent/early adult development.

Although a range of parental monitoring interventions are being developed and evaluated, few have been scaled up to be disseminated to a broader population of American parents and youth. Dissemination of efficacious parental monitoring interventions is critical to helping parents become more effective at monitoring their children. It also is a primary way to bridge the gap between research and practice. In chapter 6, Jennifer Galbraith and Bonita Stanton describe the research-to-practice path of *Informed Parents and Children Together*, a video-based, HIV prevention, parental monitoring intervention developed for African American parents of adolescents. Together, they describe the qualitative research activities conducted to develop the intervention as well as the logistical and content considerations undertaken to ensure that the intervention was feasible and appealing to a wide range of parents. In addition, the randomized controlled trials conducted to evaluate the intervention are described. Readers interested in learning more about how interventions are prepared for dissemination will welcome their discussion of the efforts and challenges necessary to package the intervention for national dissemination.

Part I closes with the introduction of a broader framework of parental monitoring and supervision that builds on the work presented in chapters 1–6. James Jaccard, Vincent Guilamo-Ramos, Alida Bouris, and Patricia Dittus draw upon the literature on parental monitoring to present a framework of monitoring and supervision that proposes three overarching constructs: *parental behavioral expectations, parental behavioral monitoring,* and *parental behavioral inducement and enforcement.* These constructs provide readers with a framework that can be used in empirical research with diverse families to study the range of health and behavioral outcomes of interest to parental monitoring researchers. In addition, the chapter discusses how this framework can be used in the development of applied monitoring interventions and supplements the arguments highlighted in chapters 5 and 6.

The decision to depart from the traditional edited volume and to use a Q & A format for the second part of the book grew out of the CDC-sponsored workshop. At the meeting, one day was devoted to presentations traditionally found at workshops and the second day was devoted to a participant Q & A session where each participant answered the same set of questions about the field more generally. The results of this session were insightful and stimulating. For example, one of the questions the group was asked to address was how to define and measure parental monitoring. A distinction is sometimes made in the literature between parental monitoring behaviors and perceived parental monitoring knowledge. There are numerous measures of parental monitoring available in the literature as well. This was one area in which the group of experts to a large extent reached consensus. The group agreed that the distinction between monitoring behaviors and parents' perceived knowledge of children's whereabouts, activities, and companions is important—one implies an active process, whereas the other may not. Both may be important constructs, but it is typically perceived knowledge that is measured. The group generally agreed that the Brown, Mounts, Lamborn, and Steinberg (1993) measure of general monitoring knowledge is a viable overall measure, but that behavior-specific measures also are useful, despite the fact that there is so little research on them.

Another question the group was asked to discuss was what specific messages about monitoring should parents be given in the context of a brief intervention. Although the participating group of experts had limited experience in developing or testing interventions, they came up with numerous creative suggestions based on their research experience.

This type of discussion is represented in the second part of the book, where our contributors give us their thoughts about a number of important issues related to parental monitoring. Each team of contributors was provided with six questions and asked to provide their expert opinion. The specific questions focus on the following issues of central import to the field of parental monitoring: (a) defining parental monitoring, (b) measuring parental monitoring, (c) factors influencing parental monitoring, (d) factors influencing adolescent compliance, (e) parental monitoring as an influence of adolescent risk behavior, and (f) designing interventions to impact monitoring.

In summary, we feel that this volume is a useful contribution to the field of parental monitoring. It fills an important gap in the existing literature on parental monitoring and provides readers with an accurate overview of what we currently know, what remains to be known, and concrete suggestions to improve our knowledge base. It will be valuable for both researchers and practitioners working on parental monitoring in a wide range of disciplines and contexts. We hope that this book not only contributes to the next wave of innovative research, but that it also plays a tangible role in all of our ongoing efforts to help keep children, adolescents, and young adults safe from harm.

References

Brown, B. B., Mounts, N., Lamborn, S. D., & Steinberg, L. (1993). Parenting practices and peer group affiliation in adolescence. *Child Development, 64,* 467–482.

Stattin, H., & Kerr, M. (2000). Parental monitoring: A reinterpretation. *Child Development, 71,* 1072–1085.

Parental Monitoring of Adolescents

Part I

Contemporary Issues in
Parental Monitoring

Parental Monitoring

A Critical Examination of the Research

HÅKAN STATTIN, MARGARET KERR, and LAUREE TILTON-WEAVER

In most Western societies, as children move through adolescence they spend increasing amounts of time away from home. At about the same time in development, rates of delinquency, alcohol drinking, and drug use rise precipitously. In the quest to understand why this increase happens and to find ways to prevent problem behavior, it has been logical and intuitively appealing to examine the role parents play. For almost three decades, the strongest results coming from studies connecting adolescent problem behavior with parenting have been for what has been called *parental monitoring*.

Our knowledge about what is called parental monitoring and its role for adolescent adjustment is mostly recent. More than 350 studies on the topic have been published in peer-reviewed journals, and most of them have been within the last few years. From 1984, when the first monitoring study appeared, to 1992, only a handful of articles were published each year. During the mid-1990s that number rose, but more than 7 out of 10 studies on monitoring have been published between 1999 and 2005. This increase over time is steeper than the overall annual increase in articles in Psycinfo during the same time, which suggests that parental monitoring is a "hot" area of research today.

Measures that have been called monitoring have been linked to delinquency, drug use, risky sexual activity, deviant friends, and poor school performance (for reviews, see Crouter & Head 2002; Dishion & McMahon 1998). The findings are robust and the conclusions are similar across studies and over two decades: "good supervision fosters appropriate parental reaction to antisocial and delinquent behaviors, and indirectly minimizes the adolescents' contact with delinquency-promoting circumstances, activities, and peers" (Snyder & Patterson 1987:227); "It may be plausibly inferred that monitoring affects boys' delinquency by preventing them from associating with [other delinquents], which may be a critical factor" (Weintraub & Gold 1991:279); "Strong parental monitoring helps to deter adolescents from using alcohol and drugs themselves and . . . from associating with drug-using peers" (Fletcher, Darling, & Steinberg 1995:270); "There is growing evidence that monitoring of adolescent children is an age-appropriate parental control practice that could decrease the likelihood that adolescents would associate with peers who consume illegal substances and engage in antisocial behavior" (Barrera et al. 2001:150). Thus, one of the most widely agreed-upon conclusions in the literature on adolescent problem behavior is that parental monitoring steers youths away from risky situations and deviant peers.

Despite the consensus that exists in the literature about this conclusion, most of these studies share conceptual and methodological problems that call into question the interpretations that have been made of the findings. In this chapter we will describe these problems. We will focus on four problems in the literature: (a) the conceptualization of monitoring does not seem to match the measures; (b) the mechanisms through which monitoring should affect youths' behaviors away from home have not been specified, operationalized, and tested; (c) correlational results have been interpreted as causal and reverse causality has seldom been considered; and (d) recently, the monitoring construct has been reformulated in ways that make it less precise.

The Conceptualization Does Not Match the Measures

What is meant by parental monitoring? The ordinary person hearing this term would probably think of something similar to the dictionary definition of monitoring: "to watch, keep track of, or check usually for a special purpose" (*Merriam-Webster*'s online dictionary: see www.m-w.com) or "to keep watch over or check as a means of control" (Read et al. 1995:822). The term assumes that there is an active agent—the monitor—who keeps track of or watches over something or someone. The conceptualization of monitoring in research has been similar, as revealed in the definitions given and the interpretations of findings. Monitoring has been defined as "attention to and tracking of the child's whereabouts, activities, and adaptations" (Dishion & McMahon 1998:61), and the interpretations of findings in the monitoring literature are consistent with a conceptualization of parents as active agents keeping track of their youths' activities. This can be seen in monitoring studies from the beginning of research on the construct to the present: "Parents must set rules and then 'check up' or track compliance with those rules, and take effective disciplinary action when the rules are violated" (Snyder & Patterson 1987:227); "parental monitoring *is* an appropriate strategy . . . helps to deter adolescents from using alcohol and drugs themselves and . . . prevents [them] from associating with drug-using peers" (Fletcher, Darling, & Steinberg 1995:270); and "parents who know what their children are doing are able to detect when the child is drifting into activities that might pose a risk. They are able to reduce opportunities for problems by steering their children away from risky situations" (Biglan 2003:155). Conceptually, then, monitoring is something that parents do. It is a parental activity.

How, then, has monitoring been operationalized? For the most part, parental activity has not been part of the operationalization. Rather, the measures have focused on parents' knowledge of youths' daily activities or youths' activities that provide information to parents.

The Earliest Measures

To our knowledge, the first study to use the term *parental monitoring* in this way appeared in *Child Development* in 1984 (Patterson & Stouthamer-Loeber 1984). This has been and continues to be an important study. According to PsycInfo, it has been cited 248 times, and the vast majority of those citations are from the past five years. According to one recent review article (Boyer 2006), the study is one of several that theoretically attribute good effects to "use of superior monitoring strategies (e.g., surveillance techniques used to obtain information regarding where their child is, who their child is with, and what their child is doing)" (p. 324). According to another recent study (Soenens, Vansteenkiste, Luyckx, & Goossens 2006), the 1984 study "operationalized different components of active behavioral control—such as monitoring, discipline, problem-solving, and reinforcement of rules—by means of multiple indicators and diverse informants" (p. 305). These current studies lead one to believe that the monitoring measure used in the 1984 study operationalized active parental control and surveillance.

In fact, it is difficult to determine how the measure of monitoring was constructed in the first monitoring study (i.e., Patterson & Stouthamer-Loeber 1984) or what the measures tap. For details, reference is given to two manuscripts that were listed as submitted, but do not currently appear in a database search (i.e., Patterson et al. 1983; Stouthamer-Loeber, Patterson, & Loeber 1982). Reportedly, a large set of measures that were thought to define the monitoring construct were taken as the starting point, and a correlation matrix including those and "four criterion variables" was examined (Patterson & Stouthamer-Loeber 1984:1303). A submitted manuscript on antisocial behavior was cited after this statement (i.e., Patterson et al. 1983), which raises the question whether antisocial behavior was included in the matrix and whether the monitoring measures might have been selected in part for their correlations with antisocial behavior. The final measures were described in a vague way: "from the child interview (four questions relating to child's whereabouts and amount of information shared with parent), the mother interview (two questions relating to importance of supervision and supervision after school), the child interviewer impressions (a rating as to how well the child seemed supervised by the parents), and the telephone interview (a comparison between the child and the parent telephone report showing how well the parent is informed about the child's activities)" (Patterson & Stouthamer-Loeber 1984:1303). From the information available, few of the items sound like measures of parents' monitoring efforts. It should be noted that in a later comment on scale construction, Patterson and colleagues explained that because this was the first attempt to develop a good measure of monitoring, "the assessment devices were rather primitive" (Patterson, Reid, & Dishion 1992:64). Nonetheless, in this seminal study, which is widely cited today, it seems that the measures did not match the conceptualization of monitoring.

Several years later, a clearer description of an attempt to operationalize monitoring was reported in an edited volume describing the measures used in the Oregon Youth Study (Capaldi & Patterson 1989). More sophisticated analyses than in the earlier study were used, but the procedure was similar in that a wide variety of indicators were taken as a starting point, and then the large number was narrowed down to three. The indicators that were retained involved parents' reports, staff impressions, and children's reports. The parent report was a question about the number of hours parents spent with the child, but since monitoring deals conceptually with parents' attempts to track the youth's whereabouts when they are away from home, this does not seem to be a measure of monitoring. The interviewer's reports were their impressions of how well the child was monitored, but there was no information about what those impressions were based on, and it is not clear how interviewers would form accurate impressions about something parents do at home on a day-to-day basis. Most of the items were children's reports, all of which measured the child's disclosure and other efforts to inform parents rather than any parental activity (e.g., How often do you tell parents when you'll be home? How often do you leave a note about where you are going? How often do you check in after school? How often do you talk to parents about daily plans?). These youth behaviors do not necessarily imply any monitoring effort on the part of parents. There were a number of measures that were originally assumed to define the construct but had to be excluded from the final monitoring measure because they did not load with these measures. Notably, the measures of parents' rules and expectations were among the ones that were excluded. Thus, this scale ended up being primarily a measure of time spent together and youths' efforts to keep parents informed rather than a measure of parents' monitoring efforts.

Later Measures: A Focus on Parental Knowledge of Daily Activities

Some studies have used scales that are made up solely or primarily of measures of the youths' willingness to keep parents informed, which does not match the conceptualization of monitoring as parents' active tracking (e.g., Barnes & Farrell 1993; Barnes, Koffman et al. 2006; Barnes, Reifman et al. 2000). Other attempts to operationalize parental monitoring have focused solely on parents' knowledge of their youths' daily activities, and these measures are the most widely used in the literature that exists today. Some of these used youths' estimations of their parents' knowledge. For instance, in 1993 a five-item scale appeared that has been used widely in the developmental literature as a measure of parental monitoring (Brown et al. 1993).

Adolescents rated, on a three-point response scale (don't know, know a little, know a lot), how much their parents *really* knew about who their friends were, how they spent their money, where they were after school, where they went at night, and what they did with their free time. Somewhat earlier, similar measures had been used in the criminology literature: "Do your parents know where you are when you are away from home? Do your parents know who you are with when you are away from home?" (Weintraub & Gold 1991:272); and "In my free time away from home, my parents know who I'm with and where I am" (Cernkovich & Giordano 1987:303). Other measures have assessed knowledge by asking parents and their children the same questions about the child's activities and then assessing agreement between the two sets of answers (Crouter, MacDermid et al. 1990; Crouter, Manke, & McHale 1995). Thus, all of these widely used operationalizations of parental monitoring assess mainly parents' knowledge of youths' daily activities or youths' activities that provide information to parents. None assesses monitoring activities that parents might have engaged in. In contrast, the definitions given and the conclusions drawn in studies using these measures reveal a conceptualization of monitoring as parents' active monitoring efforts. To the extent that operationalizations rely on parental knowledge and youths' provision of information, the conceptualization of monitoring in the literature does not match the operationalizations.

This is a question of construct validity. If the measures of a construct are not face-valid indicators of the construct, one must question the conclusions that have been drawn from studies using those measures. Concerning monitoring, hundreds of studies are involved. Before reinterpreting the conclusions of these studies, however, one should ask whether parental knowledge or a youth's willingness to provide information might *indicate* that parents have engaged in tracking or checking up, even if they do not tap them directly. If they do, then these measures might be seen as markers of parental monitoring, and the conclusions from studies that have used these measures might be correct despite problems with the measures.

Does Knowledge Come from Monitoring?

The question whether knowledge of a youth's daily activities indicates monitoring efforts was examined in two studies published in 2000 (Kerr & Stattin 2000; Stattin & Kerr 2000). Stattin and Kerr constructed measures of the types of monitoring efforts that had been discussed in the literature: (a) asking for information from different sources and (b) setting rules and tracking compliance. The measure of asking for information was called *solicitation*. It included the following items: "In the last month, have your parents talked with the parents of your friends? How often do your parents talk with your friends when they come to your home (ask what they do or what they think and feel about different things)? During the past month, how often have your parents started a conversation with you about your free time? How often do your parents initiate a conversation about things that happened during a normal day at school? Do your parents usually ask you to talk about things that happened during your free time (whom you met when you were out in the city, free time activities, etc.)?" The measure of setting rules and tracking compliance was called *control*. It included the following items: "Do you need to have your parents' permission to stay out late on a weekday evening? Do you need to ask your parents before you can decide with your friends what you will do on a Saturday evening? If you have been out very late one night, do your parents require that you explain what you did and whom you were with? Do you have to tell you parents where you are at night, who you are with, and what you do together? Before you go out on a Saturday night, do you have to tell your parents where you are going and with whom?" Thus, they attempted to operationalize parental behaviors that represented the conceptualization of monitoring in the literature.

Stattin and Kerr (2000) reasoned that if parents' monitoring efforts lie behind parental knowledge, then control and solicitation should be so highly correlated with parental knowledge that they would seem to be measuring the same thing. The results showed significant correlations in the .2 to .3 range. Although these measures of monitoring efforts were definitely related to parental knowledge, the correlations were not so high that they seemed to be measuring the same thing. Stattin and Kerr also reasoned that if parental knowledge comes from monitoring efforts, then knowledge and monitoring efforts should correlate with adjustment to about the same extent; they did not. Various measures of externalizing and internalizing problems correlated more strongly with parental knowledge (.25 to .48) than with control and solicitation (.00 to .18). All of these findings were about the same for parents' reports as for adolescents' reports. Thus, parental monitoring efforts did not explain much of what parents knew and they were not robustly linked to adolescent adjustment. It seems that parental knowledge measures do not primarily tap monitoring efforts; consequently, knowledge measures are not valid operational definitions of parental monitoring. In other words, the conceptualization of monitoring in the literature does not match the most commonly used operationalization.

In fact, parental knowledge seems to be more a function of youths' actions than parents' actions. Stattin and Kerr (2000) considered that youths might freely provide whatever knowledge parents have about their daily activities. They measured youth disclosure with questions such as: "If you are out at night, when you get home, do you tell what you have done that evening," "Do you usually tell how school was when you get home (how you did on different exams, your relationships with teachers, etc.)," and "Do you keep a lot of secrets from your parents about what you do during your free time?" The correlation between this measure and parental knowledge was high enough to suggest that they might be measuring much the same thing (around .65). Furthermore, in regression analyses in which disclosure was entered along with the two measures of parents' monitoring efforts (control and solicitation), youth disclosure was the strongest unique predictor of parental knowledge ($\beta = .59$, $p < .001$, and $\beta = .64$, $p < .001$ for parents' and youths' reports, respectively). Parental control and solicitation contributed little in comparison ($\beta = .19$, $p < .001$, and $\beta = .15$, $p > .05$ for parent-reported control and solicitation, respectively, and $\beta = .22$, $p < .001$, and $\beta = .03$, $p > .05$ for youth-reported control and solicitation, respectively). In a follow-up study, this pattern was replicated on another sample (Kerr & Stattin 2000). In addition, unlike the measures of parental actions, youth disclosure was linked to various measures of internal and external adjustment in the same way that knowledge was. Thus, it appeared that the two measures were so closely linked that knowledge measures could be seen more as a proxy for youth disclosure than as a proxy for parental monitoring.

Using similar constructs, Crouter and colleagues (Crouter et al. 2005) later examined the sources of parental knowledge (i.e., measured by comparing telephone reports of daily events). They concluded that multiple sources inform parents; however, closer examination of their clusters reveals that the primary source of information is child disclosure. That is, mothers in relational clusters and fathers in relational and spouse-informed clusters were those that perceived knowing more about their adolescents' activities, with this knowledge, in turn, being related to low levels of risk behaviors. The primary difference between mothers' relational clusters and the others was that relational clusters were significantly higher in child disclosure, as was also true for fathers' clusters. Moreover, "spouse-informed" fathers were more often informed by "relational" mothers, suggesting that the driving force behind fathers' knowledge was, again, child disclosure.

Other recent research supports the idea that parental knowledge is gained primarily through youth disclosure. Marshall, Tilton-Weaver, and Bosdet (2005) asked adolescents about their decisions to divulge or withhold information. The study demonstrated, again, that parents' knowledge was gained primarily through disclosure (standardized path coefficients were .60 for mothers and .66 for fathers). Lying was also independently predictive of what mothers knew (standardized path coefficient was −.19 for mothers). Through qualitative analyses, they also found that youths purposefully managed the flow of information to their parents. Thus, not only does parents' knowledge come mainly from the adolescents themselves, adolescents actively control that knowledge. This is very different from the assumption that knowledge represents parents' active tracking of adolescents' activities and associations.

There is one recent study in which voluntary disclosure by adolescents did not turn out to be the most important source of parental knowledge once active parental efforts were controlled (Waizenhofer, Buchanan, & Jackson-Newsom 2004), but there were features of the sample and measures that limit the comparability of this study with the others that have examined this issue. First, the sample was a convenience sample recruited from YMCA sports programs in an affluent, suburban area. As the authors explained, the youths in the study led very structured lives. For instance, most of the girls in the study were involved in swimming programs, and they attended practices almost every day and competitions once a week. Thus, their free time was very much constrained by the activity. Furthermore, the families were 100% intact and many mothers were not employed outside the home, which presumably left them with time to attend the youths' practices and competitions. Second, the measure of active parental efforts was not restricted to monitoring efforts, but included time spent together. One might expect time spent together to be an important source of knowledge in this sample, but although this is something that parents actively do that will result in their knowing what happened to the youth that day, it cannot be considered a method of monitoring youths' free time away from home. Thus, the features of this sample limit the generalizability of the findings, and the inclusion of time spent together as an active strategy limits the comparability with other research on disclosure versus active monitoring efforts as sources of knowledge. In other words, the relevance of this study can be questioned. Apart from this study, there is converging evidence that parental knowledge comes mainly from youth disclosure and that youths are active agents in deciding what information parents should get. This is very different from the assumption that lies behind using parental knowledge as a measure of monitoring.

Are Knowledge and Disclosure Measuring the Same Thing?

Given the close link between knowledge and disclosure and the additional evidence of the active steps that youths take to manage the knowledge that their parents get, one might ask whether youths' reports of parental knowledge are actually tapping the same phenomenon as their reports of disclosure. We investigated this by examining whether the items measuring the youth's willingness to disclose information and the items measuring parents' knowledge make up a common factor that is distinguishable from the measures of parents' monitoring efforts.

PARTICIPANTS

The data for these analyses and all of the other empirical examples in this chapter are from a 5-wave longitudinal study called "10 to 18," which took place beginning during the 2001–02 school year in a community of 26,000 inhabitants in central Sweden. The aims were to assess the joint roles of parents, peers, and individual characteristics in the development of adjustment problems and criminality. The design was cross-sequential, targeting at each wave all students in grades 4 through 12, which corresponds to ages 10 to 18. We were targeting all youths in the community so that when youths named peers who are important to them, those peers were also likely to be in the study and to have self-reported on their own behavior and relationships. In this way, data on peers' behaviors or relationships are independent of the youth who named them and are not affected by the youth's own perceptions and biases, which tends to inflate similarity (e.g., Iannotti, Bush, & Weinfurt 1996). In this city, the unemployment rate was similar to that in Sweden as a whole (6%). The mean income was somewhat lower than the rest of the country (214,000 Swedish kronor per year compared with 223,000 for the rest of the country). Twelve percent of the inhabitants in the community had a foreign background. Around 90% of the target sample participated at each wave ($N \approx 2,900$ at each wave, with roughly equal numbers of boys and girls). Parents participated at Waves 1, 3, and 5 by returning questionnaires by mail. Only parents of 4th through 10th graders were asked to participate, because many youths in 11th and 12th grades have reached the legal age of independence in Sweden (18), are living on their own, or both. Those with more than two children in the target sample were asked to report on only two, which we selected randomly at Wave 1. At each wave, parents reported on about 70% of youths in the sample. Approximately 70% of the questionnaires were filled out by mothers at each wave, and the rest were about equally divided between fathers and both parents working together, apart from about 1%, which were filled out by a nonparental guardian.

Youths were recruited in their classrooms during school hours. They were told what kind of questions would be included in the questionnaires and how long it would take to fill them out. They were informed that participation was voluntary and that, if they chose not to participate, they were free to do something else instead of filling out the questionnaires. They were assured that if they did participate, their answers would not be revealed to their parents, teachers, the police, or anyone else. Parents were informed about the study ahead of time in meetings held in the community and by mail. Parents were told they could withdraw their child from the study at any time by returning a postage-paid card that was mailed to them each year before the data collection or by phoning. Thus, youths participated if they voluntarily chose to do so and if their parents did not object to their participation. They filled out the questionnaires during regular school hours in sessions administered by trained research assistants. Teachers were not present. Youths were not paid for their participation, but for each of the classes in grades 4 through 6 we made a contribution to the class fund, and in each of the classes in grades 7 through 12 we held a drawing for movie tickets. All those who stayed in the room, whether they filled out questionnaires or not, were eligible for the drawing. The study was approved by the school's ethics review board at the outset and again at the midpoint of the 5 years. For these analyses, we selected youths in grades 7 to 10 (i.e., ages 13 to 16) at the first wave.

MEASURES

Twenty-four items were entered into factor analyses for youths' and parents' reports separately. The items represent parental knowledge, youth disclosure of information, and two measures of parents' monitoring efforts: control and solicitation. These measures have been reported earlier (Kerr & Stattin 2000). Youths and parents answered the same questions with only minor changes in wordings to direct the questions to the relevant reporter (e.g., "Do your parents" versus "Do you"). The items given are from the youths' questionnaires.

Parental control. Parents and youths answered five questions about youths being required to inform parents where they would be and whom they would be with when away from home. All items were measured on a scale ranging from 1 (*no, never*) to 5 (*yes, always*). The five items from this parental control scale were: "Do you need to have your parents' permission to stay out late on a weekday evening? Do you need to ask your parents before you can decide with your friends what you will do on a Saturday evening? If you have been out very late one night, do your parents require that you explain what you did and whom you were with? Do you have to tell your parents where you are at night, who you are with, and what you do together? Before you go out on a Saturday night, do you have to tell your parents where you are going and with whom?" Alpha reliabilities were adequate for parent-reported ($\alpha = .73$) and youth-reported ($\alpha = .79$) scales.

Parental solicitation. Five items assessed parents' solicitation of information from various sources. Items were measured on a scale ranging from 1 (*no or almost never*) to 5 (*very often or always*). The five items from the parental solicitation scale were: "In the last month, have your parents talked with the parents of your friends? How often do your parents talk with your friends when they come to your home (ask what they do or what they think and feel about different things)? During the past month, how often have your parents started a conversation with you about your free time? How often do your parents initiate a conversation about things that happened during a normal day at school? Do your parents usually ask you to talk about things that happened during your free time (whom you met when you were out in the city, free time activities, etc.)?" Alpha reliabilities were adequate for parent- ($\alpha = .69$) and youth-reported ($\alpha = .73$) scales.

Youth disclosure. Five items assessed youths' disclosure of information. Items were measured on a scale ranging from 1 (*never* or *not at all*) to 5 (*always* or *very much*). The items were: "Do you talk at home about how you are doing in the different subjects in school? Do you usually tell how school was when you get home (how you did on different exams, your relationships with teachers, etc.)? Do you keep much of what you do in your free time secret from your parents? Do you hide a lot from your parents about what you do at night and on weekends? If you are out at night, when you get home, do you tell what you have done that evening?" Alpha reliabilities were adequate for parent- ($\alpha = .78$) and youth-reported ($\alpha = .79$) scales.

Parental knowledge. Nine items assessed parental knowledge of the youth's whereabouts, activities, and peers. Items were measured on a scale ranging from 1 (*no, not at all,* or *never*) to 5 (*yes, fully,* or *almost always*). The items were: "Do your parents know what you do during your free time? Do your parents know which friends you hang out with during your free time? Do your parents usually know what type of homework you have? Do your parents know what you spend your money on? Do your parents usually know when you have an exam or paper due at school? Do your parents know how you do in different subjects at school? Do your parents know where you go when you are out with friends at night? Do your parents normally know where you go and what you do after school? In the last month, have your parents ever had no idea of where you were at night?" Alpha reliabilities were adequate for parent ($\alpha = .82$) and youth ($\alpha = .84$) scales.

RESULTS

To examine whether knowledge and disclosure would be separate from solicitation and control, we performed a principal axis factor analysis with promax rotation. We did the same for parent reports. From the theoretical viewpoint that knowledge and disclosure are separate from monitoring efforts, we extracted two factors both for youth and parent reports. As reported in table 1.1, for youth reports all knowledge and all disclosure items loaded on the first factor. The second factor involved all solicitation and control items. For parent reports, all knowledge and disclosure items loaded on the first factor, and the solicitation and control items loaded on the second. Although the first solicitation item for parent reports had a low loading on the second factor, the overall pattern of these results suggests that the items measuring

TABLE 1.1

Factor analyses of knowledge, disclosure, solicitation, and control measures for 13- to 16-year-olds at Wave 1 (loadings of .4 or higher are italicized)

	YOUTH REPORTS		PARENT REPORTS	
	FACTOR 1	FACTOR 2	FACTOR 1	FACTOR 2
Knowledge: parents know what you do during your free time	.64	.01	.60	-.13
Knowledge: parents know what type of homework you have	.60	-.04	.53	.07
Knowledge: parents know what you spend your money on	.69	.01	.58	-.03
Knowledge: parents know when you have an exam or paper due at school	.67	-.13	.53	-.02
Knowledge: parents know where you go with friends at night	.72	.12	.68	-.00
Knowledge: in last month, have parents had no idea where you were at night	.74	-.14	.63	-.10
Knowledge: parents know where you go and what you do after school	.67	.10	.59	-.03
Disclosure: talk at home about how you are doing in different subjects in school	.58	-.03	.53	.07
Disclosure: keep much of what you do during free time secret from parents	.60	-.03	.58	-.01
Disclosure: hide a lot from parents about what you do on nights and weekends	.74	-.11	.68	-.13
Disclosure: usually tell how school was when you get home	.48	.20	.48	.16
Disclosure: if out at night, tell about what you did during the evening	.52	.30	.54	.22
Solicitation: in the last month, have parents had contact with your friends' parents	-.02	.35	.13	.16
Solicitation: how often do parents talk to your friends when they come to your home	.07	.38	.09	.39
Solicitation: how often have parents started a conversation with you about free time	-.05	.54	-.00	.45
Solicitation: how often do parents ask you about what happened at school	.08	.51	.20	.45
Solicitation: do parents ask you to talk about things that happened during free time	.05	.65	.06	.61
Control: if out very late, have to explain what you did and with whom	-.19	.69	-.16	.49
Control: need to have parents' permission to stay out late on a weekday evening	-.04	.55	-.13	.57
Control: need to ask parents before going out Saturday evenings	.06	.47	-.04	.53
Control: have to tell parents where you are in evenings, who with, and what you are doing	-.13	.83	.01	.60
Control: on Saturday nights, have to tell parents where you are going and with whom	.12	.62	-.02	.60

Note: Principle axis factor analysis with promax rotation. Results from the pattern matrix are presented.

parental knowledge are tapping much the same phenomenon as the items measuring disclosure, and that knowledge and disclosure measure something different from parents' monitoring efforts. It should be noted that for both youth and parent reports, extracting three factors produced a solution in which the disclosure and knowledge items still made up one factor, but the solicitation and control items loaded on different factors.

Taken together then, the results of the present analyses and previous studies (Crouter et al. 2005; Kerr & Stattin 2000; Marshall, Tilton-Weaver, & Bosdet 2005; Stattin & Kerr 2000) suggest, first, that knowledge is not a good operational definition of parental monitoring and, second, that knowledge represents youth disclosure more than parenting. In other words, the operationalization of parental monitoring that is most often used in the literature represents youth activity more than parental activity. As such, it does not match a conceptualization of monitoring as parents' tracking of the youth's whereabouts and activities. If measures of parental knowledge and youth disclosure do not adequately capture parental monitoring, then the studies that have been conducted using measures of knowledge or youth disclosure must be reexamined. Conclusions about parental agency must be questioned if the measures do not capture parental agency, and so far, the evidence suggests that knowledge and disclosure measures do not capture parental agency.

One other possibility should be considered, however. Perhaps the measure of youth disclosure used here and in the previous studies (Kerr & Stattin 2000; Stattin & Kerr 2000) does not tap free, willing disclosure, as intended. For instance, we asked youths questions such as whether they tell their parents when they get home what they have done while out in the evening. When youths endorse items such as this, it might be because when they get home their parents *ask* them what had happened. In other words, it is possible that we have been measuring disclosure that is *elicited* by parental monitoring efforts. This possibility should be examined using longitudinal data to infer directions of effects between monitoring efforts and youth disclosure.

Do Parents' Monitoring Efforts Elicit Youth Disclosure?

To examine the possibility that parents' attempts to gain information about their youths' daily activities elicit youths' disclosure of information, we used cross-lagged models with youth disclosure and parental monitoring efforts at two points in time. We used three measures of monitoring efforts—the control and solicitation scales described above and youths' judgments of how much their parents tried to know about their activities.

PARTICIPANTS

For these analyses, we selected youths in grades 7 to 9 at Wave 3, which corresponds roughly to ages 13 to 15. We used youth- and parent-reported data from Waves 3 and 5, because these waves included the most complete measures of monitoring efforts and because both parents and youths participated at these waves. The youths were 509 boys and 470 girls ($N = 979$), and they constituted 88% of all students registered in grades 7–9 (there were 1,116 registered pupils in these grades). Two years later, 743 of the 979 youths (75.8%) participated again. The main reason for nonparticipation was that in the switch from middle school (grade 9) to high school (grade 10) youths selected high school programs that did not exist in the town, and they had to attend a school in a neighboring town. We compared the Wave 4 respondents and nonrespondents on the main measures used in this study at Wave 3, as well as on delinquency and drug use. They did not differ significantly in any of these comparisons. Parents participated in the study by completing and sending in questionnaires that they had received in the mail. Of the 1,116 adolescents who were registered at school, parent data were available for 746 (67%) at Wave 3. This figure understates parents' participation, however, because for families in the target sample with two or more adolescents, we only asked parents to report about one randomly selected adolescent.

MONITORING EFFORTS

We used three youth-report measures of parents' monitoring efforts: (a) setting rules and tracking compliance (*control*); (b) asking for information from various sources (*solicitation*); and (c) unspecified attempts to know about the youth's activities (*trying to know*). The trying-to-know measure was brought into the study at Wave 3. Parents reported on control and solicitation. For control and solicitation, the items were described above in conjunction with the factor analyses. For youths' reports of control, the alpha reliabilities were .80 at both times. The year-to-year stability was .60, $p < .001$. For parents' reports of control, the alpha reliabilities were .81 and .78 for the two time points. The correlation between times, which was over 2 years, was .50, $p < .001$. The correlation between youths' and parents' reports at Wave 3 was .30, $p < .001$. For youths' reports of solicitation, the alpha reliabilities were .74 and .71 at the two times. The year-to-year stability was .55, $p < .001$. For parents' reports, the alpha reliabilities were .70 and .66 for the two time points. The correlation between times was .53, $p < .001$. The correlation between youths' and parents' reports at Wave 3 was .22, $p < .001$.

Trying to know. This was used as a monitoring measure by Fletcher, Steinberg, and Williams-Wheeler (2004), and we included it at Wave 3 to capture any monitoring efforts youths might have perceived that were not covered by the specific behaviors in the control and solicitation measures. The youths were asked: "How much do your parents TRY to find out about the following things . . . Who your friends are, What places you go to when you are out with friends at night, What you spend money on, What you do in your free time, and Where you hang out and what you do in the afternoon directly after school?" The response scales were (a) doesn't try to find out at all, (b) tries a bit, and (c) tries to find out as much as possible. The alpha reliabilities were .85 and .83 for the two times. The year-to-year stability was .39, $p < .001$, which was significantly lower than for control and solicitation, $(r = .60, p < .001,$ and $r = .55, p < .001$ for control and solicitation, respectively).

The three youth-reported measures of parental monitoring efforts were significantly related to each other (r's from .35 to .46) and they formed one factor in factor analyses at both times (principal axes factoring with oblimin rotation). The two parent-reported measures were also significantly correlated, $r = .35, p < .001$.

YOUTH DISCLOSURE AND PARENTAL KNOWLEDGE

The items for both these measures were described above in conjunction with the factor analyses. For youths' reports of disclosure, alpha reliabilities were .75 and .68 for the two times. The year-to-year stability was .58, $p < .001$. For parents' reports, alpha reliabilities were .81 and .78 for the two times. The time-to-time correlation was .55, $p < .001$. For youth reports of parental knowledge, alpha reliabilities were .85 and .82 for the two times. The year-to-year stability was .63, $p < .001$. For parents' reports, alpha reliabilities for the two time points were .85 and .81. The correlation between times over two years was .52, $p < .001$. The correlation between youths' and parents' reports of disclosure at Wave 3 was .42, $p < .001$, and it was .44, $p < .001$ for knowledge.

Results

We used autoregressive structural path models with cross-lagged effects to study changes over time (two years). Missing data were addressed by using full information maximum likelihood estimation. Each model included concurrent correlations between the measures at both time points, as well as autoregressive stability paths and cross-paths between measures (i.e., each model was saturated, containing as many parameter estimates as there were available degrees of freedom). Figure 1.1 presents the significant paths for each model (i.e., nonsignificant paths are included in the models, but omitted from the figure).

From the results shown in figure 1.1, parents' monitoring efforts do not seem to be responsible for youth disclosure. Of the three youth-reported measures of parental monitoring efforts and the two parent-reported measures, there was no case in which monitoring efforts significantly predicted an increase in disclosure over time. What is most striking about these findings, however, is the robust predictive effect of youth disclosure on changes in parental monitoring efforts. In four cases out of five, including youths' and parents' reports, youth disclosure predicted changes over time in monitoring efforts. From youths' reports, disclosure predicted more solicitation over time, and more attempts by parents to know about the youths' activities away from home. From parents' reports, disclosure predicted more parental control and more solicitation over time. Overall, then, the results do not support the idea that parents by their monitoring efforts elicit youth disclosure. Rather, it seems as if the more youths disclose, the more parents will try to find out, or expressed differently, the less youths disclose, the less parents will try to find out.

Youths' Reports

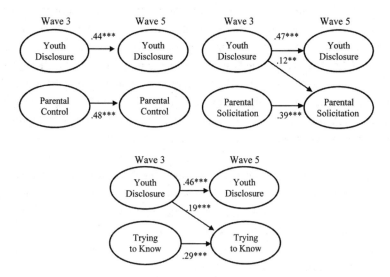

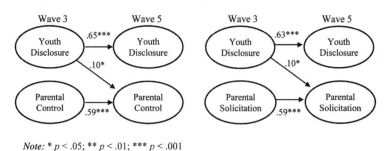

Parents' Reports

Note: * *p* < .05; ** *p* < .01; *** *p* < .001

Figure 1.1   Significant paths from autoregressive structural path models with cross-lagged effects involving parents' monitoring efforts and youth disclosure

Discussion

Why would having an adolescent who discloses a lot prompt parents to keep making active efforts to get information about the youths' activities, and why would having an adolescent who does not offer information prompt parents to make fewer efforts to gain information? Elsewhere, Kerr and Stattin have shown changes over time in parental monitoring efforts as a function of the youth's secretive, defiant behavior toward parents or lying, manipulative personality predispositions (Kerr & Stattin 2003; Kerr, Stattin, & Pakalniskiene, in press). In the second of these studies, Kerr and colleagues developed a normal-social-response explanation for these findings that might also explain the present findings. The idea is that parents respond to their adolescents the same way that we as people respond to each other, in general. If people seem warm and inviting—they seem to welcome our attention—we tend to approach them and give them our attention. On the other hand, if people seem cold and distant, we tend to leave them alone. In other words, we respond to the social cues that people give us. Kerr and colleagues reasoned that parents might respond to the social cues they get from their adolescents. Following this reasoning, they hypothesized that if parents perceive their adolescents as warm and open, they tend to approach them, including to ask them about the details of their activities away from home and to track compliance with rules that require them to give information—to monitor them. Cluster analyses of parents' ratings of their youths' warmth and openness resulted in four clusters: (a) a "warm-open" cluster; (b) an "average" cluster; (c) a "closed" cluster; and (d) a "cold-closed" cluster. These clusters differed on parent-reported monitoring efforts (F (3, 1158) = 35.03, $p < .001$), with parents who perceived their youths as warm and open having the highest standardized levels of monitoring ($M = .44$) and those who perceived their youths as cold and closed having the lowest mean levels ($M = -.51$). Over the following two years, parents who saw their youths as warm and open increased their monitoring efforts relative to the rest of the sample ($\Delta M = .17$), whereas those who perceived their youths as closed or cold and closed decreased their monitoring efforts ($\Delta Ms = -.15$ and $-.10$, respectively). Although these results are not conclusive about directions of effects, they do suggest that parents' monitoring efforts might be partly driven by their responses to the child's social signals. Together with the cross-lagged analyses reported above, these findings suggest that youth disclosure is not elicited by parents' monitoring efforts. On the contrary, disclosure and other signals that youths welcome parents' approach may actually encourage monitoring efforts. If disclosure is the primary source of parental knowledge as several studies have now shown (Crouter et al. 2005; Kerr & Stattin 2000; Marshall, Tilton-Weaver, & Bosdet 2005; Stattin & Kerr 2000), then knowledge cannot be considered a proxy for parents' monitoring efforts.

Summary

To summarize concerning the measures not matching the conceptualization, monitoring has been discussed in the literature since the middle of the 1980s as parental tracking of a youth's activities and associations when the youth is away from home. The measures of monitoring that have been used in the literature, however, do not seem to have tapped this parental behavior. First, they are largely face-valid measures of time spent together, youth disclosure of information, and parents' knowledge of the youths' activities. Although youth disclosure and parents' knowledge of the youth's daily activities seem to be measuring much the same thing, they are not the same as parents' attempts to track the youth's activities. Parents do not seem to be intentionally driving a monitoring process, because their monitoring efforts do not seem to elicit disclosure or contribute substantially to their knowledge. On the contrary, their monitoring efforts seem to reflect their perceptions of the youth's openness. All of this suggests that the findings reported in the literature should be reinterpreted in light of these new insights about what the measures really capture. For instance, in results concerning parental knowledge, one should be very aware of the close association between knowledge and the youth's disclosure of information when reinterpreting the results. When reading the conclusions from these studies, one might replace the term *parental monitoring* with *parental knowledge, much of which may have come from the youth him/herself.* We believe that the evidence suggests that conclusions about parents' active, intentional monitoring efforts should be viewed with skepticism if the measures of monitoring involve youth disclosure or parental knowledge.

Even apart from these problems with measures, however, the literature on parental monitoring is limited in at least three other ways. One concerns a lack of clear conceptualizations of the mechanisms through which monitoring should work; another concerns assumptions that have been made about causal directions; and a third concerns recent efforts to reformulate the construct, which raise a number of new problems.

Mechanisms Not Clearly Conceptualized and Tested

The original idea about why monitoring should work was clearly conceptualized. The theoretical idea discussed in the seminal paper by Patterson and Stouthamer-Loeber (1984) was based on the clinical observation that parents who do not track their youth's activities also fail to consistently punish any instances of misbehavior that they find out about, which would prevent it from recurring. The proposed mechanism, then, was punishment in the form of consistently applied consequences such as taking away money or privileges or requiring the youth to do extra chores at home. The assumption was that parents who monitor will find out about bad behavior, and when they do, they will apply appropriate punishments. In later studies, however, Patterson and colleagues included discipline and monitoring as two independent, proximal determinates of antisocial behavior (i.e., Bank et al. 1993; Dishion et al. 1991; Patterson, Reid, & Dishion 1992). To our knowledge, the original idea that punishment, discipline, or applying consequences mediates the link between monitoring and antisocial behavior has not been tested.

In fact, we are unaware of any studies that spell out and test the mechanisms through which parents' tracking of adolescents' activities should steer adolescents away from risky situations and deviant peers. The descriptions of mechanisms are usually quite vague. Monitoring is thought to be a process by which parents get knowledge, but getting or having knowledge cannot be protective in and of itself. Parents would have to do something with that knowledge in order to have a protective effect. Many studies mention steering youths away from bad influences and risky situations. The quotes from the literature that we gave earlier are representative: "It may be plausibly inferred that monitoring affects boys' delinquency by preventing them from associating with [other delinquents], which may be a critical factor" (Weintraub & Gold 1991:279); and "Strong parental monitoring helps to deter adolescents from using alcohol and drugs themselves and . . . from associating with drug-using peers" (Fletcher, Darling, & Steinberg 1995:270). "There is growing evidence that monitoring of adolescent children is an age-appropriate parental control practice that could decrease the likelihood that adolescents would associate with peers who consume illegal substances and engage in antisocial behavior" (Barrera et al. 2001:150). But how would parents prevent, deter, or decrease the likelihood of associations with delinquent or drug-using peers just by tracking their youths' activities? Some other action would be necessary—denying permission to go certain places or with certain peers, for instance, or expressing disapproval of certain peers. These or other things that parents might do to prevent bad behavior or steer a youth away from bad influences have not been spelled out or operationalized and tested in the monitoring literature.

Assumptions about Causality and Changes Over Time

A negative correlation between parental monitoring and youth problem behavior can be interpreted in at least two ways, each with a different causal explanation. One interpretation is that parents' monitoring efforts have reduced youth problems. Another is that when parents have faced problems, they have given up trying to monitor their youth. From cross-sectional data, it is not possible to tell which of these very different interpretations is correct. Nonetheless, the first—that parents affect the youth's behavior—appears very often in the literature. What is more, not only do these causal interpretations appear in the empirical studies that report the original cross-sectional results, they appear later when new studies review the literature and describe the results of past cross-sectional studies in causal terms. Thus, these causal conclusions based on cross-sectional data increase exponentially as the literature grows.

Most published studies on monitoring have been cross-sectional, showing concurrent associations. In virtually all of these studies, however, the assumption is that parental monitoring prevents problem behavior. This can be obvious, such as in the examples that we quoted at the beginning of this chapter, or it can be less obvious, in cases where the authors are careful to use terms such as *association* in most of the paper, but draw conclusions or state implications of their findings that clearly show that they have inferred causality in their findings. Another variant of this problem is when cross-sectional, correlational findings are described using terms such as *increase* or *decrease*, which imply changes over time.

Even more problematic, these misinterpretations can continue or surface in the literature decades after a study was published. For example, the oft-cited Patterson and Stouthamer-Loeber (1984) article was cross-sectional, and the findings reported were group means and zero-order correlations between parenting measures and delinquency. Yet in a recent review paper, the main findings were summarized in a way that implied that the original study had shown changes over time: "Decreased parental monitoring (which concurs with age) was associated with greater adolescent delinquency" (Boyer 2006:330). The findings from another oft-cited cross-sectional study mentioned above (Brown et al. 1993) are being cited today in causal terms as well. To take one example, in a recent article (Siebenbruner et al. 2006) the study was cited to support three different statements, all of which were about causal effects of parents on children. The authors claimed that "active parental monitoring appears to discourage substance use" (p. 553); "Parents, through their actions or, in this case, nonactions, appear to have an effect on their children's substance use" (p. 556); and "Decreased monitoring by parents in adolescence may increase the likelihood of greater substance use involvement" (p. 567). In examples such as these, the original causal interpretations from cross-sectional findings are retold again and again.

Other studies have used longitudinal designs, perhaps more often than in other areas of research in developmental psychology. In fact, 80 prospective, longitudinal studies were reported in journals and books up to 2005. Although longitudinal studies offer opportunities to test alternative directional hypotheses, in the monitoring literature this has seldom been done. For example, Fletcher and coworkers (2005) tested a path model where parents' monitoring (how much they try to know), warmth, and control affected their knowledge about their children's whereabouts, and parental knowledge was associated with problem behavior of the child concurrently and one year later. All measures in the model were concurrent except for a problem behavior measure taken one year after all of the other measures. Their conclusion was that parents directly and indirectly *affect* their adolescents' adjustment. This conclusion, however, rested mainly on the cross-sectional portion of their data. Even though the larger dataset apparently included the measures needed to test alternative directions of effects longitudinally, the authors did not test the possibility that problem behavior might affect parents' monitoring, warmth, and control. From what is reported in the study, they took for granted that parents' behaviors drive youths' behaviors. This study is just one recent example of many that have taken a unidirectional approach in analyzing longitudinal data.

There are exceptions. As far back as the early 1990s, Patterson and coworkers found in a longitudinal study that children's antisocial behavior predicted decreases in parental knowledge and parental discipline over two years controlling for the earlier knowledge and discipline measures (Patterson, Bank, & Stoolmiller 1990). A few other studies have attempted to examine bidirectionality, looking at youth problem behavior and measures of parental knowledge (Fite et al. 2006; Jang & Smith 1997; Kandel & Wu 1995; Laird et al. 2003; Stice & Barrera 1995). A strength of these studies is that they attempted to conceptualize alternative directions of effects. Because knowledge measures mostly capture youth disclosure, however, one can neither say that the results show a parental reaction to youth behavior *nor* that they show a youth reaction to parental behavior. It is worth noting, however, that all of these studies showed that youth problem behavior predicted changes over time in parental knowledge, either alone or in addition to effects in the opposite direction. This is consistent with a number of experimental and longitudinal studies outside of the monitoring literature that have shown effects of children or adolescents on the behavior of parents or other adults (e.g., Anderson, Lytton, & Romney 1986; Buss 1981; Dix et al. 1986; Mulhern & Passman 1981; Passman & Blackwelder 1981) or have shown bidirectional effects (e.g., Hastings & Rubin 1999; Kochanska 1998; Mink & Nihira 1986; Stice & Barrera 1995). These studies and several of the monitoring studies cited above have been in the literature long enough to have altered the unidirectional focus that characterizes most research on parental monitoring, but there is little evidence for this. With only a few exceptions, parental monitoring is conceptualized in the literature as a proactive strategy of parents.

To our knowledge, only two studies (Dishion, Nelson, & Bullock 2004; Kerr & Stattin 2003) have addressed the longitudinal association between parents' monitoring efforts and child problem behavior, avoiding relying on parental knowledge as a proxy for parents' monitoring actions. Dishion and colleagues (2004) reported a study linking deviant friendships to family management, including monitoring, over three years for a high-risk sample of 200 mid-adolescent boys. Their results showed that deviant peer processes produced degradation of family management over time. In this study, monitoring was operationalized by interviewers' impressions of parental monitoring. Because they reported the findings only for the broader family management measure, however, it is not possible to discern the specific role of monitoring.

In the other study to look at bidirectional effects without relying on knowledge as a proxy for monitoring efforts, Kerr and Stattin (2003) examined whether parents change their monitoring efforts in response to delinquency and whether that has an effect on later delinquency. They used a community sample, and tested a larger model of the processes involved. For one thing, they included youth behaviors that correlate with delinquency and which parents might experience at home, behaviors such as defiance, nondisclosure, lying, and manipulation. Their reasoning was that parents might react more to these behaviors than to the delinquency itself. They also included two kinds of parents' reactions to delinquency: (a) emotionally tied, or "gut level" reactions such as worry, distrust, and lessened emotional support, and (b) monitoring efforts (control and solicitation). The findings showed that parents tended to respond to the youth's negative behavior at home more than to the delinquency itself. The same was true when a measure of having deviant peers was substituted for the delinquency measure. On the gut level, parents reacted with worry, distrust, and lessened support and encouragement. Behaviorally, they reacted by slackening their monitoring efforts. Monitoring efforts, however, did not predict changes in delinquency over time.

Assume that this study would have been cross-sectional and only involved the first data collection. Then, significant, negative correlations between parents' monitoring efforts and youth problem behavior would have been found. In line with the monitoring literature, these correlations could have been interpreted as showing that when parents monitor, they reduce negative behavior at home and delinquency. This would have been misleading.

To summarize, the bulk of the monitoring research has not directly tested the causal directions between parental monitoring behaviors and youth outcomes, either because parents' monitoring efforts were not operationalized or because reciprocal causal linkages were not tested. When the causal directions between parents' monitoring behaviors and adolescents' adjustment have been tested directly, the evidence suggests that correlational findings are better interpreted as parental *reactions to* adolescents' problem behaviors, rather than proactive *actions* that reduce problem behaviors.

Making the Monitoring Construct Less Specific

In response to empirical evidence casting doubt on the use of knowledge measures for monitoring, several attempts to reconceptualize parental monitoring have surfaced. Researchers have argued that monitoring is a complex process involving parents' actions that provide an environment conducive to adolescents' disclosure (e.g., Fletcher, Steinberg, & Williams-Wheeler 2005). From this theoretical perspective, monitoring is described as located within the parent-child relationship and family processes, and parental knowledge is a product of parenting efforts to foster positive parent-adolescent relationships while maintaining behavioral standards and rules about activities outside of parents' direct supervision (e.g., Laird et al. 2003). Some have begun to use terms such as "monitoring knowledge" and "monitoring-relevant knowledge." Thus, in this reconceptualization, knowledge is preserved as the operationalization of monitoring, but the term *monitoring* has no specific meaning in terms of parental behaviors. It is redefined as anything and everything in parents' behaviors and family interactions that have resulted in youths disclosing and parents getting information through other sources.

This approach has one main advantage. It removes the shadow of doubt from the extant literature, in which parental monitoring was operationalized as parental knowledge. One does not have to reexamine the conclusions from these studies if one accepts an amorphous definition of monitoring that can include almost anything that goes on in the family, including youth disclosure of information that results in parents getting knowledge. There are, however, several disadvantages of this reformulation.

These attempts at reconceptualizing monitoring introduce imprecision into the scientific literature on several levels, beginning with the theoretical and conceptual underpinnings. First, the new terms lack clear meanings. What is monitoring knowledge? It is an unusual grammatical construction, but it seems to specify knowledge that has come from monitoring rather than from some other source. If that is the intention, then the term is misleading, according to the empirical evidence that we have reviewed in this chapter. Monitoring-relevant knowledge seems to imply something else: knowledge that parents need in order to monitor (i.e., knowledge that is relevant for their efforts to monitor). One normally assumes that monitoring results in knowledge, however, and because of this it is unclear how parents would need knowledge to get knowledge. Thus, the new terms themselves are imprecise. It will be difficult to discover the processes and mechanisms through which parents might affect and be affected by their youths' adjustment without precision in constructs and measures.

There has also been a tendency to blur the conceptual lines between ways of obtaining knowledge and monitoring. Not all ways of obtaining knowledge can, conceptually, be considered monitoring. For instance, if parents participate in activities with a youth, they will have knowledge of those activities by virtue of experiencing them firsthand, but parental monitoring of adolescents is, conceptually, more about efforts to keep track of the youth's activities away from home—those that parents do not observe or experience firsthand. Thus, although spending time with an adolescent is a parental activity, it cannot be considered a monitoring activity. Another example is information exchanged between parents. If a father asks a mother about their youth's activities, the father has made an active effort to get knowledge, but since it came from the other parent, it was knowledge that the parents already had. Thus, getting information from a spouse cannot really be considered a parental monitoring strategy. We believe that caution should be exercised when comparing findings involving these measures with those involving parents' monitoring efforts, as has been done in some recent studies (e.g., Crouter et al. 2005; Waizenhofer, Buchanan, & Jackson-Newson 2004). Parental activities that result in knowledge should be distinguished conceptually from monitoring efforts, even though monitoring efforts might result in knowledge also.

Finally, and perhaps most important, there is a problem in not recognizing youth agency. The conceptualizations of monitoring and monitoring knowledge seem to take as an implicit assumption that parents are primarily responsible for the knowledge that they get about their youth's daily activities. By using terminology such as "monitoring knowledge," the locus of causality is on parent effects. However, there is much evidence accumulating that youths are active agents in managing the information that their parents get. For instance, Marshall and colleagues (2005) asked adolescents about their decisions to divulge or withhold information. Qualitative analyses revealed that adolescents make active choices about when and how to provide information to their parents, including designing ways in which to keep their parents uninformed. In this study, adolescents' information management strategies were driven by concerns about autonomy, safety and security, preserving the relationship with their parents, and self-presentation. In a similar line of research, Smetana and coworkers (2006) found that not only could parents overestimate the amount that youths disclosed, but youths felt less obligated to disclose information in domains where they perceived that they, not their parents, retained legitimate authority (e.g., less obligation to disclose personal issues than issues in other domains). They also found that adolescents differentially disclosed on the basis of their relationships with parents. All of these findings suggest that adolescents are actively managing the information that they disclose to their parents, and for this reason it is inaccurate to view disclosure as a parental monitoring strategy.

These studies suggest a very different view of disclosure than what is currently promoted in the monitoring literature. It is becoming clearer and clearer from research that adolescents have their own reasons for disclosing or withholding, and they strategically act on their reasons. Sometimes the reasons adolescents have for disclosing information to their parents is congruent with what their parents might want or expect. Other times it is not. More important, adolescents do not treat all information in the same way, but differentiate between information that might be revealed without compromising their own agendas and information that would, if disclosed, interfere with their aims. Thus, because measures of parental knowledge and measures of youth disclosure are tapping into the same thing, as suggested by the finding that they make up a common factor, and youth disclosure is very much determined by the youth's own agenda and little determined by parents' monitoring efforts, we see no justification for renaming knowledge measures "monitoring knowledge" and "monitoring-relevant knowledge" and assuming that they show primarily parent agency.

We argue that these other behaviors—other parenting that results in disclosure, the behavior of others, anything *other* than parents active attempts to track their adolescents activities—should not be called monitoring because it is an expansion of the construct beyond a clear and precise meaning. We see a problem in taking a word with a clear everyday meaning and using it in the scientific literature to mean something else—something with no clear meaning. This problem is compounded because the meaning of the term has been changed after a large literature has accumulated with the everyday meaning of the word. The word *monitoring* has a clear meaning: "to keep watch over or check as a means of control" (Read et al. 1995:822). When we as ordinary people read in the newspaper that the police are monitoring the situation where a large demonstration is taking place, we know intuitively what this means. The term implies a certain vigilance and an intention to impose control if the situation gets out of hand. Monitors are aware that they are monitoring and why they are monitoring. Therefore, when we as researchers read that parents are monitoring their adolescent's whereabouts and activities away from home, we assume that they are actively keeping track of or checking the youth's activities with the intended purpose of getting information that will help them control problem behavior. It is problematic to change the meaning of the word, now, to a complex family process involving everything that parents do to foster the kind of parent-child relationship in which a youth will feel free to disclose the details of his or her daily life away from home. We have no doubt that parents might foster disclosure by showing love and affection, for instance, or by listening patiently and with interest when children talk, or reacting nonjudgmentally when they disclose misdeeds (e.g., Kerr, Stattin, & Trost 1999). We doubt, however, that parents do these things solely with the intended purpose of tracking the child's behavior away from home. To develop a scientific understanding of the family processes that are linked to problem behavior, it seems that a better approach would be to (a) define the specific behaviors of interest, for instance showing love and affection, listening patiently, showing interest, and reacting nonjudgmentally to disclosure; (b) to operationalize and measure these specific behaviors; and (c) to formulate and test theoretical mechanisms through which they might work. We believe that it is a mistake to try to alter the established meaning of monitoring, which is consistent with the conceptualization in the vast majority of studies in literature and with the dictionary definition.

On the practical level, researchers also want to be able to give clear advice to parents and practitioners based on research. What would the advice be to parents about what they should do based on research that deals with an amorphous monitoring construct including anything and everything that goes on in the family that ultimately results in the youth giving information? This does not suggest any clear actions that parents can take. Indeed, it raises many questions. Do we as researchers know that knowledge per se is protective? If so, how is it protective? This goes back to the problem of not specifying mechanisms. Research cannot really answer what parents do with knowledge to protect their youths from antisocial influences. Is knowledge protective, then, or is it just that youths who are not doing bad things have no reason to hide their daily activities from their parents? Only by being more precise about the constructs and mechanisms being studied and testing directions of effects can we, as researchers, develop a solid basis for giving practical advice to parents.

In short, we believe the benefits of adjusting the monitoring construct to mean anything that parents might do to get knowledge, including knowledge from youth disclosure, do not offset the costs. The costs include imprecision on all levels: theoretical, conceptual, operational, and practical.

Conclusions

In this chapter, we have taken a critical look at monitoring research. We have questioned the typical interpretation in the literature that the negative correlation between parental monitoring and adolescent problem behavior that has usually been found in studies in this area should be interpreted as something parents do unilaterally. We have advocated that for several reasons—using measures that are not valid measures of parents' tracking efforts, not conceptualizing youths as active agents, and not specifying the mechanisms through which monitoring allows parents to steer their youths away from problem behavior—the literature has been based on ill-founded assumptions about measures and mechanisms. We have questioned the typical interpretation in the literature that causality resides with parents, and we have advocated using clear and precise meanings of the term *monitoring*.

It seems certainly to be the case that much of what parents know about their adolescents' whereabouts is information that they get from their adolescents themselves. By this we do not maintain a "child effects" approach to parental monitoring, and we do not advocate pitting "child effects" against "parent effects" or vice versa (e.g., Soenens et al. 2006). Adolescents' disclosure about their everyday lives, their whereabouts, and their thoughts and feelings to parents should be strongly connected with how they perceive their parents. It should depend on their views of their parents as legitimate authorities (e.g., Smetana et al. 2006), whether they perceive support and warmth from their parent, and how their parents react to their disclosure and actions. Spontaneous disclosure to parents is unlikely to emerge if parents respond to disclosure negatively, with temperamental outbursts, sarcasm, and guilt-inducing reactions. Vice versa, parents' attempts to gain insights into their adolescents' thoughts and feelings about themselves and their whereabouts away from home are likely to be associated with their youths' openness to their influence, their youths' personalities and temperaments, and previous experiences of soliciting information and rule-setting.

New ideas and models are needed that take bidirectionality into account. They will not be child-effects or parent-effects models, and they are likely to be models that also take into account the emotional climate in the family—all the things that help to create this climate and what it means for youths' behavior inside and outside of the family. In our view, studies are needed using measures that capture parents' and adolescents' actions and reactions to each other. Such studies should give insight into under what conditions parents' monitoring efforts are likely to be successful, what other parental actions are important for the development of problem behavior, and through what mechanisms. In our opinion, these kinds of studies, along with experimental-longitudinal studies, are likely to guide well-designed preventive work. In short, there is indeed much to be discovered about what parents can do to prevent their children from developing problem behavior and how monitoring fits into the picture.

References

Anderson, K. E., Lytton, H., & Romney, D. M. (1986). Mothers' interactions with normal and conduct-disordered boys: Who affects whom? *Developmental Psychology, 22*, 604–609.

Bank, L., Forgatch, M. L., Patterson, G. R., & Fetrow, R. A. (1993). Parenting practices of single mothers: Mediators of negative contextual factors. *Journal of Marriage and Family, 55*, 371–384.

Barnes, G. M., & Farrell, M. P. (1993). Parental support and control as predictors of adolescent drinking, delinquency, and related problem behaviors. *Journal of Marriage and Family, 54*, 763–776.

Barnes, G. M., Koffman, J. H., Welte, J. W., Farrell, M. P., & Dintcheff, B. A. (2006). Effects of parental monitoring and peer deviance on substance use and delinquency. *Journal of Marriage and Family, 68*, 1084–1104.

Barnes, G. M., Reifman, A. S., Farrell, M. P., & Dintcheff, B. A. (2000). The effects of parenting on the development of adolescent alcohol misuse: A six wave latent growth model. *Journal of Marriage and Family, 62*, 175–186.

Barrera, M., Jr., Biglan, A., Ary, D., & Li, F. (2001). Replication of a problem-behavior model with American Indian, Hispanic, and Caucasian youth. *Journal of Early Adolescence, 21*, 133–157.

Biglan, A. (2003). The generic features of effective childrearing. In A. Biglan, M. C. Wang, & H. J. Walberg (Eds.), *Preventing youth problems* (pp. 145–162). New York: Kluwer Academic/Plenum.

Boyer, T. W. (2006). The development of risk-taking: A multi-perspective review. *Developmental Review, 26,* 291–345.

Brown, B. B., Mounts, N., Lamborn, S. D., & Steinberg, L. (1993). Parenting practices and peer group affiliation in adolescence. *Child Development, 64,* 467–482.

Buss, D. M. (1981). Predicting parent-child interactions from children's activity level. *Developmental Psychology, 17,* 59–65.

Capaldi, D. M., & Patterson, G. R. (1989). *Psychometric properties of fourteen latent constructs from the Oregon Youth Study.* New York: Springer-Verlag.

Cernkovich, S. A., & Giordano, P. C. (1987). Family relationships and delinquency. *Criminology, 24,* 295–321.

Crouter, A. C., Bumpus, M. F, Davis, K. D., & McHale, S. M. (2005). How do parents learn about adolescents' experiences? Implications for parental knowledge and adolescent risky behavior. *Child Development, 76,* 869–882.

Crouter, A. C., & Head, M. R. (2002). Parental monitoring and knowledge of children. In M. Bornstein (Ed.), *Handbook of Parenting, 2nd ed., vol. 3: Becoming and being a parent* (pp. 461–483). Mahwah, NJ: Erlbaum.

Crouter, A. C., MacDermid, S. M., McHale, S. M., & Perry-Jenkins, M. (1990). Parental monitoring and perceptions of children's school performance and conduct in dual- and single-earner families. *Developmental Psychology, 26,* 649–657.

Crouter, A. C., Manke, B. A., & McHale, S. M. (1995). The family context of gender intensification in early adolescence. *Child Development, 66,* 317–329.

Dishion, T. J., & McMahon, R. J. (1998). Parental monitoring and the prevention of child and adolescent problem behavior: A conceptual and empirical formulation. *Clinical Child and Family Psychology Review, 1,* 61–75.

Dishion, T. J., Nelson, S. E., & Bullock, B. M. (2004). Premature adolescent autonomy: Parent disengagement and deviant peer process in the amplification of problem behavior. In J. Kiesner & M. Kerr (Eds.), Peer and family processes in the development of antisocial and aggressive behavior [Special Issue]. *Journal of Adolescence, 27,* 515–530.

Dishion, T. J., Patterson, G. R., Stoolmiller, M., & Skinner, M. L. (1991). Family, school, and behavioral antecedents to early adolescent involvement with antisocial peers. *Developmental Psychology, 27,* 172–180.

Dix, T., Ruble, D. N., Grusec, J. E., & Nixon, S. (1986). Social cognition in parents: Inferential and affective reactions to children of three age levels. *Child Development, 57,* 879–894.

Fite, P. J., Colder, C. R., Lochmann, J. E., & Wells, K. C. (2006). The mutual influence of parenting and boys' externalizing problems. *Applied Developmental Psychology, 27,* 151–164.

Fletcher, A. C., Darling, N., & Steinberg, L. (1995). Parental monitoring and peer influences on adolescent substance use. In J. McCord (Ed.), *Coercion and punishment in long-term perspectives* (pp. 259–271). New York: Cambridge University Press.

Fletcher, A. C., Steinberg, L., & Williams-Wheeler, M. (2004). Parental influences on adolescent problem behavior: Revisiting Stattin and Kerr. *Child Development, 75*, 781–796.

Hastings, P. D., & Rubin, K. H. (1999). Predicting mothers' beliefs about pre-school-aged children's social behavior: Evidence for maternal attitudes moderating child effects. *Child Development, 70*, 722–741.

Iannotti, R. J., Bush, P. J., & Weinfurt, K. P. (1996). Perceptions of friends' use of alcohol, cigarettes, and marijuana among urban school children: A longitudinal analysis. *Addictive Behaviors, 21*, 615–632.

Jang, S. J., & Smith, C. A. (1997). A test of reciprocal causal relationships among parental supervision, affective ties, and delinquency. *Journal of Research in Crime and Delinquency, 34*, 307–336.

Kandel, D. B., & Wu, P. (1995). Disentangling mother-child effects in the development of antisocial behavior. In J. McCord (Ed.), *Coercion and punishment in long term perspectives* (pp.106–123). New York: Cambridge University Press.

Kerr, M., & Stattin, H. (2000). What parents know, how they know it, and several forms of adolescent adjustment: Further support for a reinterpretation of monitoring. *Developmental Psychology, 36*, 366–380.

Kerr, M., & Stattin, H. (2003). Parenting of adolescents: Action or reaction? In A. C. Crouter & A. Booth (Eds.), *Children's influence on family dynamics: The neglected side of family relationships* (pp.121–151). Mahwah, NJ: Erlbaum.

Kerr, M., Stattin, H., & Pakalniskiene, V. (in press). What do parents do when faced with adolescent problem behavior? In J. Coleman, M. Kerr., & S. Stattin (Eds.), *Parenting of Adolescents*. London: Wiley.

Kerr, M., Stattin, H., & Trost, K. (1999). To know you is to trust you: Parents' trust is rooted in child disclosure of information. *Journal of Adolescence, 22*, 737–752.

Kochanska, G. (1998). Mother-child relationship, child fearfulness, and emerging attachment: A short-term longitudinal study. *Developmental Psychology, 34*, 480–490.

Laird, R. D., Pettit, G. S., Bates, J. E., & Dodge, K. A. (2003). Parents' monitoring-relevant knowledge and adolescents' delinquent behavior: Evidence of correlated developmental changes and reciprocal influences. *Child Development, 74*, 752–768.

Marshall, S. K., Tilton-Weaver, L. C., & Bosdet, L. (2005). Information management: Considering adolescents' regulation of parental knowledge, *Journal of Adolescence, 28*, 633–647.

Mink, I. T., & Nihira, K. (1986). Family life-styles and child behaviors: A study of direction of effects. *Developmental Psychology, 22*, 610–616.

Mulhern, R. K., Jr., & Passman, R. H. (1981). Parental discipline as affected by the sex of the parent, the sex of the child, and the child's apparent responsiveness to discipline. *Developmental Psychology, 17*, 604–613.

Passman, R. H., & Blackwelder, D. E. (1981). Rewarding and punishing by mothers: The influence of progressive changes in the quality of their sons' apparent behavior. *Developmental Psychology, 17*, 614–619.

Patterson, G. R., Bank, L., & Stoolmiller, M. (1990). The preadolescent's contributions to disrupted family process. In R. Montemayor, G. R. Adams, & T. P. Gullotta (Eds.), *From childhood to Adolescence: A transactional period?* (pp. 107–133). Newbury Park, CA: Sage.

Patterson, G. R., Loeber, R., Stouthamer-Loeber, M., & Dishion, T. J. (1983). "A process model for the study of antisocial behaviors in children." Manuscript submitted for publication.

Patterson, G. R., Reid, J. B., & Dishion, T. J. (1992). *Antisocial boys.* Eugene, OR: Castalia.

Patterson, G. R., & Stouthamer-Loeber, M. (1984). The correlation of family management practices and delinquency. *Child Development, 55*, 1299–1307.

Read, A. W., et al. (Eds.) (1995). *The New International Webster's Comprehensive Dictionary of the English Language* (encyclopedic edition). Chicago, IL: Trident Press International.

Siebenbruner, J., Englund, M. M., Egeland, B., & Hudson, K. (2006). Developmental antecedents of late adolescence substance use patterns. *Development and Psychopathology, 18*, 551–571.

Smetana, J. G., Metzger, A., Gettman, D. C., & Campione-Barr, N. (2006). Disclosure and secrecy in adolescent-parent relationships. *Child Development, 77*, 201–217.

Snyder, J., & Patterson, G. (1987). Family interaction and delinquent behavior. In H. C. Quay (Ed.), *Handbook of juvenile delinquency* (pp. 216–243). New York: Wiley.

Soenens, B., Vansteenkiste, M., Luyckx, K., & Goossens, L. (2006). Parenting and adolescent problem behavior: An integrated model with adolescent self-disclosure and perceived parental knowledge as intervening variables. *Developmental Psychology, 42*, 305–318.

Stattin, H., & Kerr, M. (2000). Parental monitoring: A reinterpretation. *Child Development, 71*, 1072–1085.

Stice, E., & Barrera, M., Jr. (1995). A longitudinal examination of the reciprocal relations between perceived parenting and adolescents' substance use and externalizing behaviors. *Developmental Psychology, 31*, 322–334.

Stouthamer-Loeber, M., Patterson, G. R., & Loeber, R. (1982). "Parental monitoring and antisocial behavior in boys." Manuscript submitted for publication.

Waizenhofer, R. N., Buchanan, C. M., & Jackson-Newsom, J. (2004). Mothers' and fathers' knowledge of adolescents' daily activities: Its sources and its links with adolescent adjustment. *Journal of Family Psychology, 18,* 348–360.

Weintraub, K. J., & Gold, M. (1991). Monitoring and delinquency. *Criminal Behavior and Mental Health, 1,* 268–281.

Developmental and Interactional Antecedents of Monitoring in Early Adolescence

ROBERT D. LAIRD, MATTHEW M. MARRERO,
JENNIFER K. SHERWOOD

For much of the past century, scientists from a number of disciplines have been describing and categorizing behaviors that parents engage in as they raise their children and adolescents. Numerous scholars have sought to determine whether these parenting behaviors are associated with developmental outcomes. In contrast, how parents come to engage in specific behaviors or why parents employ particular parenting techniques remains largely unexplored. Moreover, researchers have yet to identify general principles for describing optimal and less optimal shifts in parenting strategies as children become adolescents (Collins 1995; Cowan, Powell, & Cowan 1998). The purpose of this chapter is to begin to fill in the gaps in our understanding of the monitoring construct by focusing on developmental and interactional processes that have the potential to explain why and how some parents become and remain aware of their adolescents' whereabouts and activities while other parents do not.

The chapter begins with a brief discussion of how monitoring has been conceptualized and how the conceptualization informs our search for antecedents. The second section of the chapter focuses on developmental changes in monitoring and discusses how evidence of variability in developmental trajectories suggests that developmental change during middle adolescence, while common, is not universal or invariant. The next two sections of the chapter focus on antecedents of monitoring. In the third section, a heuristic model of developmental and interactional antecedents of monitoring will be presented and in the fourth section pilot data from the Baton Rouge Families and Teens Project (BRFTP) will be used to illustrate how the model can be used to guide and generate research. The final section of the chapter summarizes findings from the pilot data and suggests future directions for research.

What Is Monitoring?

Monitoring has been conceptualized traditionally as a parenting practice (Dishion & McMahon 1998). However, Kerr and Stattin (2000) noted a mismatch between the conceptual and operational definitions of monitoring in the majority of the studies in the literature. Specifically, although many researchers conceptualized monitoring as a parenting practice, the items that were commonly being used to measure the construct did not assess the behavior of parents. Rather, researchers were labeling measures of parents' knowledge of the adolescents' whereabouts and activities, or more often, adolescents' perceptions of their parents' knowledge, as parental monitoring. The widespread use of the knowledge measures is likely a result of their robust associations with problem behavior. Parents who are, or who are perceived by their adolescents to be, more knowledgeable of their adolescents' whereabouts and activities have adolescents who appear to be much better behaved than parents who are less knowledgeable. Specifically, more knowledge is associated with lower levels of conduct problems, violence, and delinquency (e.g., Kilgore, Snyder, & Lentz 2000; Luster & Oh 2001); drug, tobacco, and alcohol use (e.g., Cohen & Rice 1995; Fletcher, Darling, & Steinberg 1995; Wood et al. 2004); early initiation of sexual intercourse and risky sexual behavior (e.g., Capaldi et al. 2002; French & Dishion 2003; Jacobson & Crockett 2000); and poor school performance (e.g., Crouter et al. 1990; Shumow & Lomax 2002). Moreover, a low level of parental knowledge generalizes across European American, African American, and Latin American families as a risk factor for adolescent maladjustment (Forehand et al. 1997; Flannery et al. 1994; Fridrich & Flannery 1995; Kilgore, Snyder, & Lentz 2000; Shumow & Lowmax 2002).

Despite the strong and consistent evidence that well-adjusted adolescents describe their parents as knowledgeable, the knowledge that parents possess does not necessarily reflect parenting behavior. Nonetheless, based on the assumption that knowledge is obtained through parents' monitoring behaviors, parents have been encouraged to obtain information by asking questions and having and enforcing household rules as evidenced by the advice offered through the National Youth Anti-Drug Media Campaign's public service announcements (i.e., "The more you know") and Web page (www.theantidrug.com/advice/advice_monitor.asp). However, empirical work highlighting adolescents' willingness to disclose their whereabouts, companions, and activities as the primary contributor to both parental knowledge and adolescent behavioral adjustment has cast serious doubts as to the effectiveness of advice that emphasizes parental questioning and rule-setting (Kerr & Stattin 2000; Stattin & Kerr 2000).

Kerr and Stattin's (2000) work emphasized that what parents know and how parents obtain information are distinct, yet related, constructs, and reinforced the notion that the child should be viewed as an active participant in the monitoring process. This new framework focuses primarily on knowledge or information and emphasizes adolescents as information managers rather than parents as behavior monitors. Thus far, research indicates that adolescent disclosure of information appears to be the primary proximal source of parents' knowledge with additional information provided by parents' solicitation of information (from their children, teachers, and other parents), and family rules regarding how and where adolescents are expected to spend their time (Crouter, Bumpus et al. 2005; Crouter, Helms Erickson et al. 1999; Snyder & Patterson 1987; Stattin & Kerr 2000; Waizenhofer, Buchanan, & Jackson-Newsom 2004).

Positive parent-child relationships and effective family communication are likely to enhance the effectiveness of monitoring processes (Crouter & Head 2002; Dishion & McMahon 1998; Kerr, Stattin, & Trost 1999) and are associated with greater knowledge (Laird et al. 2003b). For example, although Stattin and Kerr (2000) conclude that child disclosure is the key proximal source of parents' knowledge; other results from their dataset indicate that such disclosure is predicated on a trusting and supportive parent-child relationship (Kerr, Stattin, & Trost 1999). Thus, consistent with Crouter and colleagues' (1990) broad conceptualization of monitoring, parental knowledge is considered in this chapter to be the outcome of a long-term, relationship-based process which requires both parents and adolescents as active participants. Moreover, this broad perspective views monitoring as an element of the family culture as expressed through parental attention and awareness of children's interests and activities as well as an implicit or explicit family philosophy regarding children and adolescents. This broad conceptualization is particularly appropriate in the quest for antecedents of monitoring because it provides a framework to consider both proximal antecedents to parents' knowledge such as adolescent disclosure, family rules, and parental solicitation, as well as more distal antecedents such as the child's behavior, the quality of the parent-child relationship, and parent and adolescent expectations for behavioral autonomy. A heuristic model of antecedents of monitoring will be presented after a review of evidence documenting developmental change and variability in parent's knowledge.

How Does Parents' Knowledge Change from Early to Late Adolescence?

Although common depictions of adolescence as a time of "storm and stress" appear to be exaggerations, adolescence is a period of great transition both for individuals and for their families (Arnett 1999; Hamburg 1974, 1985). The families' transition from childhood to adolescence brings with it a new set of issues and concerns for parents (Pasley & Gecas 1984; Small, Eastman, & Cornelius 1988), as parents approach midlife and the parent-child relationship becomes more egalitarian (Baumrind 1991; Steinberg & Steinberg 1994). Although social scientists have made considerable progress in understanding how individuals make the transition to adolescence and in understanding effective family relationships and interactions during adolescence, little progress has been made in terms of understanding how the transition from childhood to adolescence affects parenting and the parent-child relationship (Steinberg & Silk 2002).

Studies using both longitudinal and cross-sectional designs have identified reductions in monitoring-relevant knowledge during the childhood-to-adolescence transition (Barber, Maughan, & Olsen 2003; Bogenschneider et al. 1998; Frick, Christian, & Wooton 1999; Patterson & Stouthamer-Loeber 1984) and from early to later adolescence (Laird et al. 2003a), although some studies have found that reductions in knowledge were limited to boys (e.g., Laird et al. 2003a) or to parent reports (e.g., Barber, Maughan, & Olsen 2003). As an illustration of the developmental reductions in knowledge, Panel A of figure 2.1 shows the mean levels of knowledge reported by adolescents participating in the Child Development Project (CDP) from ages 12 to 16 (see

Laird et al. 2003a, 2003b, for more information on these variables and their developmental trajectories). Inspection of the means shows a modest decline in knowledge over time. Panel B of figure 2.1 adds a line obtained from a growth curve model fitted to the data. Once again, inspection of the mean growth curve shows a modest decline in knowledge over time.

Many studies of parenting or family relationship transformations focus extensively or exclusively on normative patterns of change (i.e., compared mean scores at different ages) and report data similar to that shown in Panels A and B of figure 2.1. However, these data do not provide evidence of individual differences in rates or directions of change and imply that there are no individual differences in rates or patterns of development or that those differences are not important. The few studies that have analyzed data to evaluate individual differences in growth rates have found significant variation in developmental trajectories of adolescent-reported knowledge (Laird et al. 2003b), parent-reported monitoring knowledge and behavior (Pettit et al. 2007), and the related concept of unsupervised wandering (Stoolmiller 1994). To illustrate variability in individual growth curves, the solid line in Panel C of figure 2.1 shows the mean rate of change (i.e., the growth curve line from Panel B) with dotted lines added to illustrate

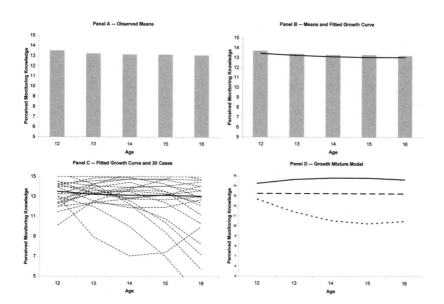

Figure 2.1   Knowledge growth curve trajectories

the variability in the trajectories found in a randomly selected subsample of 20 adolescents. This panel shows that the modest normative decrease in knowledge is not reported by all adolescents. Some report dramatic decreases in knowledge while others report stability or increases. Presumably, a substantial portion of the variability reflects true change in knowledge and not just measurement error. Predictors of growth trajectory components can be added to the growth curve models to capture some of the variability. For example, adolescent sex accounts for some of the variability in the knowledge trajectories as knowledge decreases significantly among boys but not girls (see Laird et al. 2003a: fig. 1).

An alternative approach to identifying variability in developmental trajectories is through growth mixture modeling. Growth mixture modeling differs from growth curve modeling in that it does not assume that individuals are drawn from a single population and instead allows subclasses of individuals to vary around different mean growth curves (Muthén 2004). SAS PROC TRAJ (Jones, Nagin, & Roeder 2001) was used to fit a growth mixture model to the CDP knowledge data. Models were fit specifying 2, 3, 4, and 5 group solutions with combinations of stable, linear, and quadratic shapes as recommended by Jones, Nagin, & Roeder (2001). A 3 group model with quadratic, stable, and quadratic terms for the three groups, respectively, provided the best fit to the data as shown in Panel D of figure 2.1. This panel shows that most of the sample (60.2%) fits best in the subclass characterized by stable levels of knowledge (the middle line), with other subclasses characterized by high and increasing levels of knowledge (24.1%) or by low levels of knowledge that decline over time (15.8%). Different conclusions may be drawn from the various ways the data are presented in these figures. Inspection of yearly means and the fitted mean growth curve with less attention paid to variability in growth curves may lead to the conclusion that knowledge decreases slowly across adolescence, whereas the growth mixture model may lead to the conclusion that knowledge is stable for most families with low levels and reductions over time characteristic of a small subset of families.

Both growth curve modeling and growth mixture modeling approaches identify individual differences in developmental trajectories. The identification of substantial variability in developmental trajectories, whether through attention to variation in growth curve components or growth mixture modeling, has great practical and theoretical importance because it is the variability (rather than the normative decreases) which indicates that individual and family-level processes may be responsible for change in knowledge. In other words, mean-level developmental differences provide evidence of universal *developmental processes* that are closely tied to maturation (i.e., chronological or pubertal age). Interfamily variability in developmental trajectories provides evidence that individual differences in antecedent *interpersonal processes* may underlie transformations in knowledge within individual families. Across the different analyses, the data show modest declines in perceived knowledge combined with substantial individual differences, suggesting that perceived knowledge, and monitoring more generally, are developmentally relevant phenomena. Change in perceived knowledge has been linked to a specific developmental period— in this case, mid- to late adolescence—although change in other periods has not been explored. The evidence that knowledge declines, and more importantly, that there is variability in the onset and rate of decline, indicates that it is appropriate to ask why and how perceived knowledge, or the processes that result in knowledge, change over time across and within families.

Why Are Some Parents More Knowledgeable Than Others?

Our interactional model of processes underlying monitoring was influenced by Belsky's (1984) model of determinants of parenting and by Collins's (1995) model of family adaptation to individual change. Figure 2.2 outlines the hypothesized processes. Solid lines indicate primary process pathways whereas dotted lines depict relations that are hypothesized to be mediated (partially or fully) through the primary pathways. Developmental and behavioral catalysts are expected to influence monitoring knowledge indirectly by influencing parent-adolescent relationship processes. Likewise, relationship processes are expected to influence parental knowledge through specific monitoring processes. Parent attributes and contextual factors are expected to have a direct influence on most components of the model and are expected to moderate associations among different components of the model. Catalysts, and relationship and monitoring processes, are hypothesized to predict behavior problems, but effects are hypothesized to be primarily indirect and ultimately mediated through knowledge. In a transactional manner, behavior problems are hypothesized to feed back into the system as catalysts for the next sequence of interactions.

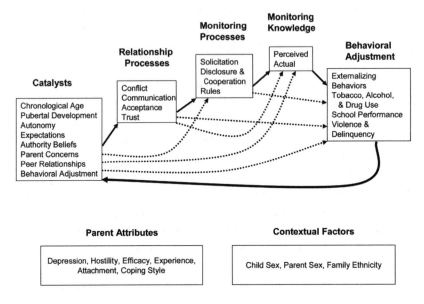

Figure 2.2   Interactional model of processes underlying monitoring

Collins (1995) identified pubertal maturation, cognitive maturation, and intensified environmental stressors resulting from age-graded transitions and expectations as the three primary factors hypothesized to provide the impetus for change in parent-child relationships across the childhood to adolescence transition. These factors, along with additional factors particularly relevant to monitoring, are reflected in the *catalysts* included in the model. Monitoring knowledge is expected to decrease as a function of chronological age and pubertal development in part because increased parent-adolescent conflict during early adolescence is expected to disrupt the monitoring processes (Holmbeck 1996; Laursen, Coy, & Collins 1998; Paikoff & Brooks-Gunn 1991). Increased parent-adolescent conflict is anticipated when parents and adolescents hold different expectations for autonomy (e.g., the adolescent expects greater freedom and the parent anticipates increased vigilance; Dekovic, Noom, & Meeus 1997). Mismatches in autonomy expectations are highest during early adolescence (Collins et al. 1997). Likewise, discrepancies in child and parent beliefs of the appropriateness of parental authority are expected to antecede reductions in monitoring knowledge. Smetana (1988, 2000) has found that parents and adolescents differ in their beliefs of the legitimacy of parental authority over personal behaviors (e.g., clothing choices) and that the discrepancies increase in early adolescence. Parents who believe they have authority over these issues are likely to exert more control and engage in more solicitation and rule setting. But when adolescents believe that parental control efforts are illegitimate, there is more parent-adolescent conflict (Bosma et al. 1996), and the adolescents are likely to resist control efforts by undermining parents' monitoring attempts or by attempting to convince parents to modify their parenting behavior. Adolescents' behavioral adjustment and peer relationships also are expected to influence monitoring knowledge through relationship and monitoring processes. High levels and increases in externalizing behavior problems have been shown to predict low levels and decreases in monitoring knowledge (Laird et al. 2003a), with the association partially mediated by the quality of the parent-child relationship and by adolescents' authority beliefs (Laird et al. 2003b). Antisocial peer involvement also has been linked to reductions in monitoring knowledge (Laird et al. 2009). Although antisocial peer involvement may initially increase parental concern and solicitation (which would presumably increase knowledge), affiliation with antisocial friends is also likely to increase parent-adolescent conflict and reduce adolescent disclosure (which decreases knowledge). In contrast, supportive friendships with well-adjusted peers may improve or maintain positive parent-adolescent relationships and lead to more monitoring knowledge.

The catalysts are hypothesized to influence monitoring knowledge primarily through their influence on the parent-adolescent *relationship processes*. As noted above, recent conceptualizations of the monitoring process have emphasized the role of the parent-adolescent relationship (Crouter & Head 2002; Dishion & McMahon 1998; Stattin & Kerr 2000). A positive parent-adolescent relationship motivates parents to stay informed (Dishion & McMahon), provides opportunities for parents to inquire about the adolescents' activities, and creates a context within which the adolescent can disclose to the parent (Kerr, Stattin, & Trost 1999; Stattin & Kerr). In contrast, relationships characterized by distrust and conflict make it difficult for parents to stay informed. Distrust may lead to greater parental solicitation (i.e., questioning), but adolescents who are not trusted may be less likely to disclose truthfully and more likely to actively deceive their parents and fail to follow family rules.

These relationship processes are hypothesized to link the catalysts to specific *monitoring processes*. Building on Stattin and Kerr's (2000) work, *monitoring knowledge* is hypothesized to be determined by parents' solicitation of information from their adolescents and other individuals (e.g., siblings, spouse, other parents), adolescents' willingness to disclose information and cooperate in monitoring situations, and family rules. It is possible that these processes are differentially influenced by the catalysts and the parent-child relationship. Specifically, the amount of solicitation may be more strongly predicted by parents' concerns (i.e., behavior problems) and beliefs about adolescence. It is also possible that changes in the catalysts and the parent-child relationship will result in changes in the individuals from whom parents seek information about their adolescents' activities and associates (i.e., concerned parents may be more likely to seek information from other parents). The amount of child disclosure may be more strongly linked to close and trusting parent-adolescent relationships. Parent-adolescent communication may contribute to parental knowledge above and beyond specific monitoring processes (Crouter & Head 2002); therefore, the model contains an additional direct link between relationship processes and monitoring knowledge. Consistent with a number of previous studies (see Crouter & Head 2002), both adolescent and parent perceptions of knowledge as well as parents' actual knowledge are expected to predict behavioral adjustment.

Parent attributes may moderate the influence of the catalysts (e.g., depressed parents are expected to be less influenced by pubertal changes). However, parent attributes are hypothesized to directly influence the parent-adolescent relationship and to have both direct and indirect influences on the monitoring processes (e.g., depression is linked to lower levels of knowledge; Patterson et al. 1992). Well-adjusted parents are expected to be able to maintain more positive relationships and engage more effectively in monitoring processes. In contrast, depressed, hostile, or insecure parents may have difficulty maintaining a positive relationship and may respond to adolescent disclosure of misbehavior with either harsh punishments or disinterest, either of which may discourage future disclosure. Parents with older children may be able to parent more effectively during the child-to-adolescent transition with subsequent children (Whiteman, McHale, & Crouter 2003). Parents who cope with distress using task-oriented strategies may be more likely to solicit information when concerned, whereas those who typically cope through emotion- or avoidance-oriented strategies may be more likely to disengage from the monitoring process when the adolescent misbehaves or when solicitation results in conflict. Overall, parent attributes are expected to contribute to the monitoring processes primarily by moderating parents' responses to the catalysts and by influencing the quality of the relationship and monitoring processes.

A number of *contextual factors* have been found to be associated with parental knowledge. Specifically, greater knowledge is reported by mothers than by fathers (e.g., Bumpus, Crouter, & McHale 2001; Crouter et al. 1990), by parents of daughters than by parents of sons (Laird et al. 2003a; Pettit et al. 2001), by parents with more rather than less education (e.g., Crouter et al. 1999; Pettit et al. 2001), and by individuals living in two-parent homes as compared to single-parent homes (Pettit et al.). On the other hand, ethnic group differences in knowledge typically are modest and not statistically significant (Dishion & McMahon 1998; Forehand et al. 1997; Fridrich & Flannery 1995; Shumow & Lomax 2002). It is unknown whether the contextual factors moderate the processes specified by the model or whether the influence of the contextual factors is limited to producing mean-level differences in the indicators of the various processes.

In summary, a sequential mediation model is proposed linking developmental catalysts, relationship processes, and monitoring processes with knowledge. Parent attributes and contextual factors are expected to moderate associations. Developmental catalysts, relationship processes, and monitoring processes are expected to be linked to behavioral adjustment indirectly through parental knowledge.

Example of Research Questions and Analyses Guided by the Model

This section illustrates how the heuristic model can be used to frame questions about monitoring and the monitoring process. The research described in this section rests on the foundation that there is a bidirectional association between parents' knowledge of their adolescents' whereabouts and activities and the adolescents' behavior problems (see Laird et al. 2003a). However, as noted above, most of the research in this area has focused on one direction—from knowledge to behavior problems—and numerous studies have reported that greater knowledge is associated with fewer behavior problems (for a review, see Crouter & Head 2002). Interpretations typically emphasize parent agency or the idea that parents are doing something—either monitoring or responding to information they obtain—that functions to prevent or inhibit behavior problems. If this is the case, then it seems reasonable to think that increases in behavior problems would be associated with increases in knowledge or, if not knowledge, at least efforts to obtain information. However, this is not what is typically found. Several studies have found that increases in behavior problems are linked to subsequent decreases in knowledge (Jang & Smith 1997; Kandel & Wu 1995; Laird et al. 2003a). This leads us to wonder "Why do behavior problems forecast reductions rather than increases in knowledge?"

We can use the heuristic model to speculate on the interpersonal processes that may result in the knowledge reduction. Given that the small pilot sample limits our ability to test interactions, we will focus on the process depicted in the top portion of figure 2.2 and not consider parent attributes and contextual factors further in this chapter. According to the model, behavior problems are hypothesized to lead to a reduction in parents' knowledge by undermining the quality of the parent-child relationship. As the parent-child relationship is weakened, adolescents are hypothesized to become reluctant to disclose information and participate in the monitoring process, and parents are hypothesized to reduce their efforts directed toward obtaining information. In the terminology of the heuristic model, behavior problems function as catalysts, and the association between behavior problems and knowledge is mediated by the quality of the parent-child relationship and by the monitoring processes.

Participants and Procedure

Pilot data from the Baton Rouge Families and Teens Project (BRFTP) were used to test the hypothesized relations. The BRFTP pilot sample includes 86 parent-child dyads (83 mother-child dyads and 3 father-child dyads) who were recruited from grades 6, 7, and 8. The sample is 59% female, and 52% of the adolescents live in a two-parent home. Forty-two percent of the adolescent are White, non-Hispanic, 52% are African American, 3.5% are Asian, and 2% are Hispanic.

Measures were derived from questionnaires administered verbally to the parents and adolescents during a visit to each family's home. Parents and adolescents were interviewed in separate parts of the home so that they could not hear one another's responses. Parents and adolescents were given a set of cards along with the possible responses for each set of items. The interviewers read the items and the adolescents responded by saying the appropriate number for their response. The primary advantages of the verbal assessment are very little missing data and the impact of illiteracy (the adult illiteracy rate in Louisiana is 28%; National Priorities Project 1999) was minimized. However, the verbal administration and responses likely biased responses toward greater social desirability. Only adolescent reports are presented in this chapter because only adolescents' self-reports of problem behavior are available and the primary analyses focus on mediators of problem behavior.

Measures

BEHAVIOR PROBLEMS

Externalizing and internalizing types of behavior problems were measured. As an assessment of externalizing problems, adolescents reported the frequency of their involvement in delinquent behavior using six delinquent behavior items (e.g., "In the last month, how many times did you steal from someone?") from the Problem Behavior Frequency Scale (Farrell et al. 2000). Each item was scored on a five-point scale from "never" (scored 0) to "7 or more times" (scored 4). The mean of the six delinquent behavior items was highly skewed, so it was dichotomized with 43% of the participants reporting some involvement in *delinquent behavior.*

As an assessment of internalizing problems, adolescents reported their *depressed mood* using six items (e.g., "In the last month, how often were you very sad?") from the Modified Depression Scale (Orpinas 1993). Each item was scored on a five-point scale from "never" (scored 0) to "always" (scored 4) and a depressed mood score was computed as the mean of the six items ($\alpha = .66$).

PARENT-ADOLESCENT RELATIONSHIP QUALITIES

Four aspects of the parent-child relationship were assessed. The parent-adolescent conflict measure weights the amount of negative affect by the frequency of conflict across 44 issues (Robin & Foster 1989). For each issue (e.g., telephone calls), adolescents reported whether the issue ever came up for discussion. If the issue did come up for discussion, adolescents reported how often the issue came up for discussion using a five-point scale (i.e., "once or twice " = 1 to "almost every day" = 5) and how hot or angry the discussions were using a five-point scale (i.e., from "calm" = 1 to "very angry" = 5). Frequency and anger scores were multiplied for each issue, and the mean of the scores across the 44 issues indexes parent-adolescent *conflict* ($\alpha = .82$).

Parent trust was measured with six items (e.g., "Does your mother trust that you will not hang out with bad people?") taken from Kerr, Stattin, and Trost (1999). Items were scored on a five-point scale from "absolutely not" (scored 0) to "completely" (scored 4). The parent *trust* score was computed as the mean of the six items ($\alpha = .80$).

Parent communication was measured with eight items (e.g., "How often do you tell your mother how you really feel about things?") also taken from Kerr, Stattin, and Trost (1999). Items were scored on a five-point scale from "never" (scored 0) to "always" (scored 4). The parent *communication* score was computed as the mean of the eight items ($\alpha = .82$).

Parental acceptance was measured using the 14 item (e.g., "Your mother is a parent who tells you that she loves you") Child Report of Parent Behavior Inventory acceptance scale (Schaefer 1965). Adolescents responded using a five-point scale from "not at all like her" (scored 0) to "a lot like her" (scored 4). The parental *acceptance* score was computed as the mean of the 14 items ($\alpha = .96$).

MONITORING PROCESSES AND KNOWLEDGE

Three monitoring processes described and tested by Stattin and Kerr (2000) were assessed using slight modifications of their items to make the items appropriate to the early adolescents. Modifications included changing items that asked about adolescents' activities at night to ask about the adolescents' free time. Parental solicitation was measured with five items (e.g., "During the past month, how often has your mother started a conversation with you about your free time?") scored on a six-point scale from "never" (scored 0) to "almost every day" (scored 5). The mean of the five items indexes parental *solicitation* ($\alpha = .68$). The child disclosure measured included eight items (e.g., "How often do you talk at home about how you are doing in different subjects in school") scored on the same six-point scale. The mean of the eight items indexes adolescent *disclosure* ($\alpha = .81$). Parental control was measured with eight items (e.g., "How often do you need to have your mother's permission to say out later than usual?") scored on a five-point scale from "never" (scored 0) to "always" (scored 4). The mean of the eight items indexes parental *control* ($\alpha = .73$).

A new measure of monitoring processes was developed for this study in an attempt to distinguish between the frequency of monitoring-relevant conversations and the initiation of such conversations. For each of seven topics common in the monitoring literature (i.e., what the adolescent is learning in school, grades, other things at school, spending money, friends, what the adolescent does with his/her friends, things that are really important to the adolescent), adolescents reported how often they talk about the topic using a six-point scale from "never" (scored 0) to "almost every day" (scored 5). Adolescents also reported who usually starts the conversation using a five-point scale (i.e., "always adolescent" = 0, "mostly adolescent" = 1, "both equally" = 2, "mostly parent" = 3, "always parent" = 4). A conversation *frequency* score was computed as the mean of the eight frequency items ($\alpha = .77$) and a conversation *initiation* score was computed as the mean of the eight initiation items ($\alpha = .76$).

We expanded the traditional measure of perceived knowledge (see Brown et al. 1993) to include ten items (i.e., "How much does your mother really know about who your friends are, where your friends live, where you go when you are not at home, how you spend your money, where you are most afternoons after school, who you are with when you are not at home, where you go at night, what you do with your free time, the names of your teachers, the names of your friends?"). Each item was scored on one of two five-point scales. Adolescents' responses to the first eight items ranged from "she doesn't know" (scored 0) to "she knows everything (scored 4). Responses to the final two items ranged from "never" (scored 0) to "always" (scored 4). A *perceived knowledge* score was computed as the mean of the ten items ($\alpha = 76$).

Analyses and Results

ANALYSIS PLAN

The analyses that follow examine individual paths in the model and then test for evidence of mediation. Analyses included bivariate correlations and multiple regressions. Point-biserial correlations and logistic regression were used to analyze delinquent behavior which had been dichotomized due to the high skew. Pearson product-moment correlations and ordinary least-squares (OLS) regression were used to analyze depressed mood.

Following Baron and Kenny's (1986) guidelines for testing mediation, we first tested for direct (i.e., non-mediated) effects between all variable domains. Specifically, we tested for a bivariate link between the independent variables (i.e., behavior problems) and the outcome (i.e., knowledge). Next, we tested the association between the independent variable(s) and the mediator(s) (i.e., monitoring and relationship processes) and, finally, to provide an estimate of indirect (i.e., mediated) effects, we tested the association between the independent variable(s) and the outcome controlling for the mediator(s). In the analyses that follow, evidence of mediation is provided by (a) a significant association between the independent variable(s) and the mediator(s), (b) a significant association between the mediator(s) and the outcome, and (c) by a reduction in the association between the independent variable(s) and the outcome after controlling for the mediator(s). As an index of the strength of mediation, we calculated, as a proportion, the reduction of the association between the independent variable and the outcome when controlling for the mediator(s).

DIRECT EFFECTS

Bivariate correlations are shown in table 2.1. Because we seek to understand the processes that link behavior problems with low levels of parents' knowledge, the first step was to determine whether the expected association between behavior problems and knowledge was found in this dataset. As anticipated, the delinquent behavior variable is negatively associated with knowledge: less knowledge was reported by adolescents in the group that reported some involvement in delinquent behavior. Adolescents reporting less knowledge also reported more depressed mood.

The next step was to examine associations between behavior problems and monitoring processes. These associations reflect the presumed indirect path from catalysts to monitoring processes in the heuristic model. Involvement in delinquent behavior is associated with less solicitation, disclosure, and frequency of monitoring-relevant conversations. Greater adolescent depressed mood also is associated with less solicitation, disclosure, control, and frequency of monitoring-relevant conversations.

TABLE 2.1

Bivariate correlations among behavior problems, relationship processes, monitoring processes, and monitoring knowledge

	1	2	3	4	5	6	7	8	9	10	11
1. Delinquent behavior											
2. Depressed mood	.42**										
3. Conflict	.29**	.36**									
4. Trust	-.36**	-.43**	-.41**								
5. Communication	-.25**	-.28**	-.47**	.63**							
6. Acceptance	-.43**	-.37**	-.46**	.67**	.69**						
7. Solicitation	-.25*	-.19	-.22*	.47**	.57**	.53**					
8. Disclosure	-.40**	-.40**	-.51**	.64**	.64**	.67**	.50**				
9. Control	-.17	-.26*	-.30**	.27*	.40**	.29**	.26*	.34**			
10. Conversation frequency	-.25*	-.22*	-.36**	.56**	.51**	.55**	.62**	.63**	.36**		
11. Conversation initiation	-.06	.02	.06	-.26*	-.13	-.04	.12	-.18	-.10	.01	
12. Perceived knowledge	-.39**	-.51**	-.57**	.65**	.53**	.57**	.46**	.64**	.53**	.57**	-.24*

Note: * $p < .05$, ** $p < .01$

Next, we examined associations between behavior problems and relationship qualities. These associations are the first link in the proposed mediation sequence. Involvement in delinquent behavior is associated with more conflict and with less trust, communication, and acceptance. Like delinquent behavior, greater teen depressed mood is associated with more conflict and less trust, communication, and acceptance. In sum, bivariate correlations provide evidence that delinquent behavior and a more depressed mood are associated with lower levels of knowledge, weaker monitoring processes, and poorer quality parent-adolescent relationships.

The next set of analyses focused on the associations between relationship qualities and monitoring processes. These associations form the second link in the proposed mediation sequence. Evidence relevant to this link is found in the multiple R when each monitoring process is regressed on the set of four relationship-quality scores. Relationship qualities are significantly associated with solicitation ($R = .60$, $p < .001$), disclosure ($R = .77$, $p < .001$, control ($R = .40$, $p < .001$), and frequency of monitoring-relevant conversations ($R = .62$, $p < .001$), but not with conversation initiation ($R = .32$, $p = .071$). Parent-adolescent communication was the only relationship quality to account for unique variance in parental solicitation and control. Trust was the only relationship quality to account for unique variance in monitoring conversations. Acceptance, conflict, trust, and communication all accounted for unique variance in child disclosure. Results indicate strong links between relationship qualities and monitoring processes.

The next set of analyses focused on the associations between monitoring processes and perceived knowledge. These associations form the final link in the proposed mediation sequence. Perceived knowledge was regressed on the set of five monitoring processes. The monitoring processes account for 57% ($p < .001$) of the variance in perceived knowledge. Disclosure, control, and conversation initiation accounted for unique portions of the variance. Note that more adolescent-initiated conversations are associated with greater knowledge.

MEDIATED EFFECTS

The next set of analyses tested the first mediation chain linking behavior problems and monitoring processes through relationship qualities. Each monitoring process was regressed on behavior problems before and after controlling for relationship qualities. The difference in the proportion of variance accounted for by behavior problems in the two analyses was computed as an index of mediation. Overall, substantial portions of the associations between delinquent behavior and the monitoring processes are mediated by the relationship qualities. Specifically, 95% of the association between delinquent behavior and solicitation is mediated by the relationship qualities; 94% of the association between delinquent behavior and disclosure is mediated by relationship qualities; and 100% of the association between delinquent behavior and conversation frequency is mediated by relationship qualities. Results were similar for depressed mood with 97% of the association with solicitation mediated, 97% of the association with disclosure mediated, and 74% of the association with conversation frequency mediated by relationship qualities.

The next set of analyses tested the second mediation chain linking relationship qualities to perceived knowledge through monitoring processes. Perceived knowledge was regressed on each relationship quality before and after controlling for the monitoring processes. Again, a substantial portion of the association between relationship qualities and perceived knowledge was mediated by the monitoring processes. Specifically, 82% of the association between conflict and perceived knowledge is mediated by the monitoring processes; 89% of the association between trust and perceived knowledge is mediated by the monitoring processes; 99% of the association between communication and perceived knowledge is mediated by the monitoring processes; and 95% of the association between acceptance and perceived knowledge is mediated by the monitoring processes. To determine whether findings differ for parent-driven and adolescent-driven monitoring processes, analyses were repeated after dividing the monitoring processes into adolescent-driven and parent-driven sets. Disclosure and conversation initiation comprised the adolescent-driven set, and solicitation and rules comprised the parent-driven set of monitoring processes. The adolescent-driven set mediated 75% (for conflict) to 92% (for communication) of the associations between the relationship qualities and perceived knowledge whereas the parent-driven set mediated 55% (for conflict) to 86% (for communication) of the associations. These analyses suggest that parent- and adolescent-driven monitoring processes appear to operate similarly within this model.

DOUBLE MEDIATION

The final set of analyses tested double mediation whereby the association between behavior problems and perceived knowledge is mediated by both relationship qualities and monitoring processes. Perceived knowledge was regressed on behavior problems before and after controlling for both the relationship qualities and monitoring processes variable sets. Again, there is strong evidence of mediation. Specifically, 96% of the association between delinquent behavior and perceived knowledge is mediated by the combination of relationship qualities and monitoring processes, and 91% of the association between depressed mood and perceived knowledge is likewise mediated by the combination of relationship qualities and monitoring processes.

Summary and Future Directions

The apparent relevance of monitoring to a broad range of problem behaviors and child outcomes has spurred researchers to focus extensively on the outcomes of monitoring. Much less attention has been devoted to antecedents of monitoring. In an attempt to provide direction in this area, this chapter focused on antecedents of parents' monitoring-relevant knowledge. Building on the frameworks offered by Kerr and Stattin (2000) and Crouter and colleagues (1990), a broad conceptualization of monitoring was emphasized. We argued that evidence of variability in developmental trajectories of parental knowledge provides a justification for considering interactional processes in addition to developmental processes as contributors to transformations in parenting and changes in parents' knowledge over the course of adolescence. A heuristic model was presented to provide a framework for considering a wide range of potential antecedent processes. Pilot data provides preliminary evidence consistent with the mediation processes incorporated into the model. Specifically, behavior problems in early adolescence were found to be associated with lower levels of knowledge, and these associations appear to be largely mediated by the parent-child relationship and specific monitoring processes.

Results from the analyses presented in this chapter reinforce the notion that monitoring is the outcome of a relationship-based process. Specifically, results indicate that parent-child relationship qualities are associated with adolescents' perceptions of their own and their parents' monitoring behaviors. When adolescents perceive that their parents are trusting and accepting and there is little parent-adolescent conflict, adolescents are more likely to disclose information to their parents and parents are more likely to obtain answers to their questions. In turn, when adolescents disclose and parents obtain answers, the adolescents perceive that their parents are more informed. Analyses suggest that the monitoring process and the outcome of monitoring processes may be strongly influenced by the quality of the parent-adolescent relationship. Longitudinal data is necessary to determine whether developmental changes in parent-child relationship qualities will be mirrored by developmental changes in monitoring processes and knowledge, and a larger sample size is necessary to test hypothesized interactions.

In addition to replicating these findings with a larger longitudinal dataset, future research guided by the model should consider a diverse set of interactional and developmental catalysts, begin to consider the relevance of parent attributes, and seek to understand how the basic interactional processes are moderated by context. A consideration of chronological (e.g., age) and biological (e.g., pubertal progression) time may help determine how knowledge and monitoring processes are influenced by development and the extent to which developmental influences are invariant. A consideration of individual differences in developmental expectations or authority beliefs, in contrast, may reveal one process through which contextual factors influence knowledge and monitoring processes, assuming that developmental expectations and authority beliefs vary across contexts. The diverse sample obtained in the pilot study provides preliminary evidence that the measures are reliable and valid across a range of families differing in demographic characteristics, but a larger sample would provide opportunities to more explicitly test whether demographic context changes fundamental interactional patterns or whether context helps to identify variations in the starting points for processes that are otherwise similar across variations in context.

Future research also should maintain an emphasis on understanding the transactional nature of many of the proposed interactional processes. For example, assuming that high levels of knowledge are protective and that adolescent disclosure is the primary source of parental knowledge, the question arises as to how might parents respond to their adolescent's disclosure of negative information (be it misbehavior of the adolescent, disagreement with parent's rules, or that a friend engages in undesirable behavior) in a manner that both guides the adolescent toward more desirable outcomes and encourages future disclosure. It is easy to imagine, for example, a scenario in which an adolescent reveals specific information, such as a romantic interest in a specific peer that leads to a parental response—perhaps discouraging the particular relationship or telling the child that they are too young to date. This may increase parent-child conflict and at least temporarily undermine the quality of the parent-child relationship and reduce child disclosure and open parent-child communication. If the parent and child had a supportive relationship before this interaction and if their relationship encourages communication and disclosure, it is possible that the agitated state will be short-lived and have little lasting impact. However, if the relationship was previously strained, or if the parent and child engage in a series of such conversations, the negative effects on the parent-child relationship, and on child disclosure, may cascade in such a way that parents loose access to information and the loss of communication further erodes the quality of the relationship. While the model presented in this chapter focuses on antecedents of monitoring, it continues to be important to learn why more knowledge is linked to better outcomes, and in doing so, research informs the antecedent model by identifying interactions that form the feedback loop between knowledge and future parent-adolescent interactions.

Greater attention to both parent and child perspectives on the factors that underlie and contribute to monitoring is also needed. Most studies have focused exclusively on adolescent perceptions of knowledge, and this may have biased our understanding of the construct. Moreover, when parent and child perspectives have been obtained, they typically have been tested in parallel, combined, or contrasted with one another. None of these approaches makes the best use of data from multiple informants who provide meaningfully different perspectives. Recent advances in statistical and methodological approaches to analyzing data from multiple informants should be used to take full advantage of the different perspectives. Furthermore, these new approaches may help to determine when processes are influenced by the differences in perspective. For example, we propose that differences in autonomy expectations will serve as a catalyst. However, measuring differences in autonomy expectations using traditional methods, such as difference scores, is problematic. Advanced methods are needed to model parent and adolescent levels and differences simultaneously as predictors of downstream processes as conceptualized in the model.

In sum, this chapter emphasizes the need to understand antecedents of monitoring and provides a heuristic model to guide the initial phases of this research. The model is innovative because it draws from several formerly distinct lines of research to specify interactional and developmental processes underlying monitoring. Moreover, the extensive focus on process and, in particular, the processes through which adolescents influence the parenting they receive, represents the forefront of contemporary parenting research in general, and of research on monitoring, in particular. The model and analyses presented in this chapter suggest that efforts to improve adolescent well-being should consider monitoring to be an element of, and contributor to, the quality of the parent-child relationship. Interventions focused too narrowly on encouraging monitoring behavior, without regard to the quality or history of the parent-child relationship or to the developmental issues faced by the family, are likely to be ineffective and unlikely to reduce adolescent involvement in problem behavior.

Note

The research described in this chapter was supported by grants from the Louisiana Board of Regents Support Fund (LEQSF-RD-A-02) and National Science Foundation (BCS 0517980) to R. D. Laird. Manuscript approved for publication by the Director of the Louisiana Agricultural Experiment Station as manuscript 06–36–0643. Robert Laird and Matthew Marrero are now at the University of New Orleans.

Arnett, J. J. (1999). Adolescent storm and stress, reconsidered. *American Psychologist, 54,* 317–326.

Barber, B. K., Maughan, S. L., & Olsen, J. A. (2003). Patterns and predictors of parenting across adolescence. In J. G. Smetana (Chair), *Changing boundaries of parental authority during adolescence: Developmental and cultural variations.* Symposium presented at the biennial meeting of the Society for Research in Child Development, Tampa, FL.

Baron, R. M., & Kenny, D. A. (1986). The moderator mediator variable distinction in social psychological research: Conceptual, strategic, and statistical considerations. *Journal of Personality and Social Psychology, 51,* 1173–1182.

Baumrind, D. (1991). Effective parenting during the early adolescent transition. In P. A. Cowan & E. M. Hetherington (Eds.), *Family Transitions* (pp. 111–163). Hillsdale, NJ: Erlbaum.

Belsky, J. (1984). The determinants of parenting: A process model. *Child Development, 55*, 83–96.

Bogenschneider, K., Wu, M-y., Raffaelli, M., & Tsay, J. C. (1998). Parent influences on adolescent peer orientation and substance use: The interface of parenting practices and values. *Child Development, 69*, 1672–1688.

Bosma, H. A., Jackson, S. E., Zijsling, D. H., Zani, B., Ciognani, E., Xerri, M. L., et al. (1996). Who has the final say? Decisions on adolescent behavior within the family. *Journal of Adolescence, 19*, 277–291.

Brown, B. B., Mounts, N., Lamborn, S. D., & Steinberg, L. (1993). Parenting practices and peer group affiliation in adolescence. *Child Development, 64*, 467–482.

Bumpus, M. F., Crouter, A. C., & McHale, S. M. (2001). Parental autonomy granting during adolescence: Exploring gender differences in context. *Developmental Psychology, 37*, 163–173.

Capaldi, D. M., Stoolmiller, M., Clark, S., & Owen, L. D. (2002). Heterosexual risk behaviors in at-risk young men from early adolescence to young adulthood: Prevalence, prediction, and association with STD contraction. *Developmental Psychology, 38*, 394–406.

Cohen, D. A., & Rice, J. C. (1995). A parent-targeted intervention for adolescent substance use prevention: Lessons learned. *Evaluation Review, 19*, 159–180.

Collins, W. A. (1995). Relationships and development: Family adaptation to individual change. In S. Shulman (Ed.), *Close relationships and socioemotional development* (pp. 128–154). Westport, CT: Ablex.

Collins, W. A., Laursen, B., Mortensen, N., Luebker, C., & Ferreira, M. (1997). Conflict processes and transitions in parent and peer relationships: Implications for autonomy and regulation. *Journal of Adolescent Research, 12*, 178–198.

Cowan, P. A., Powell, D., & Cowan, C. P. (1998). Parenting interventions: A family systems perspective. In W. Damon, I. E. Sigel, & K. A. Renninger (Eds.), *Handbook of child psychology: Vol. 4, Child psychology in practice* (5th ed., pp. 3–72). New York: Wiley.

Crouter, A. C., Bumpus, M. F., Davis, K. D., & McHale, S. M. (2005). How do parents learn about adolescents' experiences? Implications for parental knowledge and adolescent risky behavior. *Child Development, 76*, 869–882.

Crouter, A. C., & Head, M. R. (2002). Parental monitoring and knowledge of children. In M. H. Bornstein (Ed.), *Handbook of parenting, 2nd ed., vol. 3: Being and becoming a parent* (pp. 461–483). Mahwah, NJ: Erlbaum.

Crouter, A. C., Helms Erickson, H., Updegraff, K., & McHale, S. M. (1999). Conditions underlying parents' knowledge about children's daily lives in middle childhood: Between- and within-family comparisons. *Child Development, 70*, 246–259.

Crouter, A. C., MacDermid, S. M., McHale, S. M., & Perry Jenkins, M. (1990). Parental monitoring and perceptions of children's school performance and conduct in dual- and single-earner families. *Developmental Psychology, 26*, 649–657.

Dekovic, M., Noom, M. J., & Meeus, W. (1997). Expectations regarding development during adolescence: Parental and adolescent perceptions. *Journal of Youth and Adolescence, 26*, 253–272.

Dishion, T. J., & McMahon, R. J. (1998). Parental monitoring and the prevention of child and adolescent problem behavior: A conceptual and empirical formulation. *Clinical Child and Family Psychology Review, 1*, 61–75.

Farrell, A. D., Kung, E. M., White, K. S., & Valois, R. F. (2000). The structure of self-reported aggression, drug use, and delinquent behaviors during early adolescence. *Journal of Clinical Child Psychology, 29*, 282–292.

Flannery, D. J., Vazsonyi, A. T., Torquati, J., & Fridrich, A. (1994). Ethnic and gender differences in risk for early adolescent substance use. *Journal of Youth and Adolescence, 23*, 195–213.

Fletcher, A. C., Darling, N., & Steinberg, L. (1995). Parental monitoring and peer influences on adolescent substance use. In J. McCord (Ed.), *Coercion and punishment in long-term perspectives* (pp. 259–271). New York: Cambridge University Press.

Forehand, R., Miller, K. S., Dutra, R., & Chance, M. W. (1997). Role of parenting in adolescent deviant behavior: Replication across and within two ethnic groups. *Journal of Consulting and Clinical Psychology, 65*, 1036–1041.

French, D. C., & Dishion, T. (2003). Predictors of early initiation of sexual intercourse among high-risk adolescents. *Journal of Early Adolescence, 23*, 295–315.

Frick, P. J., Christian, R. E., & Wooton, J. M. (1999). Age trends in association between parenting practices and conduct problems. *Behavior Modification, 23*, 106–128.

Fridrich, A. H., & Flannery, D. J. (1995). The effects of ethnicity and acculturation on early adolescent delinquency. *Journal of Child and Family Studies, 4*, 69–87.

Hamburg, B. A. (1974). Early adolescence: A specific and stressful stage of the life cycle. In G. V. Coelho, D. A. Hamburg, & J. A. Adams (Eds.), *Coping and adaptations* (pp. 101–124). New York: Basic Books.

Hamburg, B. A. (1985). Early adolescence: A time of transition and stress. *Early Adolescence, 78*, 158–167.

Holmbeck, G. N. (1996). A model of family relational transformations during the transition to adolescence: Parent-adolescent conflict and adaptation. In J. A.

Graber & J. Brooks-Gunn (Eds.), *Transitions through adolescence: Interpersonal domains and context* (pp. 167–199). Mahwah, NJ: Erlbaum.

Jacobson, K. C., & Crockett, L. J. (2000). Parental monitoring and adolescent adjustment: An ecological perspective. *Journal of Research on Adolescence, 10,* 65–97.

Jang, S. J., & Smith, C. A. (1997). A test of reciprocal causal relationships among parental supervision, affective ties, and delinquency. *Journal of Research in Crime and Delinquency, 34,* 307–336.

Jones, B. L., Nagin, D. S., & Roeder, K. (2001). A SAS procedure based on mixture models for estimating developmental trajectories. *Sociological Methods and Research, 29,* 374–393.

Kandel, D. B., & Wu, P. (1995). Disentangling mother-child effects in the development of antisocial behavior. In J. McCord (Ed.), *Coercion and punishment in long term perspectives* (pp. 106–123). New York: Cambridge University Press.

Kerr, M., & Stattin, H. (2000). What parents know, how they know it, and several forms of adolescent adjustment: Further support for a reinterpretation of monitoring. *Developmental Psychology, 36,* 366–380.

Kerr, M., Stattin, H., & Trost, K. (1999). To know you is to trust you: Parents' trust is rooted in child disclosure of information. *Journal of Adolescence, 22,* 737–752.

Kilgore, K., Snyder, J., & Lentz, C. (2000). The contribution of parental discipline, parental monitoring, and school risk to early-onset conduct problems in African American boys and girls. *Developmental Psychology, 36,* 835–845.

Laird, R. D., Criss, M. M., Pettit, G. S., Bates, J. E., & Dodge, K. A. (2009). Developmental trajectories and antecedents of distal parental supervision. *Journal of Early Adolescence, 29,* 258–284.

Laird, R. D., Pettit, G. S., Bates, J. E., & Dodge, K. A. (2003a). Parents' monitoring-relevant knowledge and adolescents' delinquent behavior: Evidence of correlated developmental changes and reciprocal influences. *Child Development, 74,* 752–768.

Laird, R. D., Pettit, G. S., Dodge, K. A., & Bates, J. E. (2003b). Change in parents' monitoring-relevant knowledge: Links with parenting, relationship quality, adolescent beliefs, and antisocial behavior. *Social Development, 12,* 401–419.

Laursen, B., Coy, K. C., & Collins, W. A. (1998). Reconsidering changes in parent-child conflict across adolescence: A meta-analysis. *Child Development, 69,* 817–832.

Luster, T., & Oh, S. M. (2001). Correlates of male adolescents carrying handguns among their peers. *Journal of Marriage and Family, 63,* 714–726.

Muthén, B. (2004). Latent variable analysis: Growth mixture modeling and related techniques for longitudinal data. In K. Kaplan (Ed.,), *Handbook of quantitative methodology for the social sciences* (pp. 345–368). Newbury Park, CA: Sage.

National Priorities Project. (1999). The state of the states: Louisiana 2000, *Grassroots Factbook* (vol. 3). Available from the National Priorities Project Web site, www.natprior.org.

Orpinas, P. (1993). Skills training and social influences for violence prevention in middle schools: A curriculum evaluation. Unpublished doctoral dissertation, University of Texas, Austin.

Paikoff, R. L., & Brooks Gunn, J. (1991). Do parent-child relationships change during puberty? *Psychological Bulletin, 110,* 47–66.

Pasley, K., & Gecas, V. (1984). Stresses and satisfactions of the parental role. *Personnel and Guidance Journal, 2,* 400–404.

Patterson, C. J., Griesler, P. C., Vaden, N. A., & Kupersmidt, J. B. (1992). Family economic circumstances, life transitions, and children's peer relations. In R. D. Parke & G. W. Ladd (Eds.), *Family peer relationships: Modes of linkage* (pp. 385–424). Mahwah, NJ: Erlbaum.

Patterson, G. R., & Stouthamer-Loeber, M. (1984). The correlation of family management practices and delinquency. *Child Development, 55,* 1299–1307.

Pettit, G. S., Keiley, M. K., Laird, R. D., Bates, J. E., & Dodge, K. A. (2007). Predicting the developmental course of mother-reported monitoring across childhood and adolescence from early proactive parenting, child temperament, and parents' worries. *Journal of Family Psychology, 21,* 206–217.

Pettit, G. S., Laird, R. D., Dodge, K. A., Bates, J. E., & Criss, M. M. (2001). Antecedents and behavior-problem outcomes of parental monitoring and psychological control in early adolescence. *Child Development, 72,* 583–598.

Robin, A. L., & Foster, S. L. (1989). Negotiating parent-adolescent conflict: A behavioral-family systems approach. New York: Guilford Press.

Schaefer, E. S. (1965). Children's reports of parental behavior: An inventory. *Child Development, 36,* 413–424.

Shumow, L., & Lomax, R. (2002). Parental efficacy: Predictor of parenting behavior and adolescent outcomes. *Parenting: Science and Practice, 2,* 127–150.

Small, S. A., Eastman, G., & Cornelius, S. (1988). Adolescent autonomy and parental stress. *Journal of Youth and Adolescence, 17,* 377–391.

Smetana, J. G. (1988). Concepts of self and social convention: Adolescents' and parents' reasoning about hypothetical and actual family conflicts. In M. R. Gunnar (Ed.), *Development during the transition to adolescence: Minnesota Symposia on Child Psychology, vol. 21* (pp. 79–122). Mahwah, NJ: Erlbaum.

Smetana, J. G. (2000). Middle-class African American adolescents' and parents' conceptions of parental authority and parenting practices: A longitudinal investigation. *Child Development, 71,* 1672–1686.

Snyder, J. & Patterson, G. (1987). Family interaction and delinquent behavior. In H. C. Quay (Ed.), *Handbook of juvenile delinquency* (pp. 216–243). New York: Wiley.

Stattin, H., & Kerr, M. (2000). Parental monitoring: A reinterpretation. *Child Development, 71,* 1072–1085.

Steinberg, L., & Silk, J. S. (2002). Parenting adolescents. In M. H. Bornstein (Ed.), *(2002), Handbook of parenting: vol. 1: Children and parenting* (2nd ed., pp. 103–133). Mahwah, NJ: Erlbaum.

Steinberg, L., & Steinberg, W. (1994). Crossing paths: How your child's adolescence triggers your own crisis. New York: Simon and Schuster.

Stoolmiller, M. (1994). Antisocial behavior, delinquent peer association, and unsupervised wandering for boys: Growth and change from childhood to early adolescence. *Multivariate Behavioral Research, 29,* 263–288.

Waizenhofer, R. N., Buchanan, C. M., & Jackson-Newsom, J. (2004). Mothers' and fathers' knowledge of adolescents' daily activities: Its sources and its links with adolescent adjustment. *Journal of Family Psychology, 18,* 348–360.

Whiteman, S. D., McHale, S. M., & Crouter, A. C. (2003). What parents learn from experience: The first child as a first draft? *Journal of Marriage and Family, 65,* 608–621.

Wood, M. D., Read, J. P., Mitchell, R. E., & Brand, N. H. (2004). Do parents still matter? Parent and peer influences on alcohol involvement among recent high school graduates. *Psychology of Addictive Behaviors, 18,* 19–30.

[3]

Impediments to Parental Monitoring in the After-School Hours

A Qualitative Analysis

DEBORAH BELLE and BRENDA PHILLIPS

Parents who are knowledgeable about their children's activities, where-abouts, and friends are more likely than less knowledgeable parents to have well-adjusted children who avoid risky behaviors, as many studies show (Crouter & Head 2002; Dishion & McMahon 1998; Fletcher, Darling, & Steinberg 1995; Hayes, Hudson, & Matthews 2004; Laird et al. 2003a; Laird et al. 2003b). Although the positive association between parental knowledge and children's adjustment is firmly established, there is not agreement about the reasons for this association. Current debate centers on the extent to which active parental monitoring or voluntary child disclosure accounts for the larger share of the association (Fletcher, Steinberg, & Williams-Wheeler 2004; Kerr & Stattin 2000, 2003; Stattin & Kerr 2000; Waizen-hofer, Buchanan, & Jackson-Newsom 2004). Researchers also have investigated the extent to which other aspects of parental behavior or of the parent-child relationship are powerful in increasing voluntary child disclosure, thus indirectly making parents more knowledgeable about their children's lives (Smetana et al. 2006; Soenenset al. 2006). Some researchers emphasize the possibility that children already engaged in disapproved activities with disapproved peers in disapproved places will be understandably reluctant to inform parents of their misbehavior, so that the adolescent's own delinquent behaviors lead to the parents' lack of knowledge, rather than the reverse (Kerr & Stattin 2003).

Little is known about the larger context in which parental monitoring occurs (Crouter & Head 2002; Menaghan 2003), and few studies illuminate the life situations of the parents who monitor or the young people who are monitored, as these affect the monitoring process. As Menaghan (2003:157) put it,

> if one had to imagine people's lives by looking at the variables that are considered, one would get the impression that no one ever leaves the house— except possibly the child, and then only to commit delinquent acts.

Many studies of parental monitoring do not collect and analyze any information at all about family structure, parental employment, or resources available to parents. Those that do typically use the "social address" model in which families are characterized in a limited number of ways (e.g., single parent versus married parent; employed versus unemployed) with no additional information gathered about the specific characteristics of the marriage or the work that might have an impact on a parent's ability to monitor a child (Vandell & Posner 1999). The social address model points to differences between different kinds of families, but does not fully capture the richness of parental monitoring in diverse types of families. A striking exception is the work of Davis, Crouter, and McHale (2006) on shift work.

Parental monitoring is likely to be especially important during the after-school hours, when children have been released from school but many parents are not yet home from work. Maternal employment, like paternal employment, is now normative in the United States and other industrialized nations, and the typical school day is hours shorter than the full-time workday for employed parents.

Much research documents the dangers young people face during the after-school hours. This is the peak time for violent juvenile crime, with the greatest danger occurring in the first hour after school is dismissed (Stewart 2001). Drug use and risky sexual behavior also may be particularly likely when young people are unsupervised after school (Stewart 2001). Spending unsupervised time with peers, especially away from home, is associated with higher levels of delinquency, substance use, and susceptibility to peer pressure (Flannery, Williams, & Vazsonyi 1999). Spending longer hours without adult supervision increases the risks to young people's well-being (Stewart 2001). Conversely, parental monitoring, parental warmth, and a nonpermissive parenting style appear to protect unsupervised adolescents from many problem behaviors (Galambos & Maggs 1991; Stewart 2001). Not surprisingly, the risks of unsupervised time are greatest, and the benefits of after-school programs are strongest, for low-income young people and those in dangerous neighborhoods (Marshall et al. 1997).

Although many researchers refer to parental monitors undifferentiated by gender, the few studies that have addressed gender issues agree almost unanimously that in two-parent families mothers are typically more active and more successful monitors than are fathers (Bumpus, Crouter, & McHale 2001; Crouter et al. 1990; Waizenhofer, Buchanan, & Jackson-Newsom 2004) and are more often the recipients of their children's self-disclosure (Belle, Dill, & Burr 1991; Smetana et al. 2006; Younnis & Smollar 1985). An interesting exception is the work of Stattin and Kerr (2000), which finds no gender difference in parents' knowledge of their children's lives. This study was undertaken in Sweden, where, as the authors note, Swedish law encourages and facilitates father's involvement with their children in ways that U.S. law does not.

Still less is known about the actual nature of parental monitoring in action. Little research examines the real-life difficulties parents face in monitoring their children or documents the successful strategies some parents discover for staying informed about their children's lives despite such obstacles. How do parents inform themselves about their children's lives, particularly after the child reaches adolescence and spends much more time away from the parent? What specific things do parents do to keep track of their children? How do successful parental monitors overcome children's potential reticence or duplicity? How do they learn about the child's involvement in forbidden activities? How do children interpret their parents' attempts to obtain information about their unsupervised after-school activities?

Nor is there agreement about the language to use when referring to such concepts. Several researchers persist in using the phrase "parental monitoring" or "parental monitoring knowledge" when discussing what parents know about children's lives, no matter how this knowledge is obtained. As other researchers point out, monitoring is an active verb and should only be used to refer to initiatives parents take to learn about and keep track of their children (Crouter & Head 2002; Montemayor 2001; Waizenhofer, Buchanan, & Jackson-Newsom 2004). Such researchers prefer the phrase "parental knowledge" to refer to what parents know about their children. In the present chapter we follow this usage, restricting the term *monitoring* to forms of parental action, and using *knowledge* to refer to parental awareness about the child's life.

The Present Study

The purpose of the present chapter is to examine the contexts in which parents attempt to monitor their children's after-school activities and the associated impediments that negatively impact their ability to monitor successfully. Many of the limitations of the parental monitoring literature arise because that literature has been overwhelmingly quantitative, relying on forced-choice questionnaires. In contrast, the present study relies on qualitative data elicited through open-ended interviews with parents and children who spoke about their specific day-to-day experiences and concerns. A qualitative analysis permitted us to examine issues that parents and children spontaneously raised when discussing the child's after-school experiences. Themes that emerged from our analysis include issues not addressed in the existing literature on parental monitoring.

Methods

Data come from a 4-year longitudinal study of employed parents and their children. Both parents and children were interviewed annually about the child's after-school arrangements and experiences. Families were selected to be diverse in socioeconomic status, ethnicity, and family structure, and were recruited through schools, after-school programs, housing projects, and community organizations. Low-income and single-parent families were intentionally oversampled, as we anticipated that such families would have special difficulties providing desirable arrangements for their children in the after-school hours. Of the 53 families participating in the study, 15 were African American, 1 was Hispanic, 1 was Asian, and 36 were non-Hispanic White. All but three mothers had high school degrees, and over half of the mothers had completed a college education. Focus children (30 girls, 23 boys) ranged in age at the start of the study from 7 to 12 years of age, thus this is a study of preadolescent children approaching and in some cases entering adolescence.

Of the children in the study, 33 lived in single-parent households as the study began. (For further information about this study, see Belle [1999].)

Interviewers were primarily doctoral students in psychology or education, and the first author of this chapter also conducted a substantial number of interviews over the course of the study (66 interviews concentrated in 32 of the research families). Before conducting any interviews with research families, all interviewers received training and successfully completed practice interviews with families not included in the study. Interviews were not tape-recorded. Instead, interviewers were trained to write down the ideas and words of interviewees. Interviewers visited families in teams, with a separate interviewer assigned to each person to be interviewed. Research group meetings were held on a frequent basis, often weekly, to plan interview visits, correct problems, and discuss insights that arose.

Informed Consent

The first visit to each research family was arranged so that parents and children could meet together with their interviewers, discuss the nature of the study, and provide informed consent. Informed consent statements were discussed with both parents and children present so that parents could be certain their children understood and agreed to the procedures of the study. In addition to allowing family members an opportunity to read the informed consent material, interviewers verbally emphasized to children the key points of the statement, especially the child's right to end the interview at any point and to decline to answer any interview question for any reason. Families were asked to choose a code name by which their family would be known to the research group. The ensuing discussion was often fun, and helped to concretize for children our promise of privacy and confidentiality. No family was interviewed until parents had given informed consent for their own participation and that of their children, and children had given their informed assent to participate.

The Research Interviews

Family members were interviewed separately about the child's after-school routine, social support network, emotional well-being, and behavioral adjustment. Information was also gathered on the daily schedules and whereabouts of all household members. In each family, the focus child and one parent, usually the mother, were interviewed each year. Annual interviews also were conducted with interested fathers and often with those siblings who spent after-school time with the focus child. Interviews included both open-ended questions and standardized questionnaires, lasted between 1 and 2 hours, and were generally conducted in the family home. On occasion, interviews were conducted at our Boston University research offices, a parent's workplace, or another setting chosen by the research family. Interviewers did their best to assure that interviews were conducted privately, although in some cases the arrangements of small apartments made complete privacy impossible.

Open-ended questions were used to elicit rich and detailed information. Parents were asked about the child's current and past after-school arrangements, how these came about, and the advantages and disadvantages of the arrangements. One section of the interview was devoted to family rules for after-school time, including the possibility that children did not follow some or all of these rules. Other sections of the interview focused on parent-child communication and social support, with questions about the circumstances in which children could contact parents in the after-school hours or parents could contact children. Parents were also asked whether there were certain times of day when they generally found out about the child's day. Children were asked a parallel set of questions about their after-school arrangements and experiences. Interviewers encouraged parents and children to elaborate on issues of concern.

After interviews were completed, the research group met to discuss the experiences of the children in each of the research families and the salient themes that had emerged in the research interviews. In some cases similar themes were evident in interviews from many of the participating families. In other cases only one or two families reported a particular experience or concern. This chapter reports on both frequently reported themes and also on some issues that only emerged in one or two families, but may warrant study in future research.

This chapter uses our interview material to deepen our understanding of parental monitoring, raise some new questions about parental monitoring, and offer hypotheses for future research. The names of children and parents referred to in the chapter are pseudonyms, used to protect the privacy of the research participants. The chapter focuses first on the contexts in which parental monitoring occurs and the difficulties families face in optimizing after-school experiences for children when parents are employed. We next turn to some parental strategies for structuring after-school time for children and dealing with children's tendencies to break or bend after-school rules. We describe some examples of active parental monitoring and of instances in which children appear to monitor their own behavior. Voluntary self-disclosure by children and the tendency of such self-disclosure to decline with the advent of adolescence are then considered. The importance of gender in monitoring is discussed, followed by consideration of a type of monitoring that seems designed more to reassure parents than to affect the behavior of children. Next, we present an extended description of failed monitoring in one of our research families and consider the reasons for this failure. The chapter concludes with some recommendations for future research and policymaking concerning parental monitoring.

Limitations of This Study

In reading this chapter several limitations should be kept in mind. Research families were not randomly sampled from their communities but instead volunteered to participate in a time-consuming project over four years involving multiple family members. This self-selection process may well have resulted in our including families with more successful parental monitoring strategies than are typical, or, conversely, in our attracting families with heightened concerns about this aspect of family life. In addition, the original study was not designed to illuminate parental monitoring, but focused instead on related topics, such as the provision of social support to children. Some parents and children provided more information about parental monitoring than did others. Data from the study are probably least valuable in estimating the prevalence of certain behaviors or problems in the general population, and are most valuable in suggesting issues that would benefit from future study with more representative research samples. It should also be kept in mind that the sample was limited to families in which both parents or the single-parent household head were employed full time, at least at the start of the study. This study is therefore virtually silent on parental monitoring issues for non-employed parents and their children.

Results

Exploring the Context of After-School Monitoring

"All I do after 3:00 is worry," Terry Edwards says. Many parents would agree that it is stressful to be an employed parent, when the school day is shorter than the parental workday and acceptable after-school programs are often hard to find, hard to get to, or are financially out-of-reach. Adults in the United States work longer hours than do adults in any of the other industrialized nations, and increasing numbers work afternoon and evening shifts when children are not in school (Heymann 2000; Heymann, Penrose, & Earle 2006). Although parents often organize their work lives to have as much time as possible with their children, many must work long hours away from home. Some have no way to contact their children during their time at work.

When Jocelyn Williams was growing up, her parents both worked full time, but only at one job each. According to Jocelyn, life is tougher now, and you have to work more than one job to survive. Jocelyn separated from her husband some months prior to the start of the study. She is currently working two full-time jobs and says she would work four jobs if her schedule allowed it. "You're going to die anyway. It might as well be from hard work." Jocelyn works as a senior office assistant from early morning to late evening on weekdays, arriving home around 10 p.m. Without education beyond high school, Jocelyn's pay is low. Working two jobs allows her to approach a middle-class lifestyle. She is currently looking for a third, weekend job, as she is trying to save money for a house.

Jocelyn's hard work provides her children with advantages and opportunities they otherwise would not have, including residence in a pleasant apartment building in a middle-class neighborhood. Jocelyn also models the kind of devotion to hard work she would like to see in her children, and her work-impelled absence forces them to develop the self-reliance that Jocelyn values so highly. Yet with Jocelyn away most of their waking hours, her children have had to learn to take care of themselves.

At 14 years of age Gregory Polansky has an after-school job 2 or 3 days a week, but spends most of his after-school time hanging out with friends, usually at fast food restaurants, or walking around the streets. His mother notes that there are no recreational activities in town for young people after school, and unless someone can drive the kids to the roller skating rink, they can't get anywhere. Gregory says he does not really enjoy the time he spends hanging out with his friends in town. He claims the town is boring, and there is not much to do. If he had a choice, he would move to a different city with more things to do, "All there is here is a bowling alley that no one goes to."

When 8-year-old Cynthia Edwards gets home from school her mother is generally there, but she is also generally asleep because she works the midnight shift as a medical technologist. Terry Edwards works the night shift because it offers more money and because she believes that leaving Cynthia and her older brother while they are asleep at night is preferable to leaving them alone during the day. Cynthia knows not to wake her mother unless there is an emergency. She is careful to bring her key with her to school so she can let herself into the apartment without disturbing her mother, and she avoids noisy activities like playing the piano that might wake her mother during the afternoon. Cynthia understands that the after-school program costs too much, and she knows her mother needs to work. "I know that much. I wish she could just go outside and pick money off the trees."

Many of the families we studied are unable to rely on relatives to provide after-school monitoring when parents are at work. Many of the parents we interviewed were cared for as children when their parents were at work by their own grandmothers or other female relatives. Grandparents today, however, typically have jobs themselves. They rarely figure as full-time after-school caretakers to the children in our study. Some families rely on grandparents intermittently, during school vacations or when children are ill. Irene Castillo's grandmother, who lives down the street from her, takes care of her when Irene is sick or when there is a school vacation. For one year Jeffrey Wright's grandparents took care of him the one day each week his after-school program was closed. George Townsend's grandmother is a schoolteacher, so she has the same vacation days and can supervise him then. Justin Stiles' grandmother works as a housekeeper, and she has been able to bring Justin to work with her when he is sick. Most employment arrangements, however, are less flexible. Omar Jones would very much like to be with his grandmother after school. "I'd go see my grandmother every day, if she didn't have to work."

Parents who wish to be knowledgeable about their children's lives face difficulties simply because their own work schedules frequently preclude their presence at home with the children and make communication and monitoring difficult, even by proxy. The need to provide for the family economically conflicts with the need to protect and supervise children day to day.

Structuring After-School Time

Unable to be with their children in the after-school hours, and often unable to provide alternative adult supervision, many parents do find ways to structure and monitor their children's behavior. Ms. Somers leaves lists for each of her children each afternoon detailing the tasks that are to be accomplished in the after-school hours: "For example: 'Vanessa—do homework, practice piano, eat your salad, make so and so for supper.' They can check things off and when I come home, even if they're in bed, I can see what happened, what they did and didn't do."

Jocelyn Williams's rules govern and organize the time her son and daughter spend without her. The children must call her when they get home from school. They must do their homework, with the television off, before they can go outside to play. If they have no homework, they must spend some time studying. Jocelyn checks their homework when she comes home from work, and if it is not correct and neat they must do it over. After they do their homework, they are allowed to go out and play right outside their building until dark. They must call Jocelyn before they leave the building and again when they return.

Bill MacCarthy, however, is forced by his supervisor to limit his calls home to one a day, and telephone calls from his daughters must be kept to a minimum. Terry Edwards would like to speak with her daughter just as Cynthia gets out of bed in the early morning. Unfortunately, that is also the busiest time on her midnight shift, which makes calling home difficult.

Rule-breaking

In the Kelley family, parents and children are aware that unsupervised time allows the children to bend or break household rules. Yet, significantly, only some rules are broken, and these rules do not concern safety. When asked what she likes best about being home on her own, Michelle says, "I get to do things I'm not allowed to do, like eat junk food and do homework in front of the TV." She is only allowed to watch 1 hour of television a day, but when she is alone she watches more (her brother reports the same television rule and the same propensity to break it). Their mother, however, is not unaware. When asked whether the children follow the house rule forbidding television while doing homework, she says, "I think it is a safe bet to say they sneak it." Yet the children do follow their parents' rules when safety is concerned. Their father proudly reports that one day the cable television installer came and Michelle refused to violate the house rule by letting him in when neither parent was at home. The workman said to her, "Well, it's now or never," and she replied, "Well, then, I guess, it's never."

Parental Monitoring

Many parents in our study were able to keep their children's misbehaviors in check through active monitoring, sometimes involving creative detective work.

Eric Holden often fails to follow his after-school rules, but his mother generally figures this out.

> She can tell if I don't have homework done or I'm gone too long. Sometimes she knows if a friend is over. She finds evidence, like shoe prints on the floor. She'll look in my room and see the chairs were moved. She'll say, "You had a friend over." I'll say, "No." Then she'll say, "Why were the chairs moved?"

Diana Hardy's mother also successfully detects her daughter's misbehavior, particularly her failure to limit her television viewing. According to Diana, "I used to come straight home and watch cartoons. Then when I thought Mom was coming home, I'd turn it off. She used to feel the back [of the television] and find out it was warm!" Diana says she follows the rules now.

Self-monitoring

The Moores do not circumscribe their daughters' behavior very tightly when the girls are unsupervised in the after-school hours, seeing Bonita and Barbara as having already internalized most of their parents' values and concerns. The girls are free to leave the house, but usually call to tell their mother where they are going and when they will be back. When it comes to having friends visit, there are "no rules if it's friends we know, but they usually ask." About homework, "it's just expected that it's done— unvoiced expectations." Concerning the television,

> They have to monitor themselves. Barbara spends much more time reading. Bonita has to monitor herself and tells me how she'll cut back. Her conscience bothers her because she knows we don't like it.

Cooking is allowed, and the girls sometimes make dinner for the family. When answering the telephone, they avoid telling callers they are home without their parents, saying instead that their mother is busy or at the neighbor's and will be right back. According to Ms. Moore, this rule is one the girls heard somewhere and adopted themselves, not a rule imposed by either parent. As this example suggests, the girls' rules change over time, often because of suggestions from Bonita and Barbara. Their father says,

> As they grow older they request changes in the rules based on their increased levels of responsibility and maturity. Sometimes rules just stop being enforced because they are not actual anymore.

Rules are "not a big deal" in the Moore household, and neither is punishment. "We're not into punishment. We are into limit-setting. Praise is easier to give."

Although the Moores do not restrict their daughters with many rules, the girls take seriously the rules they do have. Ms. Moore tells about one time when she went to meet the girls after an evening activity. When she arrived she found they had already left, so she returned home, looking for them on the way, but missing them. The girls later reminded her that she had told them always to walk on a particular street when traveling between this activity and their house. They had done so, but their mother, having forgotten the rule, had chosen another route.

Voluntary Self-disclosure

In several families parents described children who routinely inform their parents about each day's events without parental prompting. In the Kelley family, the children gravitate to their parents in the evening hours. As their mother describes it, "They do their homework around the dining room table. They tend to want to be around us, to follow us around, to float around us and want to talk." Weining Chen says her daughter Meiguei tells her about her day "as soon as I see her. Then she never stops talking." Mrs. Moore says of her daughters, "Sometimes they're just on my bed in the morning ready to have a long, serious conversation. That's important time for us, getting the day going, cooling out any stress, getting them ready."

When problems arise during the after-school hours, Bonita Moore says she can talk about them later with family members and friends and these discussions make her feel better. Once one of the children at the day care center where she worked fell and hit her head. "I didn't know how badly hurt she was. My boss was on the phone, in the office. I was the only one with the kids." When Bonita got home she started talking about it "to everyone in my family," and "it calmed me down." In these families and others in our study, children engage in a great deal of voluntary disclosure, telling their parents about the events of the day and soliciting their responses.

The Vicissitudes of Voluntary Self-disclosure

Self-disclosure often declines during the adolescent years, however, as children pull away. Those who once sought out their parents now prefer to be apart. The early morning or after-school conversations diminish in frequency and in depth. Mary Ellen Kelliher used to enjoy spending time with her mother, but now wishes her mother worked every day "until midnight." Clara Shephard is usually at home when her son returns from school, but now he generally spends time elsewhere. According to Clara, Max "really does not want to be with me this year." Peggy Monroe does not see as much of Zack on the weekends as she did when he was younger. "We have gotten out of the habit of going to see movies together. He is getting to an age where he is just spending most of his time with his friends. He doesn't sit with me at the movies anymore even when we do go." Eric Holden, at 14, spends less and less time with his mother. She thinks it has become more difficult to tell if he has had a bad day,

> because since adolescence he's more often "grumpy" with me and I don't always know if it's for a reason or not. If I have a reason to believe that something happened, I'll try to make him talk about it. But it's not always very successful, since he's not really good at communicating his feelings.

Bernice Gates says that her 15-year-old son, Stanley, "doesn't like to do anything with me anymore unless I'm taking him to the store to buy him something. . . . Having serious affectionate conversations is not okay with him right now."

Parents try to understand the sources of such estrangement and often fight against it. Bernice Gates says,

> We both feel we are losing our closeness. We try and figure out why without blaming either of us. His interests are changing. I'm not sure if it is my work or him just maturing that has made the difference. I am having a hard time letting go. His dad is alive and doesn't give him any time. A sacrifice had to be made in order for us to keep this house. I had to work.

She even quits her evening job to spend more time with Stanley, but he generally leaves for the recreation center with his friends before she gets home from work and rarely comes home before 9 or 9:30 p.m.

Jessica Holden still tries to show her son, Eric, she loves him and cares about him, but this is a more difficult task than it was when Eric was younger.

> I say things to him, but not as much as I used to. I also am not as affectionate as I used to be, since he's older now, an adolescent male, and I think he needs his distance. I try to cook something that he really likes.

He appreciates it. I try not to show him through buying too much, because it always gets out of hand.

As a large body of research has shown, the parent-child relationship may also suffer when parents themselves are stressed, depressed, or demoralized (Belle 1982; Elder, Caspi, & Van Nguyen 1986; McLoyd 1990). Peggy Monroe faces considerable stress at work, including a workday that often lasts well into the evening. The combination of this stress and her difficulties with Zack are taking their toll.

I've been working so hard. I'd never encourage anyone to have a child alone. I just don't have the energy to deal with things. Sometimes I come home from work, tired and worn out, and I walk into the house and see he hasn't done anything—I come into my room and close the door. I'm feeling angry and depressed and Zack knows enough just to stay away.

In such circumstances, fewer opportunities exist for the child to disclose or for the parent to solicit information.

Monitoring as a Gendered Process

Monitoring also appeared a highly gendered process in our study, as mothers in two-parent families were often the designated child monitors, and boys tended to resist monitoring more than did girls. Even in families in which parents divided the after-school tasks equally, mothers often functioned as supervisors, keeping track of changing schedules and alerting fathers to their responsibilities from day to day. Jonathan Schapiro performs as many after-school tasks on a daily basis as his wife does, but when we asked him about his child's previous after-school arrangements, he said that he did not remember what the past arrangements had been and suggested we ask his wife. As he explained, his wife "takes responsibility for that part of the family." In the Somers family, both parents assist their children in the after-school hours, driving them to a wide variety of activities. Yet, according to both parents, Micah's mother, Laura, is the one responsible for orchestrating the complicated weekly after-school plans for the family.

Monitoring and Parental Anxiety

Many parents fear that something terrible will happen to their children when they must be left alone and unsupervised, and some of the monitoring parents do seems a response to these fears. Visiting the house, or speaking to a child on the telephone, can help parents cope with their own anxieties. Such visits can also convey to children that parents are concerned about them, at least if the children are made aware of these visits.

When Terry Edwards is working at night she can sometimes drop in to see her daughter Cynthia and her older son. "It's not terribly easy, but I can." She estimates she has done so about five times in the last year. These trips home are "not to visit, because she is sleeping. But just to make sure they're all right. Just to reassure myself." Terry sees these trips as "mostly for me, because they don't know I've been there."

Angela Jones, whose 8-year-old son, Omar, is sometimes at home alone with his younger siblings, says she responds to her own anxieties by telephoning home frequently. She recounts a recent, typical telephone call.

> Mother: Is everything all right?
> Omar: Yes, Mommy. Is Daddy on his way home?
> Mother: Yes, Daddy should be home soon.
> Omar: I'm hanging up now.
> Mother: No, wait! What are the kids doing? Let me talk to your brother. [*Talks to Christopher*] Is the baby hungry? Her bottle is in the fridge. Daddy will be home soon.

"I call home like crazy," Angela says, "but Omar doesn't like this." The calls provide Angela some reassurance, but do little to aid Omar in his difficult situation.

Misdirected Monitoring

The study also provides one example of disastrous, misdirected, or incomplete monitoring. As the study began, Bill MacCarthy, who had sole custody of his daughters, was unhappy about the arrangements he had for Patricia, who was 11, and her older sister, Karen, who was 12. Much of Bill's concern centered around the dangers he believed his daughters faced, especially from sexual predators. Although Bill cannot be with his daughters after school and cannot afford to provide alternate adult supervision for them, he attempts to ensure their safety through rules that are meant to govern their behavior. As he states, "I probably hold the reins a little tighter than most parents." Patricia may only leave the apartment with prior permission or after finishing all of her homework and chores. She can have friends over with her father's prior approval, although this is not often granted.

Although Bill attends closely to Patricia's physical safety and to her rule-breaking behaviors, he does not monitor the events of her daily life or her emotional responses to these events. According to Patricia, he knows very little about her. When Patricia feels worried or sad she says she will "go sit in a corner by myself and [not] talk to anybody." Does she tell people things that happen to her at school? "No. I just don't care about it. Nobody really needs to know. They have their own problems." Bill offers a similar perspective. Asked whether there are certain times of day in which he generally finds out about Patricia's day he says simply, "No." Not surprisingly, Patricia's report of her own loneliness is extremely high. However, Patricia's father does not seem to be aware of this problem. In filling out the Child Behavior Checklist, he reports that it is "not true" that Patricia complains of loneliness or is withdrawn. He says it is only "somewhat or sometimes true" that she is unhappy, sad, or depressed.

Later in the study Patricia reports several occasions on which she was scared after school when her older sister did not meet her as expected or did not come home for hours or ran away from home. Asked whether she had told her father about her fears for Karen, Patricia responds, "No, he doesn't really listen to me." Patricia sees herself as having no ability to influence family decisions because her father refuses to listen to alternative ideas. "Whatever Dad says goes. He tells us what the rules are." Patricia also admits that she flouts these rules, especially by having friends over to visit despite her father's prohibitions.

Before we returned for our final interviews with Patricia and her father, tragic events took place in the MacCarthy family. Karen ran away from home again, and then moved in with her aunt. Patricia also ran away, was raped, and attempted suicide. Her father's worst nightmare about his daughter was realized. As a result of these events, social service agencies intervened in Patricia's life and arranged for meetings with a therapist and with a therapy group. Patricia still has difficulty communicating with her father. "I try to talk to him, the phone rings and ends our conversation. He spends a lot of time on the phone. Sometimes I keep talking, but he gets angry." Once again, Patricia describes frightening levels of loneliness. This year, for the first time, her father also sees such problems, as well as the externalizing problems he had noted in previous years.

One might think about the problems in the MacCarthy family in several ways. Bill could be characterized as a highly controlling parent, as an authoritarian parent, as an unsupportive parent, and as a parent remarkably ill-informed about his own daughters. Although custodial fathers have been found to know less than custodial mothers about their female children following divorce (Buchanan, Maccoby, & Dornbusch 1996), Bill MacCarthy's lack of knowledge about his daughters is extreme. One could also think about the facets of his daughters' lives that Bill attempted to monitor. He paid great attention to their behaviors, especially their completion of chores and obedience to parental rules. He did not, however, attend closely to their emotional lives, and his ignorance of his daughters' deep unhappiness left him unable to foresee their running away and powerless to prevent it.

Discussion

In the present study, workplace demands were the most frequently encountered impediments to effective parental monitoring. Parents who worked afternoon, evening, or nighttime shifts could not be with their children when the children were out of school, and many were unable to provide alternate adult care by relatives, friends, or after-school programs. Some had difficulty as well in telephoning their children or receiving telephone calls at work. As shift work and long hours become increasingly common among U.S. workers, parental monitoring will become increasingly difficult unless compensatory actions are taken. Effective solutions will probably require government action, either to expand the availability and affordability of high-quality after-school programs or to raise the minimum wage to the point that parents need not work more than one full-time job to support a family. Living wage campaigns can raise wages locally, even without federal legislation. Reviving union strength is critical if workers are to reclaim power in their negotiations with powerful corporations.

Lengthy work hours and stressful life situations left some parents unable to mobilize the energy to monitor their children, even after they had returned home from work. Demoralized and tired, some parents withdrew physically or emotionally to regain the energy they needed. Just as parents sometimes withdrew from children, children approaching adolescence sometimes pulled away from their parents, reducing their voluntary disclosures and avoiding situations in which parents might comfortably inquire about the child's day. This pulling away occurred even with young people whose earlier relationships with parents were strong and communicative. In our study we saw this withdrawal most often with adolescent males, although it occurred with adolescent females as well. These problems of parental withdrawal and adolescent withdrawal sometimes reinforced each other, although some parents resisted this synergy. Future studies could examine ways in which effective parental monitoring may fluctuate with parental morale and energy level. Parents' strategies for coping with children's withdrawal and their reduction in voluntary self-disclosure could also be studied. It would be helpful to learn more about successful strategies parents have found for overcoming their own demoralization or for sustaining or recreating a communicative relationship with an adolescent who is inclined to withdraw.

The present study suggests, in accord with previous research, that mothers often do more parental monitoring than do fathers, and future studies should continue to examine gender differences in the amount of parental monitoring that is done. The present study also suggests that there may be gender differences in the aspects of children's lives that parents monitor. Bill MacCarthy's careful monitoring of his daughter's behaviors but lack of attention to their emotions is certainly extreme, but perhaps it reflects to some extent a gendered understanding of what should be monitored. Do mothers make more efforts than fathers to stay in touch with their children's emotional lives? Do fathers make more efforts to learn if household rules are being followed? Do mothers and fathers differ in their styles of monitoring, in the ways they seek to acquire information about their children's lives? Such research questions could provide a more nuanced account of possible gender differences in parental monitoring.

The results of this study suggest that programs for parents might give parents opportunities to speak about and reflect on the constraints that prevent them from monitoring their children as effectively as they might like. A discussion of the barriers that make effective monitoring difficult could then be followed by consideration of ways to overcome such barriers. Parents who have particularly difficult work situations might strategize with other parents and with a group facilitator about ways to move employers to make accommodations such as allowing more telephone calls in the after-school hours, or might compare notes about techniques for reenergizing oneself after a hard day at work in order to have enough energy for the children. Similarly, parents could discuss what elements of their children's behavior they attempt to monitor and why. One could then discuss the value of attending to children's emotional states as well as to their overt behavior.

Trying to elicit information from a resistant child or adolescent is a difficult task. In contrast, receiving the child's voluntary disclosures is a nearly effortless path to information and understanding of the child. The contrasting experiences in different families and even in the same families at different stages of the child's development raise again the question: why do some children voluntarily disclose so readily to their parents, while others do not? Previous research has already illuminated some of the factors associated with voluntary self-disclosure (Smetana et al. 2006; Soenens et al. 2006), and the present study suggests that further research in this area would be particularly valuable. Promoting a child's voluntary self-disclosure may well be the most effective strategy for increasing parental knowledge, even though it is not a form of parental monitoring.

Parents are often exhorted to monitor their children in order to promote positive development. Many parents already realize the value of monitoring but find it difficult to accomplish, given the constraints they face. Acknowledging the many barriers that make parental monitoring difficult is essential as we think about public policies that would make monitoring, and all of parenting, a less formidable task.

References

Belle, D. (1999). *The after-school lives of children: Alone and with others while parents work.* Mahwah, NJ: Erlbaum.

Belle, D. (Ed.) (1982). *Lives in stress: Women and depression.* Beverly Hills, CA: Sage.

Belle, D., Dill, D., & Burr, R. (1991). Children's network orientations. *Journal of Community Psychology, 19,* 362–373.

Buchanan, C. M., Maccoby, E. E., & Dornbusch, S. M. (1996). *Adolescents after divorce*. Cambridge, MA: Harvard University Press.

Bumpus, M. F., Crouter, A.C., & McHale, S. M. (2001). Parental autonomy granting during adolescence: Exploring gender differences in context. *Developmental Psychology, 37*, 163–173.

Crouter, A. C., & Head, M. R. (2002). Parental monitoring and knowledge of children. In M. H. Bornstein (Ed.), *Handbook of parenting, 2nd ed., vol. 3: Being and becoming a parent* (pp. 461–483). Mahwah, NJ: Erlbaum.

Crouter, A. C., MacDermid, S. M., McHale, S. M., & Perry-Jenkins, M. (1990). Parental monitoring and perceptions of children's school performance and conduct in dual- and single-earner families. *Developmental Psychology, 26*, 649–657.

Davis, K. D., Crouter, A. C., & McHale, S. M. (2006). Implications of shift work for parent-adolescent relationships in dual-earner families. *Family Relations: Interdisciplinary Journal of Applied Family Studies, 55*, 450–460.

Dishion, T. J., & McMahon, R. J. (1998). Parental monitoring and the prevention of child and adolescent problem behavior: A conceptual and empirical formulation. *Clinical Child and Family Psychology Review, 1*, 61–75.

Elder, G. H., Jr., Caspi, A., & Van Nguyen, T. (1986). Resourceful and vulnerable children: Family influences in hard times. In R. K. Silbereisen, K. Eyferth, & G. Rudinger (Eds.), Development as action in context (pp. 167–186). New York: Springer-Verlag.

Flannery, D. J., Williams, L. L., & Vazsonyi, A. T. (1999). Who are they with and what are they doing? Delinquent behavior, substance use, and early adolescents' after-school time. *American Journal of Orthopsychiatry, 69*, 247–253.

Fletcher, A. C., Darling, N., & Steinberg, L. (1995). Parental monitoring and peer influences on adolescent substance use. In J. McCord (Ed.), *Coercion and punishment in long-term perspectives* (pp.259–271). New York: Cambridge University Press.

Fletcher, A. C., Steinberg, L., & Williams-Wheeler, M. (2004). Parental influences on adolescent problem behavior: Revisiting Stattin and Kerr. *Child Development, 75*, 781–796.

Galambos, N. L., & Maggs, J. L. (1991). Out-of-school care of young adolescents and self-reported behavior. *Developmental Psychology, 27*, 644–655.

Hayes, L., Hudson, A., & Matthews, J. (2004). Parental monitoring behaviors: A model of rules, supervision, and conflict. *Behavior Therapy, 35*, 587–604.

Heymann, J. (2000). The widening gap: Why America's working families are in jeopardy and what can be done about it. New York: Basic Books.

Heymann, J., Penrose, K., & Earle, A. (2006). Meeting children's needs: How does the United States measure up? *Merrill-Palmer Quarterly, 52*, 189–215.

Kerr, M., & Stattin, H. (2000). What parents know, how they know it, and several forms of adolescent adjustment: Further support for a reinterpretation of monitoring. *Developmental Psychology, 36,* 366–380.

Kerr, M., & Stattin, H. (2003). Parenting of adolescents: Action or reaction? In A. C. Crouter & A. Booth (Eds.). *Children's influence on family dynamics: The neglected side of family relationships* (pp. 121–151). Mahwah, NJ: Erlbaum.

Laird, R. D., Pettit, G. S., Bates, J. E., & Dodge, K. A. (2003a). Parents' monitoring-relevant knowledge and adolescents' delinquent behavior: Evidence of correlated developmental changes and reciprocal influences. *Child Development, 74,* 752–768.

Laird, R. D., Pettit, G. S., Dodge, K. A., & Bates, J. E. (2003b). Change in parents' monitoring-relevant knowledge: Links with parenting, relationship quality, adolescent beliefs, and antisocial behavior. *Social Development, 12,* 401–419.

Marshall, N., Coll, C. G., Marx, F., McCartney, K., Keefe, N., & Ruh, J. (1997). After-school time and children's behavioral adjustment. *Merrill-Palmer Quarterly, 43,* 497–514.

McLoyd, V. C. (1990). The impact of economic hardship on Black families and children: Psychological distress, parenting, and socioemotional development. *Child Development, 61,* 311–346.

Menaghan, E. G. (2003). On the brink: Stability and change in parent-child relations in adolescence. In A. C. Crouter & A. Booth (Eds.), *Children's influence on family dynamics: The neglected side of family relationships* (pp.153–162). Mahwah, NJ: Erlbaum.

Montemayor, R. (2001). Parental monitoring. In J. V. Lerner, R. M., Lerner, & J. Finkelstein (Eds.), *Adolescence in America: An encyclopedia* (vol. 2, pp. 481–484). Santa Barbara, CA: ABC-CLIO.

Smetana, J. G., Metzger, A., Gettman, D. C., & Campione-Barr, N. (2006). Disclosure and secrecy in adolescent-parent relationships. *Child Development, 77,* 201–217.

Soenens, B., Vansteenkiste, M., Luyckx, K., & Goossens, L. (2006). Parenting and adolescent problem behavior: An integrated model with adolescent self-disclosure and perceived parental knowledge as intervening variables. *Developmental Psychology, 42,* 305–318.

Stattin, H., & Kerr, M. (2000). Parental monitoring: A reinterpretation. *Child Development, 71,* 1072–1085.

Stewart, R. (2001). Adolescent self-care: Reviewing the risks. *Families in Society: The Journal of Contemporary Human Services, 82,* 119–126.

Vandell, D. L., & Posner, J. K. (1999). Conceptualization and measurement of children's after-school environments. In S. L. Friedman & T. Wachs (Eds.), *Mea-*

suring environment across the life span: Emerging methods and concepts (pp. 167–196). Washington, D.C.: American Psychological Association Press.

Waizenhofer, R. N., Buchanan, C. M., & Jackson-Newsom, J. (2004). Mothers' and fathers' knowledge of adolescents' daily activities: Its sources and its links with adolescent adjustment. *Journal of Family Psychology, 18,* 348–360.

Younnis, J., & Smollar, J. (1985). Adolescent relations with mothers, fathers, and friends. Chicago: University of Chicago Press.

Cross-Cultural Analysis of Parental Monitoring and Adolescent Problem Behavior

Theoretical Challenges of Model Replication When East Meets West

SONIA VENKATRAMAN, THOMAS J. DISHION,
JEFF KIESNER, and FRANÇOIS POULIN

It goes without saying that the dynamics and mechanisms of childrearing are likely to vary across cultures (Whiting & Edwards 1988). A corollary of this understanding is that the more closely two cultures resemble one another, the more likely they are to share childrearing patterns and mechanisms, as compared to those that are dramatically different. Thus, it is critical that etiological research on both adolescent problem behavior and emotional adjustment within a variety of cultural contexts be conducted to provide data that would generate new theoretical understanding of human behavior and psychopathology. Many people would agree with this claim without thinking twice; yet relatively little research has been done to substantiate it.

Parent-child interactions in general and parental monitoring in particular have been studied mostly within the United States and other Western cultures (Dishion & McMahon 1998; Kerr & Stattin 2000). Even in the West, the definition of family has changed significantly in the past century, due much to an increase in the number of single-parent families, working parents, and, consequently, latchkey children. Corresponding developments in society have affected these changes and, conversely, these changes have affected society. The importance of parental involvement in a child's life and upbringing is a key issue that has surfaced repeatedly in various studies (e.g., Baumrind 1991; Patterson & Stouthamer-Loeber 1984). It is fairly well accepted that it is prudent for parents to know where their children are and what sorts of activities they engage in. Such monitoring of children by their parents has been encouraged, as there are often many beneficial outcomes for the child (e.g., Dishion & McMahon; Duncan et al. 1998).

Parenting in Different Cultures

Parenting styles have been much studied mostly in Western contexts, but there has been a fair amount of research done on parenting in other cultures. It can likely be assumed that humans universally seek to socialize their children and teach those behaviors and values that will help them fit into the larger society in which they live (Vazsonyi 2003). Most Western societies are defined by their emphasis on independence as a valued trait. Many Western parents stress individual achievement and expression, self-reliance, and competitiveness (Greenfield 1994). They impress upon their children the importance of being able to take care of oneself and upward mobility. These traits fit roughly into what many researchers characterize as "individualism"—self-worth is guided almost solely by individual achievement. On the other end of the spectrum, many Eastern cultures tend to be grouped together to fall under the heading of "collectivist," a concept that differs starkly from individualistic Western countries. According to many researchers (e.g., Berry et al. 1992; Harkness, Super, & Keefer 1992), collectivistic cultures seek to foster interdependence instead of independence; rather than emphasizing individuality and thinking "outside the box," people are encouraged to adhere to societal norms, to fit in smoothly; children are taught to respect elders, even to put the needs and desires of their families before their own.

However, it is not the case that cultures, or even subcultures, fall neatly into one of those two categorizations (Bornstein et al. 1998; Greenfield 1994; Harkness & Super 1995). Certainly, many Eastern cultures share similar values, but not all can be labeled collectivist as neatly; within collectivist countries, there may be metropolitan areas that promote individual over group welfare. Likewise, there may be several traditionally individualistic cultures that share many traits with collectivistic cultures, especially when it comes to family. Several European countries, though individualistic by definition, tend to incorporate many values of interdependence (e.g., Suizzo 2004). Kagitçibasi (1996a, 1996b) outlined different cultural models relating to the dimensions of agency (autonomy and heteronomy) and interpersonal distance (relatedness and separateness). She proposed that most cultures could fit into one of three cultural models: the model of independence, the model of interdependence, and the model of autonomous relatedness. The model of independence, which could include most Western industrialized cultures, stresses emotional and economic independence. In this model, the individual is seen to be unique and separate from others, including family, and self-reliance and competitiveness are stressed. The model of interdependence, which might include many Eastern cultures, is characterized by emotional and economic interdependence. The individual is valued by how well he or she fits into the group, in particular, the family; characteristics such as obedience and respect, especially toward elders, are valued, as is the contribution one makes toward the good of the group. The third model, the model of autonomous relatedness, combines emotional interdependence with economic independence; it is often found in societies or subcultures where there exist a mix of cultural heritages.

As mentioned above in describing collectivism, in many Eastern cultures the extended family plays a large role, but not only when it comes to influencing individual goals and actions. Extended family is often very important when it comes to monitoring children's activities, in addition to a collective sense of community that involves nonfamilial members (e.g., Atzaba-Poria, Pike, & Barrett 2004; Wakil, Siddique, & Wakil 1981). It is often the case that parents feel comfortable leaving their children, as there is usually another adult to monitor their children's activities. Parents in these cultures are often strict, placing great importance on academic achievements. Often, academic activities will take precedence over children's social activities with friends or sports teams (Chen, Dong, & Zhou 1997). Divorce is not a culturally accepted phenomenon and, as a result, there are relatively few single-parent families.

Studies of parenting styles in other cultures have suggested that these Western constructs do not always affect the same results in different cultures. One example of this is in the case of the authoritarian parenting style (Baumrind 1967). Authoritarian parenting in individualistic societies is associated with parental rejection and lack of warmth. It is also related to use of physical punishment and strictness, and is often associated with negative child outcomes. However, in many Eastern, collectivist cultures, the authoritarian parenting style is widely employed, often without the negative connotations and consequences present in the West (Ekblad 1986; Rudy & Grusec 2001). In fact, many children and adolescents in such cultures report high academic excellence (e.g., Chao 1994; Chen, Dong, & Zhou 1997).

In certain Eastern cultures, where religion and culture are so often intertwined, children are raised with the belief that obedience and acceptance of the authority of elders is expected (e.g., Stewart et al. 1999). Levels of parental control are higher in those cultures, but children also better tolerate them. For many Pakistani women, for example, the concept of "supervision" is important in the definition of the parental role. Mothers are expected to keep tabs on their children and make sure they follow what is expected of them by the culture.

A study of second-generation Indian children in Britain (Atzaba-Poria, Pike, & Barrett 2004) examined different acculturation styles. The researchers proposed two different acculturation styles: the first, the traditional acculturation style, was characterized by the retention and maintenance of many of the values and customs of the culture of origin; the second, called "Western attitudes," was characterized more by acceptance and integration of values of the host country (in this case, Britain) into daily living and parenting. It was found, in part, that those Indian children whose parents employed a more traditional acculturation style in terms of parenting, including regular use of the native Indian language, displayed lower levels of internalizing, externalizing, and total problem behavior than those children who were raised with a more Western attitude.

Existing literature such as this indicates that there do exist cultural differences in regard to parenting and family dynamics, and that this is an area in which more careful examination is required (e.g., Darling & Steinberg 1993; Heine et al. 1999).

Parental Monitoring as a Construct

The term *parental monitoring* was first used by Patterson (1982) to describe the tendency of parents of antisocial children to not track or supervise the activities of their children. Over the next decade, much research was devoted to documenting the relationship between parental monitoring practices and child problem behavior, which could include substance use, academic failure, and behavior such as fighting, arguing, and stealing. Dishion and McMahon (1998) further defined parental monitoring as the "tracking and structuring" of a child's activities and environments (p. 236); more specifically, this involves the structuring of the child's home, school, and community environments, and observing the child's behavior in these environments. They advise that such monitoring directly impacts children's safety, the development of childhood and adolescent antisocial behavior, and substance use.

As children approach adolescence, they quite naturally tend to spend more time in unsupervised activities, often only in the company of friends. This lack of parental supervision has been found to correlate strikingly with less positive outcomes. For instance, it has been found that individual differences in parents' monitoring practices correlate with levels of antisocial behavior in boys (Patterson & Stouthamer-Loeber 1984). Parental monitoring has also been found to have both direct and indirect effects on delinquent behavior (Patterson & Dishion 1985), and poor parental monitoring has been found to be a significant factor in whether or not children start developing networks of deviant peers (i.e., peers who engage in delinquent behavior) in early adolescence (Dishion et al. 1991).

Parental monitoring has been found to correlate with amounts of adolescent problem behavior and substance use (see Hawkins & Catalano 1992; Laird et al. 2003; Loeber & Dishion 1983). Chilcoat and colleagues (1995) initiated a study among a population of inner-city and urban students in Baltimore, Maryland, to establish the effects of levels of parental monitoring on starting drug use in children. They used a sample of nearly 1,000 children, aged 8 to 10, who had no history of drug use, and assessed levels of drug use, monitoring by parents, and peer drug use. One year later, over 4% of the children in the sample were found to have started using alcohol, tobacco, or other drugs. Results indicated that those children who received lower levels of parental monitoring were found to be more at risk of starting drug use than those who received higher levels of monitoring.

Low levels of parental monitoring have been linked to levels of substance use in many studies (e.g., Brown et al. 1993; Fletcher et al. 1995). Dishion and Loeber (1985) found that parental monitoring was directly and indirectly correlated with young adolescents' alcohol and marijuana use. Links between parental monitoring and adolescents' association with deviant peers have also been established (e.g., Snyder, Dishion, & Patterson 1986). Dishion and colleagues (1991) tested two samples of adolescent boys in a longitudinal study that examined how the boys' family experiences later impacted their association with antisocial peers. Participants were first assessed at age 10 to measure levels of constructs such as parental monitoring and parental discipline. In both samples, levels of parental monitoring at age 10 were significantly negatively correlated with and predictive of later association with antisocial peers.

Parental monitoring has broad implications for prevention programs that aim to benefit children (Dishion & McMahon 1998); it is something that can be generally fairly easily manipulated and measured, and which can have discernable consequences. However, while parental monitoring has been measured and studied for decades in the West, it is not as thoroughly researched a topic in countries with different cultures, particularly cultures that are considered collectivistic.

Measuring Parental Monitoring

Parental monitoring during the adolescent years can be a difficult thing to measure. The nature of monitoring itself morphs throughout a child's development, from infancy to young adulthood. When assessing parental monitoring, changes in the developmental status and the expanding ecologies of the child must be considered (Dishion & McMahon 1998). In infancy, monitoring of a child takes place mainly in the home setting. In childhood, when much of a child's day is spent at school and after school with friends, monitoring by parents might include information gained from teachers, parents of other children, or babysitters. Once a child reaches adolescence and gains a certain degree of autonomy, he or she can themselves be an important source of information for parents, along with existing sources at school and the neighborhood. Neighborhood and community activities and peer groups take on greater importance for the adolescent; tracking and structuring the adolescent's community settings are relevant to this time period (Dishion et al. 1995). The parent-adolescent relationship is also key here; it is important to maintain a good relationship. Problem-solving and negotiation skills are especially important in adolescence (Forgatch 1989); conflict during parent-adolescent discussions can lead to the adolescent choosing to spend more time with peers away from home (Forgatch & Stoolmiller 1994).

Some researchers have felt that the current methods of measuring monitoring are not consistent with the complexity of the construct. In their recent studies, Kerr and Stattin (2000; Stattin & Kerr 2000) proposed a modified definition of parental monitoring. They agreed that parental tracking and surveillance of activities is necessary to promote positive child adjustment, but that those alone will not prevent children's interactions with deviant peers. They suggested that a child's willingness to share and disclose information is equally important. As such, an important component of the influence of parental monitoring in the prevention of adolescent problem behavior or association with deviant peers is the ability for parents to elicit willingness to disclose from their children, without making the children feel controlled. Their version of a parental monitoring measure, administered to both parents and children, assessed levels of child disclosure and parental solicitation, in addition to levels of parental control.

A potential issue with cross-cultural research is the measurement of constructs in different countries. Many assessments used on populations in different cultures were originally created for and based on European and Western populations. The efficacy of these measures and methodologies on non-Western populations has been challenged by many researchers (e.g., Marsella et al. 1985). Also, it may well be the case that different cultural groups have different community structures that take the place of "parental monitoring." In many Eastern cultures, extended family and community members play a large role in a child's or adolescent's upbringing. The concept of "parental monitoring" might be too restricting in these cases; that is to say, just because a parent does not know what a child is doing, it does not mean that the child is not being held accountable to and monitored by another adult or authority figure.

Model for Parental Monitoring and Adolescent Problem Behavior

The function of an empirically based model is to guide the design of effective intervention practices that both prevent and treat problem behavior in childhood and adolescence. Patterson and colleagues (1992) outlined a model describing the development of adolescent antisocial behavior. They indicated that family management practices, including levels of family conflict, family involvement, and parental monitoring, could have a significant bearing on adolescents' future associations with deviant peers and engagement in antisocial behavior. Parental mismanagement, such as engaging in inconsistent discipline, can trigger a cycle, whereby aversive parent-child encounters serve to reinforce children's aggressive or problematic behavior. Such behavior is not limited to the home environment; when children enter the school environment, these behavior patterns continue. Antisocial behavior in school can lead to rejection by peers; this can initiate association with deviant peers, who, in turn, are likely to reinforce antisocial behavior. This model takes into consideration the influence deviant peers have on adolescent antisocial behavior, but also proposes that these associations with deviant peers are themselves predicted by poor family management practices.

In the formative years of developing an empirical model, Dishion and Loeber (1985) noted that family management in general, and parental monitoring in particular, was associated with substance use in adolescence. Indeed, the model seemed quite simple: parental monitoring predicted both deviant peer association and substance use. Dishion, Capaldi, and colleagues (1995) expanded this work into a longitudinal model, showing that early adolescent problems in monitoring predicted involvement with deviant peers and drug use in middle adolescence. At this stage of the research, direct observations of friendship dynamics were included in the model, identifying a process referred to as "deviancy training" to be particularly predictive. Later, the joint contribution of peer deviance and monitoring over the course of adolescence was considered, and it was found that as youth became more involved in deviant peer networks, parents often relinquished their monitoring practices (i.e., negative longitudinal slope), and that both developmental dynamics predicted long-term patterns of problem behavior that reached into young adulthood (Dishion, Nelson, & Bullock 2004; Dishion & Owen 2002).

Most of the work on parental monitoring confirms the linkage between deviant peer involvement and problem behavior. However, there has been less work considering how well the construct holds across cultural groups, where patterns of childrearing may vary enough that parental monitoring may be of less importance. Surprisingly, when comparing various ethnic groups in the United States, it appears that parental monitoring holds up rather well as an explanatory construct (Chilcoat & Anthony 1996; Chilcoat, Dishion, & Anthony 1995). For example, in a study involving different ethnic groups in the United States, the replicability of a similar model was assessed (Barrera et al. 2001). The researchers discovered that there existed good consistency across Native American and Latino youth populations with regard to family influences in the prediction of adolescent problem behavior.

Current Study

The current study analyzed data collected from India, Italy, and Quebec (Montreal), Canada. India was chosen as a site since, culturally, it is notably different from Western populations such as those in Europe and North America; it is also a country that has not been heavily researched in this area thus far. This study had two main goals. The first goal was to assess the applicability of a model similar to that identified by Patterson and colleagues (1992). This model looks at the associations between parental monitoring and problem behavior, with deviant peer association as a suggested mediator, among Indian adolescents, in comparison to Italian and French Canadian adolescents. To our knowledge, the efficacy of this type of model had not been tested in non-Western populations outside of the United States. The second goal was to compare Indian adolescents to their Italian and French Canadian counterparts with respect to parental monitoring, deviant peer association, problem behavior, and substance use; it was hypothesized that Indian adolescents would report higher levels of positive parental monitoring and lower levels of deviant peer association, problem behavior, and substance use than either Italian or French Canadian adolescents.

Method

PARTICIPANTS AND DEMOGRAPHICS

The total sample consisted of 398 adolescents between the ages of 13 and 15 from three separate and distinct regions of the world: India, Italy, and Quebec, Canada. The Indian sample consisted of 58 males and 37 female adolescents (*Mage* = 14.5 years) in the 9th standard (age equivalent of 8th grade in Western countries) from the southern Indian city of Coimbatore, Tamil Nadu. All participants were born and raised in India and of Indian ethnicity and were fluent in both English and their native Indian language. The Italian sample consisted of 83 male (55%) and 69 (45%) female adolescents (*Mage* = 14 years), attending 8th grade in Padua, Padua province. Ninety-six percent of the adolescents were born in Italy and listed Italian as their native language. The French Canadian sample consisted of 61 (40%) male and 90 (60%) female adolescents (*Mage* = 14.6 years) attending 8th grade in Montreal, Quebec. Although most participants (82%) indicated that they were born in Canada, reported native language varied more so than in either the Indian or Italian samples—64% of participants reported French as their native language, 11% Spanish, 6% Creole, 3% English, and the rest other assorted languages.

Both Coimbatore and Montreal are medium-sized cities, each having populations of nearly two million people. Padua is included in the Padua-Venice Metropolitan Area, which has a population of about 1.6 million people. Demographically, 44% of the Indian households were considered middle- or lower-middle class, 97% were two-parent households, and 27% of parents had at least a bachelor's degree (15.8% had a two-year diploma). Forty-six percent of Italian households were middle-class, 90% were two-parent households, and 37.2% of parents had a professional qualification or technical degree. For the French Canadians, 41% of households were considered middle class, 63% were two-parent households (this included households in which a parent was cohabiting with a partner), and 26% of parents had a baccalaureate or university degree.

PROCEDURE

For all three samples, area middle schools were invited to participate. Materials explaining the nature of the study were sent to parents of 8th and 9th grade standard children who were interested in participating. These materials also invited parents to sign a letter of informed consent if they chose to let their child participate. Assent was also obtained from students who wished to participate and who had signed letters of consent from their parents. Of the 96 families approached in India, 95 (99%) students participated. In the Italian sample, signed parental consents and assents were obtained from 152 students (62% of all potential participants). Of the 260 potential participants in the French Canadian sample, signed parental consent and assent forms were obtained from 151 students (58% of all potential participants).

Research assistants initially approached students in classrooms (with the permission of principals and teachers) to describe the study. The research assistants returned to the classrooms several days later to administer questionnaires to students who had signed assent forms and whose parents had given informed consent. The questionnaires took anywhere from 60 to

90 minutes to complete; upon completion of the questionnaire, students were given the equivalent of $10 in cash or gift certificates. The questionnaires were written and administered in English for the Indian sample, as children in India are fluent in English from the time they start school. The questionnaires were translated into and administered in Italian for the Italian sample, and into French for the French Canadian sample. Both sets of measures were back-translated to English to ensure accuracy.

MEASURES

A full description of the measures can be found in table 4.1. These measures have been used, thus far, only on Western populations. Data on the reliability coefficients for each sample are presented in the next section.

Youth report. A self-report survey was adapted from previous research (Biglan, Ary, & Metzler 1995; Biglan, Metzler, & Ary 1994) to assess a variety of elements in the respondent's life in school, at home, and in the neighborhood. The survey assesses, among other things, problem behavior (e.g., *"In the last week, I purposely damaged or tried to damage property"*; *"I skipped school without an excuse"*), parental monitoring (e.g., *"How often does a parent know where you are after school?" "How often does a parent know what you are doing away from school?"*), parental rule-monitoring (e.g., *"My parents have a rule about me doing homework every day"*; *"My parents have a rule on being in the house without adult supervision"*), family positive relations (e.g., *"My parents and I get along really well"*; *"There's a feeling of togetherness in our family"*), and deviant peer groups and interactions (e.g., *"In the last week, I spent time with friends who fight a lot"*; *"I spent time with friends who take things that are not theirs"*). Each of the above scales was used for analysis in this study: parental monitoring, parental rule-monitoring, deviant peer association, and problem behavior (e.g., Dishion, Nelson, & Kavanagh 2003).

Parental monitoring. The child-report version of the Parental Monitoring Scale (Kerr & Stattin 2000; Stattin & Kerr 2000) is a standardized, validated, and reliable means of assessing levels of parental monitoring and control in the family. It consists of four different scales created using the mean scores: parental control (e.g., *"Do you need your parents' permission before you spend money?" "Do you need to have your parents' permission to stay out late on a weekday evening?"*); parental solicitation (e.g., *"In the last month,*

TABLE 4.1

Construct Items and Standardized Alphas

CONSTRUCT AND ITEMS	STANDARDIZED ALPHA (OVERALL)
Parental Monitoring	.75

Parental Monitoring

How often does a parent know what you are doing away from home?

How often does a parent know where you are after school?

How often does a parent have an idea about your plans for the next day?

How often does a parent know your interests, activities, and whereabouts?

In the last 2 days, how often did a parent know where you were and what you were doing?

Parental Rule-Monitoring

On a scale of 1-4, how true are each of these for you:

My parents have a rule about me doing homework every day.

My parents have a rule on not smoking cigarettes or using tobacco.

My parents have a rule on being in the house without adult supervision.

My parents have a rule on checking in with them if I come home late.

Family Relations

On a scale of 1-4, how true are each of these for you:

I really enjoy being with my parents.

My parents and I get along really well.

My parents trust my judgment.

There's a feeling of togetherness in my family.

My family members back each other up.

The things we do together are fun and interesting.

(continued)

TABLE 4.1 (*continued*)

CONSTRUCT AND ITEMS

STANDARDIZED ALPHA (OVERALL)

Parental Control

Do you need to have your parents' permission to stay out late on a weekday evening?

Do you need to ask your parents before you decide what you and your friends will do on a Saturday evening?

Do your parents always require that you finish your homework before going out with your friends?

Do you need your parents' permission before you spend money?

Do you need your parents' permission before going to a friend's house?

Parental Solicitation

In the last month, how often have your parents talked with the parents of your friends?

How often do your parents ask your friends what they like to do or what they think about different things?

During the past month, how often have your parents started a conversation with you about what you do during your free time?

How often do your parents ask you about things that happened during school?

How often do your parents ask you to talk about your friends and what you do together?

Self-disclosure

How often do you tell your parents how you are doing in school, without them asking?

Do you keep secrets from your parents about what you do during your free time?

Do you hide a lot from your parents about what you do during nights and weekends?

How often do you spontaneously tell your parents, without them asking you, what you do when you go out during the evening?

How often do you spontaneously tell your parents, without them asking you, about your friends and what you do together?

(*continued*)

TABLE 4.1 (*continued*)

CONSTRUCT AND ITEMS	STANDARDIZED ALPHA (OVERALL)

Trust

Do your parents trust you to be careful with money?
Do your parents trust you to take responsibility for your life?
Do your parents trust you to do their best in school?
Do your parents trust you when you're home alone?

Deviant Peer Association   .67

In the last week:

I spent time with friends who get in trouble.
I spent time with friends who fight a lot.
I spent time with friends who take things that are not theirs.
I spent time with friends who smoke cigarettes or chew tobacco.

Problem Behavior   .71

In the last week:

I lied to my parents about my whereabouts or whom I was with.
I stayed out all night without my parents' permission.
I intentionally hit or threatened someone at school.
I skipped school without an excuse.
I stole something worth more than $5.
I purposely damaged or tried to damage property.
I panhandled.
I carried or handled a weapon (gun or knife).
I spent time with gang members as friends.

how often have your parents talked with the parents of your friends?" *"How often do your parents ask you about things that happened during school?"*); self-disclosure (e.g., *"How often do you tell your parents how you are doing in school, without them asking?"* *"Do you hide a lot from your parents about what you do during the day?"*); and trust (e.g., *"Do your parents trust you to be careful with money?"* *"Do your parents trust you when you're home alone?"*).

Substance use. The substance-use section of the questionnaire was based on the Child Interview (CINT-S; Oregon Social Learning Center 1984), which consists of questions dealing with adolescent substance use. This measure asked adolescents to report how often in the past month the youth had smoked cigarettes, drank beer, drank wine (for the Italian sample, the term *"spritz,"* which is similar to a wine cooler, was used), drank hard alcohol, and smoked marijuana. Responses were given on a 14-point scale ranging from *"0"* to *"41 or more times"* in the past month. Adolescents were also asked whether they had *ever* used any of those substances.

ANALYTIC STRATEGY

Construct Formation. Three constructs (parental monitoring, deviant peer association, and problem behavior) were selected for use in the evaluation of the replication of the model of development of adolescent problem behavior in the Indian, Italian, and Canadian samples (see figure 4.1), as well as in the general comparison of the three samples regarding the constructs. Levels of substance use were assessed separately.

Parental monitoring. The monitoring construct was created by computing the standardized mean of items concerning adolescents' perceptions of parental monitoring, positive family relations, and parental rule-making (see table 4.1) from the Youth Report, as well as the parental control, parental solicitation, self-disclosure, and trust scales of the Parental Monitoring Scale (Kerr & Stattin 2000; Stattin & Kerr 2000). The standardized item alphas for this construct for the Indian, Italian, and Canadian samples were .68, .73, and .80, respectively; the standardized item alpha for the three samples combined was .75.

Deviant peer association. The deviant peer association construct was created by computing the mean of four items from the Youth Report, includ-

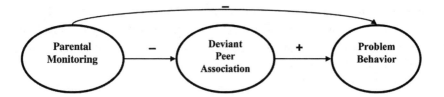

Figure 4.1   Constructs used in the meditational model of adolescent problem behavior

ing questions about friends who got in trouble or fought frequently. The standardized item alphas for this construct were .55 in the Indian sample, .71 in the Italian sample, and .72 in the Canadian sample.

Problem behavior. This construct was created by computing the mean of eight items from the Youth Report dealing with adolescent antisocial behavior, such as lying, hitting, damaging property, carrying weapons, and skipping school. For the Indian sample, the question regarding time spent with gang members was removed, due to the fact that the word *gang* is commonly used for the word *group* in India. The standardized item alphas for this construct were .61 in the Indian sample, .77 in the Italian sample, and .75 in the Canadian sample.

DATA ANALYSIS

For the replication portion, an examination to determine whether this model could be measured and identified in the three samples was first conducted. This was achieved by assessing bivariate correlations of the three constructs (parental monitoring, deviant peer association, and problem behavior). Then, standard multiple regression procedures were used to evaluate whether parental monitoring directly predicted adolescent problem behavior or was mediated by involvement with deviant peers. For these analyses, the predictor variables consisted of the parental monitoring and deviant peer association constructs; the criterion variable was the problem behavior construct.

The comparison of differences between the Indian, Italian, and Canadian samples with regard to parental monitoring, deviant peer association, and problem behavior was accomplished using one-way analyses of variance (ANOVA). Substance use in the Indian sample compared to substance use in the Italian and Canadian samples was extremely low; comparisons were made using percentages.

Results

The first part of the study involved assessing a model of development of adolescent problem behavior. The constructs of parental monitoring, deviant peer association, and problem behavior were assessed to determine the applicability of this model in the three samples, particularly among Indian adolescents. The second was to conduct a comparison between Indian, Italian, and Canadian adolescent samples of levels of those three constructs, as well as levels of substance use.

REPLICATION

Bivariate correlations. In order to determine the applicability of the model of the development of adolescent antisocial behavior among Indian, Italian, and Canadian adolescents; analyses of Pearson correlations of the three constructs (parental monitoring, deviant peer associations, and problem behavior) were first assessed for each of the three groups.

For the Indian group, only the correlations between parental monitoring and deviant peer association ($r = -.284$, $p < .01$) and between parental monitoring and problem behavior ($r = -.298$, $p < .01$) were significant. The correlation between deviant peer association and problem behavior was not significant, however, though the direction of the correlation was as expected (see table 4.2).

For the Italian sample, correlations between the constructs were found to be significant. There was a significant negative correlation between the parental monitoring and deviant peer association constructs ($r = -.319$, $p < .01$) and the parental monitoring and problem behavior constructs ($r = -.426$, $p < .01$). There was also, as predicted, a significant positive correlation between the deviant peer association and problem behavior constructs ($r = .425$, $p < .01$).

TABLE 4.2

Bivariate Correlations for Regression Model Constructs, by Country

	PARENTAL MONITORING	DEVIANT PEER ASSOCIATION	PROBLEM BEHAVIOR
Indians			
Parental monitoring	1	−.284**	−.298**
Deviant peer association	−.284**	1	.104
Problem behavior	−.298**	.104	1
Italians			
Parental monitoring	1	−.319**	−.426**
Deviant peer association	−.319**	1	.425**
Problem behavior	−.426**	.425**	1
French Canadians			
Parental monitoring	1	−.218**	−.458**
Deviant peer association	−.218**	1	.509**
Problem behavior	−.458**	.509**	1

Note: ** $p < .01$

Similarly, the Canadian sample showed significant correlations between the constructs in the expected directions. Significant negative correlations were present between the parental monitoring and deviant peer
association constructs ($r = −.218$, $p < .01$) and between the parental monitoring and problem behavior ($r = −.458$, $p < .01$). A significant positive correlation was found between the deviant peer association and problem behavior
constructs ($r = .509$, $p < .01$).

Multiple regression analysis. Multiple regression analyses were performed
on the Indian, Italian, and Canadian samples using the parental monitoring, deviant peer association, and problem behavior constructs to determine
whether parental monitoring would directly predict adolescent problem behavior or was mediated by adolescent deviant peer associations.

Regression analyses showed that the model partially predicted with the
Indian sample (see figure 4.2); analyses suggested that parental monitoring alone significantly contributed to the prediction of adolescent problem
behavior ($F (1, 91) = 8.64$, $p < .01$), with 8.7% of the variance in the prediction of problem behavior being explained by the model (see table 4.3).
When the deviant peer association construct was added into the model,

Contemporary Issues in Parental Monitoring

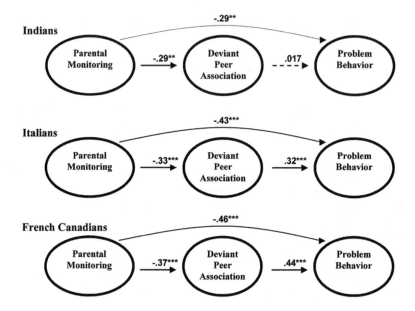

Figure 4.2   Results of model predicting problem behavior using parental monitoring and deviant peer association: Standardized beta coefficients.

however, R^2- and F-change statistics showed that parental monitoring did not continue to contribute uniquely to the prediction of problem behavior (F *change* (1, 90) = .026, p = .873). The full model, however, was significant in predicting adolescent problem behavior (F (2, 90) = 4.28, p < .017).

The model did significantly predict among Italian youth. Analyses suggested that parental monitoring significantly contributed to the prediction of adolescent problem behavior (F (1, 149) = 33.35, p < .001), with 18.3% of the variance in the prediction of problem behavior being explained by the model. When the deviant peer association construct was added into the model, R^2- and F-change statistics showed that parental monitoring continued to contribute uniquely to the prediction of problem behavior (F *change* (1, 148) = 18.87, p < .001), with 9.2% of the variance being explained by association with deviant peers. The full model significantly predicted adolescent problem behavior (F (2, 148) = 28.11, p < .001), with 27.5% of the variance being explained by parental monitoring and association with deviant peers.

Likewise, the model predicted adolescent problem behavior among Canadian youth. Regression analyses revealed that parental monitoring

TABLE 4.3

Summary of Model Predicting Problem Behavior Using Parental Monitoring and Deviant Peer Association

INDIANS

MODEL	R	R^2	SE	R^2 CHANGE	F CHANGE	UNSTANDARDIZED β	STANDARDIZED β	T
1. (Constant)	.294	.087	.965	.087	8.636**	.014		
Parental monitoring						-.507	-.294	-2.939**
2. (Constant)	.295	.087	.970	.000	.026	.013		
Parental monitoring						-.498	-.290	-2.757**
Deviant peers.						.017	.017	.160

ITALIANS

MODEL	R	R^2	SE	R^2 CHANGE	F CHANGE	UNSTANDARDIZED β	STANDARDIZED β	T
1. (Constant)	.428	.183	.910	.183	33.345***	.002		
Parental monitoring						-.684	-.428	-5.77***
2. (Constant)	.525	.275	.860	.092	18.869**	.002		
Parental monitoring						-.521	-.325	-4.41***
Deviant peers						.322	.321	4.34***

FRENCH CANADIANS

MODEL	R	R^2	SE	R^2 CHANGE	F CHANGE	UNSTANDARDIZED β	STANDARDIZED β	T
1. (Constant)	.458	.210	.893	.210	39.28***	-.003		
Parental monitoring						-.683	-.458	-6.27***
2. (Constant)	.619	.384	.791	.174	41.46***	.001		
Parental monitoring						-.544	-.365	-5.50***
Deviant peers						.427	.427	6.44***

Note: ** $p < .01$; *** $p < .001$

significantly contributed to the prediction of adolescent problem behavior in this population (F (1, 148) = 39.28, $p <$ .001), with 21.0% of the variance in the prediction of problem behavior being explained by the model. With the addition of the deviant peer association construct into the model, R^2- and F-change statistics indicated that parental monitoring still contributed uniquely to the prediction of problem behavior (F *change* (1, 147) = 41.46, $p <$ .001), with 17.4% of the variance being explained by association with deviant peers. As with the Italian youth, the full model significantly predicted adolescent problem behavior (F (2, 147) = 45.74, $p <$ .001), with 38.4% of the variance being explained by parental monitoring and deviant peer association.

MEAN LEVEL COMPARISON

In order to determine whether or not levels of parental monitoring, deviant peer association, and problem behavior differed among Indian, Italian, and Canadian adolescents, a series of ANOVA were performed (see table 4.4).

Parental monitoring. Contrary to the hypothesis, no significant differences were found between the Indian sample and either the Italian ($p =$ .994) or Canadian ($p =$ .983) samples in regard to parental monitoring.

Deviant peer association. Consistent with the hypothesis, Indian adolescents ($M =$ 0.51, $SD =$ 0.68) reported lower levels of deviant peer association than both Italian adolescents ($M =$ 0.88, $SD =$ 1.12; F (1, 243) = 8.49, $p =$ .004) and Canadian adolescents ($M =$ .77, $SD =$ 1.00; F (1, 243) = 5.13, $p =$ .002).

Problem behavior. With regard to levels of problem behavior, no significant differences were found between the Indian sample ($M =$ 1.22, $SD =$ 0.29) and the Italian sample ($M =$ 1.26, $SD =$ 0.40; F (1,245) = .80, $p =$ .371). However, consistent with the hypothesis, significant differences were found between the Indian sample and the Canadian sample (F (1, 244) = 9.63, $p =$ .002), with the Canadian adolescents ($M =$ 1.40, $SD =$ 0.51) reporting higher levels of antisocial behavior than the Indian adolescents.

Substance use. Levels of substance use among the three groups were compared using percentages (see tables 4.5 and 4.6). Substance use in

TABLE 4.4

Analysis of Variance Comparison by Construct

	Indian (N=95)	
	F	p
Italian (N=152)		
Parental monitoring	.000	.994
Deviant peer association	8.49	.004
Antisocial behavior	.80	.371
French Canadian (N=151)		
Parental monitoring	.000	.983
Deviant peer association	5.13	.024
Antisocial behavior	9.63	.002

TABLE 4.5

Amount of Substance Use (in Percentages) Used
by Adolescents in the Past Month

	CIGARETTES	ALCOHOL	MARIJUANA
Indian	1%	4%	0%
Italian	21%	59%	2%
French Canadian	22%	57%	26%

TABLE 4.6

Amount of Substance Use (in Percentages) Ever Used by Adolescents

	CIGARETTES	BEER	WINE	WINE COOLERS	HARD ALCOHOL	MARIJUANA
Indian	2%	2%	12%	3%	1%	0%
Italian	32%	54%	59%	35%	30%	3%
French Canadian	49%	66%	72%	56%	46%	39%

general among Indian adolescents was low. Of the 95 participants, only 1 (<1%) had used cigarettes in the past month. Only 4 participants (<4%) had used alcohol, and none had used marijuana.

Among Italian and Canadian adolescents, however, the numbers were markedly higher. Of the 152 Italian participants, 32 (21%) had used cigarettes, 89 (59%) had used alcohol, and 3 (2%) had used marijuana within the past month. Of the 152 Canadian youth, 33 (22%) had used cigarettes, 86 (57%) had used alcohol, and 39 (26%) had used marijuana in the past month.

It should also be noted that there were fairly large differences across the groups in terms of the percentage of adolescents who reported having *ever* used specific substances. In all cases, a larger percentage of the Canadian adolescents reported having ever used specific substances than either Italian or Indian adolescents, with between 12 to 36 percentage points higher than Italians and 38 to 64 percentage points higher than Indians. Specifically, for the Canadian sample, 49% had smoked cigarettes, 66% had had beer, 72% had drunk wine, 56% had had wine coolers, 46% had drunk hard alcohol, 39% had smoked marijuana; in the Italian sample, 32% had smoked cigarettes, 54% had had beer, 59% had drunk wine, 35% had had wine coolers (*spritz*), 30% had drunk hard alcohol, 3% had smoked marijuana. Finally, in the Indian sample, 2% had smoked cigarettes, 2% had had beer, 12% had drunk wine, 3% had had wine coolers, 1% had drunk hard alcohol, and none reported having smoked marijuana.

Discussion

A mediational model of adolescent problem behavior was assessed, similar to one identified by Patterson and colleagues (1992) that has been shown to replicate well among American adolescent populations (e.g., Ary et al. 1999; Barrera et al. 2001). This model was only partially replicated in the Indian sample. In the Italian and French Canadian samples, the model replicated perfectly. The Indian sample, however, only partially replicated. Parental monitoring uniquely predicted adolescent problem behavior and deviant peer association separately, but the full model was only near significant, as the development of problem deviant peer association did not significantly mediate behavior.

The partial replication may be due to the differences in mean levels of deviant peers across cultures. Consistent with our hypothesis, Indian adolescents in fact displayed lower levels of deviant peer association than their Italian and French Canadian counterparts, and lower levels of problem behavior than French Canadian adolescents. However, there were no significant differences among the three samples in terms of parental monitoring, or between Indians and Italians with regard to problem behavior. Support was found, however, for the assertion that lower levels of substance use would be found among Indian adolescents, as compared to Italian and French Canadian adolescents; Indian adolescents reported markedly lower levels of substance use, including cigarette, alcohol, and marijuana use. The results concerning deviant peer association and problem behavior are similar to those suggested by other studies (e.g., Greenberger et al. 2000).

The findings related to levels of adolescent substance use are more straightforward to interpret. Of note are seeming differences in cultural acceptance of drug and alcohol use. In Italy, for example, drinking wine with dinner is something that is done in many households; parents are frequently aware and tolerant of their children's consumption. As such, care needs to be taken when interpreting the substance use differences, as certain types of substance use may, in fact, be sanctioned by the parents and/or community, and may not be simply a delinquent behavior.

Cross-Cultural Measurement

As mentioned earlier, the potential issue with cross-cultural research is that measurements of constructs may vary from country to country. The fact that the mediational model of adolescent problem behavior did not replicate smoothly in the India sample might have come about in part because some of the constructs and measures used were too specific to European or Western populations. It may well be the case that in order for a model to replicate, exact measures do not need to be used at each site. Conger, Patterson, and Ge (1995) conducted a study in which the efficacy of a model assessing the influence of parental stress on adolescent adjustment was tested at two different research sites. Many of the indicators were specific to each site; the investigators relied on the assumption that multiple indicators of equivalent theoretical constructs would create models that were generalizable.

The model did, indeed, replicate across sites, including differences in geographic location, social contexts, gender, and developmental age of the respondent. This finding suggests that, in relation to the present study, perhaps the same measures need not have been used at all three sites; it might have been more fruitful to use measures that specifically addressed each construct in each cultural context. To this end, more collaboration between researchers in different countries needs to occur, so that aspects of different constructs relevant to each cultural context can first be assessed for reliability before use in research studies.

As mentioned before, in contrast to the findings in the Indian sample, the model did replicate well in Native American, Latino, and African American populations in the United States (Barrera et al. 2001). The fact that the same smooth results were not found in India only justifies the overarching premise of this study: to see whether adolescent groups of different ethnicities, especially those in an Eastern culture, would respond the same as those in Western cultures. It is quite possible that the reason the model replicated in ethnic groups in the United States is because those groups were influenced by the larger social context—American culture. Studies have shown the effects of the larger social context on areas such as family functioning (Biglan 1992). Native American and Latino children often go to the same schools as European American children, watch many of the same TV shows and movies, and shop at many of the same stores. They have much more interaction with European Americans and the American "way of life" than many children in many Eastern cultures ever will; inadvertently, they are influenced by the dominant, mainstream culture.

Additionally, though many measures are translated and back-translated, there is often a loss of linguistic equivalence (e.g., Tsai et al. 2001), whereby identical phrases can mean very different things. Such was the case with some terms used in measures in this study. For instance, the term *gang* or *gang member* in the United States has distinctly negative connotations, especially in association with violence. This, apparently, is not the case with other societies. Many children in the India sample, when asked whether or not their friends were gang members, indicated they were, often with the explanation that yes, those individuals were members of their "gang of friends." In Indian English, "gang" is synonymous with "group."

Cultural Issues of Monitoring

The fact that there were no differences in levels of parental monitoring among the groups is somewhat puzzling. Although monitoring levels do not vary when comparing these three contexts, levels of problem behavior do. If findings such as these replicate, it suggests there may be different mechanisms for influencing problem behavior across cultures, and the construct of monitoring may need further refinement.

Cross-cultural studies have indicated that parents in Eastern cultures often employ a stricter, more authoritarian parenting style (e.g., Rudy & Grusec 2001; Stewart et al. 1999) than their Western counterparts, often allowing their children less freedom. Several of the children in the India sample reported being in school, tutoring, or other organized activities for approximately 12 hours each day, leaving little time for unstructured social activities. It was expected, then, that children would be subjected to more monitoring in India. However, certain cultural trends have come to light that may impact the way constructs are measured.

The construct of "monitoring" in psychology is often synonymous with "parental monitoring." In Western cultures, where nuclear families are emphasized, parents are often the only ones who monitor their children. Other adults in other situations may monitor children, such as in school or at other activities, but such monitoring is discontinuous; children are passed from the supervision of one adult to the next or, as is the case with many teens, left unsupervised at times.

In many Eastern cultures, children are expected to disclose information regarding academics and activities voluntarily to their parents or other members of their extended family, who play a much larger role (e.g., Chen et al. 2003). Households often consist not only of parents, but often grandparents, aunts, uncles, and cousins, to many of whom children are answerable. If the parents are not home, it is likely that some other relatives are in the home. Thus, the definition of family and the constitution of the living space have rather powerful consequences for youth and how they spend their time. Dishion, Bullock, and Kiesner (2008) recently analyzed data suggesting that the operative factor in parental monitoring is simply the average number of hours a child spends with friends without an adult present. Thus, it may well be that the measurement of parental monitoring promoted by Kerr and Stattin (2000) does not really tap the key dynamic, despite its improvement of incorporating child effects in the monitoring process. Some contexts, such as in Indian culture, simply may not be structured in a way as to afford adolescents with predictable and extended periods of time when they can explore new behaviors such as substance use or other problem behaviors without a caregiving adult present.

Community involvement and membership is quite important in many cultures (Wakil, Siddique, & Wakil 1981). Families are aware of what happens in other families in the community and, conversely, are very aware that other families will know what happens in theirs (e.g., Burr & Chapman 2004; Chew-Graham et al. 2002). Thus, monitoring in this context extends beyond the immediate family, to the community; parents are not the only ones doing the monitoring. In fact, those being monitored are not only children, but adults and families as well, and not always with positive intentions (e.g., Chew-Graham et al. 2002).

Another mechanism that may be influential is a sense of familial collectivism with respect to shame and pride. In collectivist cultures, appearances in the community are especially important and might be a deterrent to problematic behavior by adolescents (Jessor et al. 2003). This might be in part why Indian adolescents reported markedly lower levels of substance use. In such contexts, to limit measurement of how monitored a child is to just the parents would be to seriously underestimate the actual amount of monitoring occurring. Simply changing the wording of a question from, for instance, "How often do you tell your parents where you are after school?" to "How often do you tell an adult where you are after school?" might have elicited some very different answers. One main limitation in this study was the fact that only child-report data were used; given that children are often monitored by other adults, it would have been useful to have been able to use data from parents, teachers, and other relatives in the home.

Finally, lower levels of problem behavior may simply be a function of lower thresholds in problem behavior that are culturally bound. Thus, Indian caregivers of adolescents may tolerate far less problem behavior, and these differences were not measured in the present study. Differences in thresholds have to be directly measured, as it is not reflected in the measurement strategy used in this report. Similar anomalies were observed in a study comparing levels of problem behavior among young Thai and American children (Weisz et al. 1995). This could play out in several ways, one being that Indian adolescents are simply more accustomed to being highly monitored, and therefore adjust their responses to the kinds of questions asked from the frame of their experiences and culture.

Future Directions

These hypotheses suggest the importance of cross-cultural research in understanding mechanisms and dynamics of youth-positive adjustment as well as problem behavior. Studies in similar Eastern cultures should be sure to accurately measure other sources of monitoring than the parents, and also measure how much influence the community has on childrearing practices and the prevention of problem behavior.

To make progress on these issues, there are at least two basic steps. First, in cross-cultural studies in general, it is imperative to gain enough knowledge of the culture, by collaborating with researchers within that culture, to ensure that the measures used will adequately assess the constructs they are meant to assess. Investigators cannot automatically assume that their interpretations of a given construct or item will match the interpretations of their study's subjects.

The second step is to consider measurement strategies and indicators that may better directly observe actual behaviors that underlie the psychological constructs we measure and use to test theoretical models. Direct-observation strategies of parent-adolescent communications have been used with some success in previous research (Dishion, Nelson, & Bullock 2004; Dishion, Nelson, & Kavanagh 2003). These strategies offer opportunities for ratings of parental monitoring based on observed interactions between the child and the parent. We have used the following as a prompt to elicit relevant discussions: "Tell your parent(s) about a time when you were with friends and there were no adults present. Tell them who you were with, where you were, and what you were doing." It is often obvious the variability in the amount of free time with friends some adolescents have, as well as parental thresholds and norms, and the communication dynamics between the parent and child. Another promising measurement strategy is a brief periodic assessment, which assesses specific behaviors rather than inferential constructs. For example, as noted previously, we have used the following: "How many hours was ——— with peers in the last day when there were no adults present?" We have asked the youth a similar question, and found excellent conversation in their reports of "Hours Unsupervised." Measures that are less ambiguous require fewer inferences and are less vulnerable to cultural variation; they are also more likely to unveil important differences and similarities between cultural contexts.

As these data hint, an important aspect of model testing is to branch out to cultures that are more radically different than our own industrialized Western cultures. The fact remains that the understanding of Eastern cultures is often yet elusive to Western researchers. The effects of a culture, especially one that is more cohesive than those of many Western cultures, on family dynamics are not to be underestimated. The inclusion of greater cultural sensitivity is only the first step toward understanding the psychology of families in other cultures.

Note

This research was supported by grants DA 07031 and DA 018760 from the National Institute of Health. We are grateful for the active support of P. R. Krishna Kumar and Parvathy Varier at the Ayurvedic Trust, in Coimbatore, India.

References

Ary, D. V., Duncan, T. E., Biglan, A., Metzler, C. W., Noell, J. W., & Smolkowski, K. (1999). Development of adolescent problem behavior. *Journal of Abnormal Child Psychology, 27,* 141–150.

Atzaba-Poria, N., Pike, A., & Barrett, M. (2004). Internalising and externalising problems in middle childhood: A study of Indian (ethnic minority) and English (ethnic minority) children living in Britain. *International Journal of Behavioral Development, 28,* 449–460.

Barrera, M., Jr., Biglan, A., Ary, D., & Li, F. (2001). Replication of a problem behavior model with American Indian, Hispanic, and Caucasian youth. *Journal of Early Adolescence, 21,* 133–157.

Baumrind, D. (1967). Child care practices anteceding three patterns of preschool behavior. *Genetic Psychology Monographs, 75,* 43–48.

Baumrind, D. (1991). The influence of parenting style on adolescent competence and substance use. *Journal of Early Adolescence, 11,* 56–95.

Berry, J. W., Poortinga, Y. P., Segall, M. H., & Dasen, P. R. (1992). *Cross-cultural psychology: Research and applications.* New York: Cambridge University Press.

Biglan, A. (1992). Family practices and the larger social context. *New Zealand Journal of Psychology, 21,* 37–43.

Biglan, A., Ary, D. & Metzler, C. (1995). CASY: Community action for successful youth. Eugene: Oregon Research Institute.

Biglan, A., Metzler, C., & Ary, D. (1994). Increasing the prevalence of successful children: The case for community intervention research. *Behavior Analyst, 17,* 331–335.

Bornstein, M. H., Tamis-LeMonda, C. S., Tal, J., Ludeman, P., Toda, S., Rahn, C. W., et al. (1992). Maternal responsiveness to infants in three societies: The United States, France, and Japan. *Child Development, 63,* 808–821.

Brown, B. B., Mounts, N., Lamborn, S. D., & Steinberg, L. (1993). Parenting practices and peer group affiliation in adolescence. *Child Development, 64,* 467–482.

Burr, J., & Chapman, T. (2004). Contextualizing experiences of depression in women from South Asian communities: A discursive approach. *Sociology of Health and Illness, 26,* 433–452.

Chao, R. K. (1994). Beyond parental control and authoritarian parenting style: Understanding Chinese parenting through the cultural notion of training. *Child Development, 65,* 1111–1119.

Chen, C., Dong, Q., & Zhou, H. (1997). Authoritative and authoritarian parenting practices and social and school performance in Chinese children. *International Journal of Behavioral Development, 21,* 855–873.

Chen, C., Greenberger, E., Farruggia, S., Bush, K., & Dong, Q. (2003). Beyond parents and peers: The role of important non-parental adults (VIPs) in adolescent development in China and the United States. *Psychology in the Schools, 40,* 35–50.

Chew-Graham, C., Bashir, C., Chantler, K., Burman, E., & Batsleer, J. (2002). South Asian women, psychological distress, and self-harm: Lessons for primary care trusts. *Health and Social Care in the Community, 10,* 339–347.

Chilcoat, H. D., & Anthony, J. C. (1996). Impact of parent monitoring on initiation of drug use through late childhood. *Journal of the American Academy of Child and Adolescent Psychiatry, 35,* 91–100.

Chilcoat, H. D., Dishion, T. J., & Anthony, J. C. (1995). Parent monitoring and the incidence of drug sampling in urban elementary school children. *American Journal of Epidemiology, 141,* 25–31.

Conger, R. D., Patterson, G. R., & Ge, X. (1995). It takes two to replicate: A mediational model for the impact of parents' stress on adolescent adjustment. *Child Development, 66,* 80–97.

Darling, N., & Steinberg, L. (1993). Parenting style as context: An integrative model. *Psychological Bulletin, 113,* 487–496.

Dishion, T. J., Bullock, B. M., & Kiesner, J. (2008). Vicissitudes of parenting adolescents: Daily variations in parental monitoring and the early emergence of drug use. In M. Kerr, H. Stattin, & R. C. M. E. Engels (Eds.), *What can parents do? New insights into the role of parents in adolescent problem behavior* (pp. 113–133). Chichester, Eng.: Wiley.

Dishion, T. J., Capaldi, D. M., Spracklen, K. M., & Li, F. (1995). Peer ecology of male adolescent drug use. *Development and Psychopathology, 7,* 803–824.

Dishion, T. J., & Loeber, R. (1985). Adolescent marijuana and alcohol use: The role of parents and peers revisited. *American Journal of Drug and Alcohol Abuse, 11,* 11–25.

Dishion, T. J., & McMahon, R. J. (1998). Parental monitoring and the prevention of child and adolescent problem behavior: A conceptual and empirical formulation. *Clinical Child and Family Psychology Review, 1,* 61–75.

Dishion, T. J., Nelson, S. E., & Bullock, B. M. (2004). Premature adolescent autonomy: Parent disengagement and deviant peer process in the amplification of problem behavior. In J. Kiesner & M. Kerr (Eds.), Peer and family processes in the development of antisocial and aggressive behavior [Special Issue]. *Journal of Adolescence, 27,* 515–530.

Dishion, T. J., Nelson, S. E., & Kavanagh, K. (2003). The Family Check-Up for high-risk adolescents: Motivating parenting monitoring and reducing problem behavior. In J. E. Lochman, & R. Salekin (Eds.), Behavior oriented interventions for children with aggressive behavior and/or conduct problems [Special Issue]. *Behavior Therapy, 34,* 553–571.

Dishion, T. J., & Owen, L. D. (2002). A longitudinal analysis of friendships and substance use: Bidirectional influence from adolescence to adulthood. *Developmental Psychology, 38,* 480–491.

Dishion, T. J., Patterson, G. R., Stoolmiller, M., & Skinner, M. L. (1991). Family, school, and behavioral antecedents to early adolescent involvement with antisocial peers. *Developmental Psychology, 27,* 172–180.

Duncan, S. C., Duncan, T. E., Biglan, A., & Ary, D. (1998). Contributions of the social context to the development of adolescent substance use: A multivariate latent growth modeling approach. *Drug and Alcohol Dependence, 50,* 57–71.

Ekblad, S. (1986). Relationships between child-rearing practice and primary school children's functional adjustment in the People's Republic of China. *Scandinavian Journal of Psychology, 27,* 220–230.

Fletcher, A., Darling, N., Steinberg, L., & Dornbusch, S. (1995). The company they keep: Relation of adolescents' adjustment and behavior to their friends' perceptions of authoritative parenting in the social network. *Developmental Psychology, 31*, 300–310.

Forgatch, M. S. (1989). Patterns and outcome in family problem solving: The disrupting effect of negative emotion. *Journal of Marriage and Family, 51*, 115–124.

Forgatch, M. S., & Stoolmiller, M. (1994). Emotions as contexts for adolescent delinquency. *Journal of Research on Adolescence, 4*, 601–614.

Greenberger, E., Chen, C., Beam, M., Whang, S., & Dong, Q. (2000). The perceived social contexts of adolescents' misconduct: A comparative study of youths in three cultures. *Journal of Research on Adolescence, 10*, 365–388.

Greenfield, P. (1994). Independence and interdependence as developmental scripts: Implications for theory, research, and practice. In P. M. Greenfield & R. R. Cocking (Eds.), *Cross-cultural roots of minority child development* (pp. 1–37). Hillsdale, NJ: Erlbaum.

Harkness, S., & Super, C. M. (1995). Culture and parenting. In M. H. Bornstein (Ed.), *Handbook of parenting: Biology and ecology of parenting, vol. 2* (pp. 211–234). Mahwah, NJ: Erlbaum.

Harkness, S., Super, C. M., & Keefer, C. H. (1992). Learning to be an American parent: How cultural models gain directive force. In R. D'Andrade & C. Strauss (Eds.), *Human motives and cultural models* (pp. 163–178). New York: Cambridge University Press.

Hawkins, D. J., & Catalano, R. F., Jr. (1992). *Communities that care: Action for drug abuse prevention.* San Francisco: Jossey-Bass.

Heine, S., Lehman, D., Markus, H., & Kitayama, S. (1999). Is there a universal need for positive self-regard? *Psychological Review, 106*, 766–794.

Jessor, R., Turbin, M. S., Costa, F. M., Dong, Q., Zhang, H., & Wang, C. (2003). Adolescent problem behavior in China and the United States: A cross-national study of psychosocial protective factors. *Journal of Research on Adolescence, 13*, 329–360.

Kagitçibasi, C. (1996a). The autonomous-relational self: A new synthesis. *European Psychologist, 1*, 180–186.

Kagitçibasi, C. (1996b). Family and human development across countries: A view from the other side. Mahwah, NJ: Erlbaum.

Kerr, M., & Stattin, H. (2000). What parents know, how they know it, and several forms of adolescent adjustment: Further support for a reinterpretation of monitoring. *Developmental Psychology, 36*, 366–380.

Laird, R. D., Pettit, G. S., Dodge, K. A., & Bates, J. E. (2003). Change in parents' monitoring knowledge: Links with parenting, relationship quality, adolescent beliefs, and antisocial behavior. *Social Development, 12*, 401–419.

Loeber, R., & Dishion, T. (1983). Early predictors of male delinquency: A review. *Psychological Bulletin, 94,* 68–99.

Marsella, A. J., Sartorius, N., Jablensky, A., & Fenton, F. R. (1985). Cross-cultural studies of depressive disorders: An overview. In A. Kleinman & B. Good (Eds.), *Culture and depression: Studies in the anthropology and cross-cultural psychiatry of affect and disorder* (pp. 299–324). Los Angeles: University of California Press. Oregon Social Learning Center. (1984). Oregon Social Learning Center Child Interview. Eugene: Oregon Social Learning Center.

Patterson, G. R. (1982). *Coercive family process.* Eugene, OR: Castalia.

Patterson, G. R., & Dishion, T. J. (1985). Contributions of families and peers delinquency. *Criminology, 23,* 63–79.

Patterson, G. R., Reid, J. B., & Dishion, T. J. (1992). *Antisocial boys.* Eugene, OR: Castalia.

Patterson, G. R., & Stouthamer-Loeber, M. (1984). The correlation of family management practices and delinquency. *Child Development, 55,* 1299–1307.

Rudy, D., & Grusec, J. E. (2001). Correlates of authoritarian parenting in individualist and collectivist cultures and implications for understanding the transmission of values. *Journal of Cross-Cultural Psychology, 32,* 202–212.

Snyder, J., Dishion, T. J., & Patterson, G. R. (1986). Determinants and consequences of associating with deviant peers during preadolescence and adolescence. *Journal of Early Adolescence, 6,* 29–43.

Stattin, H., & Kerr, M. (2000). Parental monitoring: A reinterpretation. *Child Development, 71,* 1072–1085.

Stewart, S. M., Bond, M. H., Zaman, R. M., McBride-Chang, C., Rao, N., Ho, L. M., et al. (1999). Functional parenting in Pakistan. *International Journal of Behavioral Development, 23,* 747–770.

Suizzo, M. (2004). French and American mothers' childrearing beliefs: Stimulating, responding, and long-term goals. *Journal of Cross-Cultural Psychology, 35,* 606–626.

Tsai, J. L., Butcher, J. N., Munoz, R. F., & Vitousek, K. (2001). Culture, ethnicity, and psychopathology. In P. B. Sutker & H. E. Adams (Eds.), *Comprehensive handbook of psychopathology* (pp.105–127). New York: Kluwer Academic/ Plenum.

Vazsonyi, A. T. (2003). Parent-adolescent relations and problem behaviors: Hungary, the Netherlands, Switzerland, and the United States. *Marriage and Family Review, 32,* 161–187.

Wakil, S. P., Siddique, C. M., & Wakil, F. A. (1981). Between two cultures: A study in socialization of children of immigrants. *Journal of Marriage and Family, 43,* 929–940.

Weisz, J. R., Chaiyasit, W., Weiss, B., Eastman, K. L., & Jackson, E. W. (1995). A multimethod study of problem behavior among Thai and American children in school: Teacher reports versus direct observations. *Child Development, 66,* 402–415.

Whiting, B. B., & Edwards, C. P. (1988). *Children of different worlds: The formation of social behavior.* Cambridge: Harvard University Press.

[5]

When Is Parenting Over?

Examining Parental Monitoring and High-risk Alcohol Consumption in Young Adult College Students

ROB TURRISI, ANNE E. RAY, and CAITLIN ABAR

During childhood, parental monitoring can take on different forms such as direct behavioral observation or communication. For example, parents may watch their children play at a park or near a busy street or they may want to know where they are going and with whom after school hours. Both types of monitoring are intended to make sure that children are safe and away from situations where there is danger. Early on, there is more of the former monitoring approach and less of the latter. However, as children develop into their teen years, this trend reverses. Although there are still opportunities to engage in direct observation, such as encouraging teens to have their friends over, bringing food or other tangible goods as ways of "checking in" when friends are over, or volunteering to chaperone a school event or coach a team, in adolescence parental monitoring primarily shifts from observation to communication.

For the most part, parental monitoring communication practices consist of parents asking their teens where they are going, what they are doing, and with whom. The purpose of the monitoring has not changed from making sure that children are safe and away from danger, but the process, quantity, and quality has changed. Lastly, as teens develop into the stage of late adolescence—emerging adulthood, when there is greater emphasis on part-time jobs, driving, graduating from high school, and starting college—there are even fewer occasions where parents have the chance to engage in direct observation. At this point, monitoring shifts almost entirely into communication about what the teens are doing, when, and with whom. It is during this time that many parents believe, at this point in their child's life, their primary role is to provide physical-tangible resources such as food, shelter, and money. The familial values have already been conveyed and reinforced over numerous occasions and now, by and large, it is the responsibility of teens, not their parents, to keep themselves away from harm. Although most parents would argue that they are not truly done parenting, many would concede that their roles have diminished greatly. The questions beg then, are they done or close to being done? Do they need to know about what their young adult children are up to?

It is a complicated philosophical and empirical question when consideration is given to the high rates of drug and alcohol abuse, sexually transmitted diseases, sexual assaults, and unintended pregnancies during this phase of the developmental period. The focus of this chapter is to examine whether parenting, in the form of parental monitoring, has a continued and important role in terms of preventing harm even at this late stage of development in the parent-teen relationship. Our examination draws from our own research program exploring the relationship between parenting and high-risk alcohol use in college students. We could only locate two published studies to guide our conceptualization of parental monitoring after teens leave home to attend college (e.g., Turrisi et al. 2001; Wood et al. 2004), both of which used adaptations of items from Barnes (1990). In our current research, monitoring was conceptualized as parental monitoring activity (e.g., How often do your parents try to know where you go at night? How often do your parents try to know what you do with your free time? How often do your parents try to know where you are most afternoons after school?).

Background

Studies conducted over the last decade reveal that the highest proportion of heavy drinkers and individuals with diagnosable alcohol substance disorders are 18 to 29 years of age, the ages encompassing over 92% of all enrolled college students (Dawson et al. 2004; Grant 1997; Hurlbut & Sher 1992; Johnston, O'Malley, & Bachman 1991; Newman, Crawford, & Nellis

1991; O'Malley & Johnston 2002; Schall, Kemeny, & Maltzman 1992; Wechsler, Davenport et al. 1994; Wechsler, Issac et al. 1994; Wood, Nagoshi, & Dennis 1991). A number of individually based factors have been implicated in the etiology of alcohol misuse among college students. These include gender, ethnicity, personality, and family history (Baer, Kivlahan, & Marlatt 1995; Sher et al. 1991; Wechsler, Davenport et al., 1994), alcohol expectancies and motives for drinking (Carey & Correia 1997; Goldman, Greenbaum, & Darkes 1997; Johnson & Fromme 1994; Stewart, Zeitlin, & Samoluk 1996; Wood, Sher, & Strathman 1996), availability and attractiveness of alternative activities (Turrisi 1999; Vuchinich & Tucker 1988), and perceptions of risk for negative consequences (Mallet et al. 2006). Other external factors such as alcohol availability and pricing, alcohol offers, social modeling, and perceived descriptive and injunctive norms have also been found to be related to heavy drinking outcomes (Carey 1993, 1995; Graham, Marks, & Hansen 1991; Hawkins, Catalano, & Miller 1992; Larimer et al. 1997; Wood et al. 2001).

College is also a time where individuals make great strides into adulthood. For example, data from the *Chronicle of Higher Education* indicate that 85.7% of individuals attending undergraduate institutions in 2006 lived away from home (Chronicle of Higher Education, 2007). Many of these students support themselves by part- or full-time jobs while attending classes (47.2 %) and establish many new friendship networks (Borsari & Carey 2001; Epstein et al. 1995; Scheier & Botvin 1997). This new independence forces the adolescent to make daily decisions regarding time use and lifestyle choices without direct adult input (Maggs 1997; Schulenberg et al. 1996). These same decisions are also required about the use of alcohol. Unfortunately, the data suggest that between 20 and 40% of students make decisions to drink in a frequent heavy episodic manner (four drinks or more in a sitting for females, five or more for males) (Wechsler, Davenport et al. 1994). Thus, it has been argued that alcohol poses the greatest risk to the health of university students (Hingson et al. 2002; Prentice & Miller 1993).

The widespread prevalence of collegiate alcohol abuse has underscored the need for empirically supported interventions (Hingson, Berson, & Dowley 1997; Marlatt, Baer, & Larimer 1995). Numerous approaches to preventive interventions with college student drinkers have been forwarded, including universal (Haines & Spear 1996), selective (Larimer et al. 2001; Turrisi et al. 2001) and indicated preventive efforts (Marlatt et al. 1998). In addition to policy-based approaches (Bormann & Stone 2001; Cohen & Rogers 1997; O'Hare & Sherrer 1999), suggested modalities for these interventions have included environmental, group-based, and individual-level interventions (for a review, see Larimer & Cronce 2002). Each unique approach carries with it both advantages and disadvantages, and the scope of college drinking requires that it be addressed across multiple domains, through the integration of various empirically validated approaches.

Until recently, one notable gap in current prevention efforts for college drinking has been parent-based interventions. Parent interventions have a long and distinguished history in the psychology literature, addressing a variety of health, social, academic, and behavioral problems of children and adolescents (Borkowski, Ramey, & Bristol-Power 2002; Bornstein 2002; Fine 1989; Socha & Stamp 1995). In addition, a substantial body of literature has underscored the importance of parental involvement in adolescent substance use, even among those in late adolescence or early adulthood (Duncan, Duncan, & Hops 1994; Reifman et al. 1998; Turrisi, Wiersma, & Hughes 2000; Windle 2000). Studies have reported relationships between teen drinking and parent attitudes and beliefs (Barnes & Welte 1986; DiBlaso 1986; Hawkins, Catalano, & Miller 1992; McDermott 1984), and parent behaviors (Ary et al. 1993; Beck & Lockhart 1992; Dielman 1995; Hansen et al. 1987). For example, Turner, Larimer, and Sarason (2000) found parent-child conflict at entrance to college was positively related to heavier alcohol consumption and negative consequences one year later for fraternity and sorority members. Wood and colleagues (2000) found that parental modeling and monitoring were related to lowered use, problems, and moderated peer influences on drinking outcomes.

In light of the literature pointing to the continued importance of parental influences on the alcohol use of adolescents (Barnes 1990; Dishion, Kavanagh, & Reid 1989; Hawkins, Catalano, & Miller 1992; Johnson et al. 1990; Peterson et al. 1995), a number of parent-based interventions have been developed to prevent or reduce early and mid-adolescent alcohol misuse. These interventions have generally been efficacious in increasing parental concern and awareness of adolescent alcohol use, parent-child communication, and parental involvement regarding decision making around drugs and alcohol and, subsequently, decreased adolescent alcohol use (Johnson et al. 1990; McPherson & McKnight 1987; Rohrbach et al. 1995).

Despite the positive findings of parent-based interventions for adolescent substance abuse, these approaches have not been readily applied to the area of excessive drinking among college student populations. A review of the universal, selective, and targeted prevention programs shows a downward trend in interventions for 16- to 20-year-olds for parent-involved programs (Spoth, Greenberg, & Turrisi 2008). This probably derives from the widespread assumption that parents have minimal influence on their children at this late stage of adolescent development. Our program of research was designed to empirically test this and other assumptions regarding parental influence on college students, through conducting randomized trials of a parent-based intervention delivered in the summer prior to college entrance (Turrisi, Padilla, & Wiersma 2000; Turrisi et al. 2001). As described in our published studies, results indicate our parent intervention produced significant differences in consumption and negative consequences in comparison to controls (D'Amico et al. 2005; Lange et al. 2002; Turrisi et al. 2001).

Theoretical Approach

The theoretical model guiding our research program, using constructs from social psychological theories of decision making and parent-teen relationships, is shown in figure 5.1. According to the model, parents exposed to our intervention are more likely to have specific communications about alcohol with their teens (identified under the column labeled *Distal Mediators*). Particularly, the parent attempts to persuade or convince a teen to perform or not perform a behavior. Thus, we are in a classic "persuasion" situation as conceptualized in the field of attitude change in social psychology. The parent is the "source" of a "message" and the teen is the "recipient" of that message. Specific parental attributes that help convey the information in these focused communications include (a) perceived expertise (e.g., parents give good advice to their teens), (b) perceived trustworthiness of the source (e.g., looking out for the teen's best interests), (c) availability, (d) dealing with conflict, and (e) listening as opposed to lecturing (see Guilamo-Ramos et al. 2006). It is believed that with our parent materials, parents learn to develop communications that maximize these dimensions, which, in turn, greatly increases the effectiveness of discussions with their teens.

The second column, labeled *Proximal Mediators*, has variables from our theoretical models of decision making (specific beliefs about the positive/

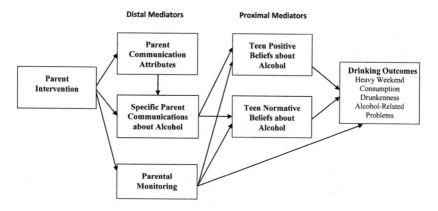

Figure 5.1   Theoretical Mediation Model

negative consequences of drinking and normative beliefs about drinking). These represent constructs that the parent is trying to persuade or influence. In turn, the proximal mediators have a direct influence on drinking outcomes. In our theoretical model we propose that parental monitoring has both a direct and an indirect impact on drinking outcomes. The direct influence is presumed to function through teens' perceptions that their parents will know if they engage in drinking activities and will not approve of them. By engaging in active monitoring activities, parents are implicitly or explicitly sending a message to their teens that they are taking responsibility for knowing their teens' whereabouts and activities. As parents communicate and discuss the teens' "comings and goings" (e.g., How often do your parents try to know where you go at night?), teens are less likely to engage in activities that might result in not being trusted or receiving parental sanctions. The indirect influence is presumed to be mediated by teens' alcohol-related beliefs. As parents engage in monitoring activities, this gives them greater opportunities to reinforce values regarding safe versus risky behaviors, affect change on teens' beliefs about drinking, and assist teens in making safer choices about drinking behaviors.

Finally, our theoretical model suggests the potential for parental monitoring to moderate the relationship between proximal mediators (drinking beliefs) and drinking outcomes (path not shown in fig. 5.1). For example, when there is below-average parental monitoring, it is plausible to expect that as the perceptions about drinking become more positive, more drinking will occur (a positive slope). In this case, parents show little interest in their teens' whereabouts and behaviors, and the teens' beliefs have more influence, for better or worse, on their behaviors. However, as the degree of parental monitoring increases to average or above-average levels, it is plausible to expect that perceptions about drinking will have less influence on drinking (flatter slope). In this case, parents show greater interest in their teens' whereabouts and behaviors, and the teens' beliefs have less influence on their behaviors.

Although some reports have suggested that the salience of parental influences is proposed to recede (Hawkins, Catalano, & Miller 1992; Kandel & Andrews 1987; Windle 2000; Wood et al. 2001), there are others that indicate that parents are active in helping their teens prepare for and adjust to college (American College Health Association 2003; Amerikaner et al. 1994; Brack, Gay, & Matheny 1993; Galotti & Mark 1994; Kashubeck & Christensen 1995). For example, Galotti and Mark (1994) found that high school seniors consulted with their parents significantly more often than peers and teachers in evaluating academic (type of school, programs) and institutional factors (location, dorms/off-campus housing, and distance from home). Langhinrichsen-Rohling, Larsen, and Jacobs (1997) observed that adolescents who reported more cohesion with their parents had smoother transitions to college and in developing new relationships. Taken together, these studies suggest the potential importance of parents in their sons' and daughters' lives even when they have achieved young adulthood and/or moved away from home.

Study Design

The data we used were from a larger study examining the efficacy of parent interventions on college freshmen. The respondents in the present analyses of parental monitoring and drinking behaviors consisted of 433 incoming freshmen attending colleges in the United States and who resided near the University at Albany, State University of New York (SUNY), and Boise State University just prior to attending college that were in the control conditions.[1] Only control students were utilized in the present study to assess the relationships that naturally occur between parent and student variables in college and universities in the United States, independent of any unique program effects. As described by Turrisi and colleagues (2001), parents of the students of high schools surrounding the two universities were contacted initially by telephone and asked whether they had a son or daughter who was a senior in high school who would be attending college in the fall. If they did, their teens were mailed a letter which described the study and invited them to participate. A follow-up phone call was made to confirm students' willingness to complete the survey. Once teens expressed a verbal interest in completing the survey, they were mailed a consent form, the survey, and a postage-paid return envelope. Individuals who completed the survey received a small monetary incentive. Our response rate using this approach was 97%.

Teens completed a battery of measures assessing drinking tendencies and consequences, perceptions about drinking, normative perceptions about drinking, and measures of parental monitoring and the perceptions of parenting constructs during the summer prior to college and approximately 90 days into their first semester in college. The measures were all drawn from the general literature on college drinking and our own program of research described in detail in our published studies (e.g., Turrisi 1999; Turrisi, Padilla, & Wiersma 2000; Turrisi, Wiersma, & Hughes 2000; Turrisi et al. 2001). Those selected for our analyses of parental monitoring and drinking behaviors are reported in table 5.1. All measures are from the teens' perceptions. Thus, parental monitoring is conceptualized from the standpoint of how much teens perceive their parents' monitor their behavior.

The demographic composition of the sample was 44% male, 56% female; 38% liberal, 45% moderate, and 17% conservative; 92% Caucasian, 1% African American, 1% Asian, and 4% other; 25% Catholic, 11% Protestant, 4 % Jewish, 17% Church of Latter Day Saints, and 25% other. Despite the fact that all teen respondents were below the legal age for drinking at baseline (mean age = 18.12), 70% indicated that they had gotten drunk at least one time in the past year, 30% indicated that they had consumed five or more drinks two weeks prior to the data collection period, and 30% indicated that they drank alcohol weekly.

Analytic Approach

Our analyses are organized into three sections. First, we examined the relationship between parental monitoring and high-risk drinking using linear regression models. Second, we examined the mediational relationships

TABLE 5.1

Measures Used in the Analyses

VARIABLE LABEL		QUESTION	RESPONSE OPTIONS
pmonit1	yougo1	How often do your parents try to know where you go at night?	3 point scale including "don't try," "try a little," and "try a lot"
	yourtim1	How often do your parents try to know what you do with your free time?	3 point scale including "don't try," "try a little," and "try a lot
	aftersc1	How often do your parents try to know where you are most afternoons after school?	3 point scale including "don't try," "try a little," and "try a lot"
drinking1	thurs1	Given that it is a typical week, please write the number of drinks you probably would have on a Thursday	Open-ended
	friday1	Given that it is a typical week, please write the number of drinks you probably would have on a Friday	Open-ended
	sat1	Given that it is a typical week, please write the number of drinks you probably would have on a Saturday	Open-ended
	drunk1	During the past 30 days (about 1 month), how many times have you gotten drunk, or very high from alcohol?	6 point scale including "Never," "1–2," "3–4," "5–6," "7–8," and "9 or more"
pmonit2	yougo2	How often do your parents try to know where you go at night?	3 point scale including "don't try," "try a little," and "try a lot"
	yourtim2	How often do your parents try to know what you do with your free time?	3 point scale including "don't try," "try a little," and "try a lot"
	aftersc2	How often do your parents try to know where you are most afternoons after school?	3 point scale including "don't try," "try a little," and "try a lot"

(continued)

positive beliefs2	specocc2	Having a few drinks is a nice way to celebrate special occasions	5 point scale ranging from "Strongly disagree" to "Strongly agree"
	feelgoo2	Drinking makes me feel good	5 point scale ranging from "Strongly disagree" to "Strongly agree"
	addsfun2	Alcohol adds fun and excitement to an otherwise boring life	5 point scale ranging from "Strongly disagree" to "Strongly agree"
norm beliefs2	peerpre2	It would be difficult for me not to drink alcohol because most of my friends do	5 point scale ranging from "Strongly disagree" to "Strongly agree"
	friends2	Most of my friends drink	5 point scale ranging from "Strongly disagree" to "Strongly agree"
	phase2	Everybody goes through the drinking phase	5 point scale ranging from "Strongly disagree" to "Strongly agree"
drinking2	thurs2	Given that it is a typical week, please write the number of drinks you probably would have on a Thursday	Open-ended
	friday2	Given that it is a typical week, please write the number of drinks you probably would have on a Friday	Open-ended
	sat2	Given that it is a typical week, please write the number of drinks you probably would have on a Saturday	Open-ended
	drunk2	During the past 30 days (about 1 month), how many times have you gotten drunk, or very high from alcohol?	6 point scale including "Never," "1–2," "3–4," "5–6," "7–8," "9 or more"

involving parental monitoring as described earlier in figure 5.1 using structural equation models in AMOS 7.0. Last, we examined variables that moderated effects of parental monitoring on drinking using moderated regression approaches suggested by Jaccard and Turrisi (2003).

Parental Monitoring and Alcohol Consumption

Our first premise was that parental monitoring at baseline would be related to drinking at time 2 (fall assessment). Our analyses regressed a latent variable for drinking tendencies having three indicators onto a latent variable for baseline parental monitoring having three indicators. The results revealed a nonsignificant relationship between baseline parental monitoring and drinking ($b = .268$, $SE = .169$, $t = 1.583$, $p = .113$). Our second premise was that parental monitoring at time 2 (fall assessment) would be related to drinking at time 2 (fall assessment). These analyses used the same approach only substituting time 2 parental monitoring and resulted in a significant negative relationship ($b = -.258$, $SE = .111$, $t = -2.324$, $p < .02$). As parental monitoring increased in the fall semester, drinking tendencies were lower. These findings suggest parental monitoring does make a difference in terms of drinking tendencies of sons and daughters even at this stage of late adolescence/early adulthood. However, it only seems to be influenced by the most recent parental monitoring activity that occurs during the fall rather than the monitoring that occurred prior to college matriculation. Thus, the results support the notion that only sustained monitoring tendencies have an impact on drinking tendencies. Taken another way, parents' work is not done at the point at which their children leave for college.

Mediation Processes

The second focus of the analyses was to examine the process by which parental monitoring influenced drinking tendencies. We tested the model shown in figure 5.2. This model depicts a more specific examination of the relationships between parental monitoring and drinking tendencies than the heuristic model in figure 5.1 in that it takes into account changes that occur before and after college matriculation. According to this theoretical

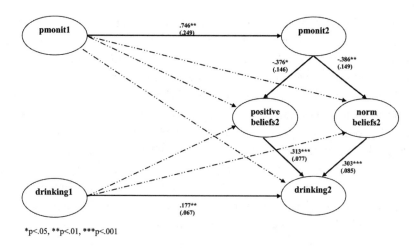

Figure 5.2 Positive and normative beliefs as mediators of the relationship between parental monitoring and alcohol use

model, we hypothesize that the monitoring behaviors of parents' post-matriculation (pmonit2) are influenced by their monitoring behavior prior to college matriculation (pmonit1). These post-matriculation monitoring tendencies in turn have an influence on the positive beliefs that teens hold about drinking in the fall (positive beliefs2) as well as their normative beliefs about drinking in the fall (norm beliefs2). Finally, drinking tendencies in the fall are influenced by prior drinking experiences (drinking1), personal beliefs teens hold about drinking in the fall as well as their normative beliefs about peer drinking in the fall. Monitoring prior to college matriculation is hypothesized to have an indirect effect on the teens' beliefs in the fall and subsequent fall drinking tendencies via the impact on parental monitoring in the fall. Finally, monitoring after college matriculation (i.e., during the fall) is reported to have an indirect effect on fall drinking tendencies via the impact on the teens' beliefs in the fall.

The overall fit of the model was adequate (X^2 (df = 159) = 309.37, CFI = .931, RMSEA = .071, CIl90 = .059, CIh90 = .083). Figure 5.2 shows the paths in bold that were significant and the paths in dashed lines that were not significant. As anticipated, drinking tendencies in the fall semester were influenced indirectly by parental monitoring in the fall, which in turn was influenced by parental monitoring prior to college. These effects were mediated by the beliefs teens held about drinking in the fall and their normative beliefs about peer drinking in the fall. As parental monitoring prior to college matriculation increased, parental monitoring post–college matriculation was found to increase as well. Further, as monitoring post–college matriculation increased, individuals held less positive beliefs about drinking (their own and normative) and as these beliefs decreased in magnitude, so did subsequent drinking tendencies. These results provide additional support that sustained parental monitoring tendencies after college matriculation have an impact on drinking tendencies. Thus, once again there was little support for the notion that parents are done parenting, as defined by parental monitoring communication practices, at the point at which their children leave home for college.

Moderation

The final focus of the analyses examined variables that moderated the effects of parental monitoring on drinking. We were interested to see if under certain conditions the effects of parental monitoring on drinking could be stronger or weaker. For these analyses, composite variables were created by summing the items within a construct (coefficient alphas were > .80). Our analyses regressed drinking tendencies onto parental monitoring subsequent to college matriculation, a moderator, and a product term using the logic described in Jaccard and Turrisi (2003). We found no significant effects for the moderator's gender, location of residence when at college (home versus dorms), Greek membership, athletic status, and parental approval of alcohol consumption. We did find evidence of a moderating effect of perceived friend-alcohol use on the relationship between parental monitoring and drinking ($b = -.165$, SE $= .052$, $t = -3.188$, $p = .002$, Lower CI $= -.268$, Upper CI $= -.063$). Examination of the means in table 5.2 revealed the nature of the interaction effect seemed to be that when friend-alcohol use was at the mean (typical friend use), parental monitoring had less of an influence on drinking than when friend use tended to be heavy. High monitoring under the latter conditions reduced drinking tendencies to levels comparable to when friend use was typical. However, lower monitoring when friend use was high resulted in much heavier consumption. These analyses suggest that the impact of monitoring is greater as friend use increases. Given the reports of heavy peer influences in the

TABLE 5.2

Means for the moderating effect of friend-alcohol use on the relationship
between parental monitoring and weekend drinking

	AVERAGE FRIEND -ALCOHOL USE	HIGH FRIEND-ALCOHOL USE (1 SD ABOVE THE MEAN)
Low parental monitoring (1 SD below the mean)	5.192	10.120
Average parental monitoring	4.344	8.085
High parental monitoring (1 SD above the mean)	3.496	6.050

drinking literature (Larimer et al. 1997), these findings underscore the importance of continued parental monitoring following college matriculation.

Summary

Previous reports that parental influence on teen drinking diminishes as teens develop into later adolescence and early adulthood may be premature. The results from our own research program support the role of parental monitoring into the college years. Interestingly, our results suggest that sustained efforts of monitoring from pre- to post–college matriculation were associated with reduced high-risk drinking. This has important implications for parents whose teens have not initiated into high-risk drinking patterns when in high school who may inaccurately perceive themselves to be "out of the woods" or that their teens are not interested in drinking so they do not need to continue to monitor later. Our data suggest that continued monitoring into the first year will result in lower drinking outcomes above and beyond earlier efforts.

Our findings are not at odds with those of Kandel and Andrews (1987), Hawkins, Catalano, & Miller (1992), and Windle (2000), so much as they are consistent with other reports that indicate that parents are active in helping their teens prepare for and adjust to college (American College Health Association 2003; Amerikaner et al. 1994; Brack, Gay, & Matheny 1993; Galotti & Mark 1994; Kashubeck & Christensen 1995; Wood et al. 2004) and our own preventative intervention research showing that parental efforts can reduce heavy consumption and consequences (Turrisi et al. 2001). It must be emphasized that the earlier reports that showed parents to have less influence on teen drinking and risk behaviors were all conducted prior to the widespread use of communication channels such as cell phones, text messaging, instant messaging, and email. These have undoubtedly increased the quantity and frequency of communications between parents and teens and subsequently increased the degree of parental involvement.

On a practical level, not much is known about how the increased communications between parents and teens affect high-risk behaviors or transitions into adult roles and responsibilities. On the positive side, increased parent-teen communications permit parents greater opportunities to reinforce family values regarding safe versus risky behaviors, affect change on teens' beliefs about drinking, and assist teens in making safer choices about drinking behaviors. The data from the present analyses suggest that there is a benefit from sustained monitoring activity well into the freshman year.

Our analyses are not without limitations. First, further work is clearly needed to examine how to best motivate parents to engage in sustained monitoring activity. Parents who feel that monitoring their adolescents is unnecessary are going to be less likely to monitor, all things being equal. In recruiting parents for our studies related to alcohol use and parent-teen communication, a common response from some parents is that they do not feel the need to participate in a study about alcohol use or communicating with their teen because their teens do not drink and/or they already have a great relationship. Their response runs counter to epidemiological data that shows by the time teens' graduate from high school, the majority have already tried alcohol and that almost one-third are drinking five or more drinks per occasion on a weekly basis. One challenge we face in prevention efforts is to find the best way to change the underlying assumptions parents hold so they are more likely to engage in sustained monitoring activity in their teens' first years of college when high-risk drinking and alcohol-related consequences are at their peak.

Second, more research is needed to understand what are the optimal dosages of parental interventions for college-aged individuals. Our present research program has already begun to conduct studies that examine some of these issues, but the empirical evidence thus far demonstrating that parental efforts have a beneficial effect on reducing high-risk drinking is encouraging. Third, even with the most active monitoring tendencies, there are serious limits to how much parents can actually know when teens are living away at college without honest and open communications. Successful parental monitoring involves engaging in positive parenting practices that serve to build trust and positive communication avenues with teens, as well as engaging in monitoring activity. Our research program attempts to increase positive communications and trust, but there are limits if teens are highly motivated to engage in risk behaviors such as heavy drinking. For the latter, take the situation where parents engage in the habit of asking their teens where they are going at night, but their teens are highly motivated to drink heavily. More often than not, these teens will deliberately conceal their true intentions and behaviors from their parents. More research is needed to examine how parents can be successful for teens that have already engaged in heavy drinking patterns prior to college and are motivated to continue these patterns while living away.

In sum, the present study has demonstrated that the role of parenting does not end with graduation from high school. Although more research is needed, the evidence suggests that sustained parental monitoring can be an effective approach to reducing high-risk drinking tendencies even when teens have moved away to college.

Notes

Acknowledgements: This research was supported by grants R01 AA012529 and R01 AA015737 from the National Institute on Alcohol Abuse and Alcoholism.

1. Approximately 30% of the students did matriculate at Boise State and SUNY Albany. Past analyses have not revealed significant differences in drinking outcomes between those who attended these schools versus those that did not or between data collected at the different sites.

References

American College Health Association. (2003). *National college health assessment: Reference group report Spring 2003*. Baltimore: American College Health Association.

Amerikaner, M., Monks, G., Wolfe, P., & Thomas, S. (1994). Family interaction and individual psychological health. *Journal of Counseling and Development, 72,* 614–620.

Ary, D. V., Tildesley, E., Hops, H., & Andrews, J. (1993). The influence of parent, sibling, and peer modeling and attitudes on adolescent use of alcohol. *International Journal of the Addictions, 28,* 213–228.

Baer, J. S., Kivlahan, D. R., & Marlatt, G. A. (1995). High-risk drinking across the transition from high school to college. *Alcoholism: Clinical and Experimental Research, 19,* 54–61.

Barnes, G. M. (1990). Impact of the family on adolescent drinking patterns. In R. L. Collins, K. E. Leonard, & J. S. Searles (Eds.), *Alcohol and the family: Research and clinical perspectives* (pp. 137–161). New York: Guilford.

Barnes, G., & Welte, J. (1986). Predictors of driving while intoxicated among teenagers. *Journal of Drug Issues, 18,* 367–384.

Beck, K. H., & Lockhart, S. J. (1992). A model of parental involvement in adolescent drinking and driving. *Journal of Youth and Adolescence, 21,* 35–51.

Borkowski, J. G., Ramey, S. L., & Bristol-Power, M. (2002). *Parenting and the child's world: Influences on academic, intellectual, and social-emotional development.* Mahwah, NJ: Erlbaum.

Bormann, C. A., & Stone, M. H. (2001). The effects of eliminating alcohol in a college stadium: The Folsom Field beer ban. *Journal of American College Health, 50,* 81–88.

Bornstein, M. H. (2002). *Handbook of parenting, vol. 1: Children and parenting.* Mahwah, NJ: Erlbaum.

Borsari, B., & Carey, K. B. (2001). Peer influences on college drinking: A review of the research. *Journal of Substance Abuse, 13,* 391–424.

Brack, G., Gay, M. F., & Matheny, K. B. (1993). Relationships between attachment and coping resources among late adolescents. *Journal of College Student Development, 34,* 212–215.

Carey, K. B. (1993). Situational determinants of heavy drinking among college students. *Journal of Counseling Psychology, 40,* 217–220.

Carey, K. B. (1995). Alcohol-related expectancies predict quantity and frequency of heavy drinking among college students. *Psychology of Addictive Behaviors, 9,* 236–241.

Carey, K. B., & Correia, C. J. (1997). Drinking motives predict alcohol problems in college students. *Journal of Studies on Alcohol, 58,* 100–105.

Chronicle of Higher Education. (2007, January 26). Housing plans during fall term. In *Statistical profile: This year's freshmen at four-year colleges.* Retrieved May 7, 2007, from http://chronicle.com/premium/stats/freshmen/2007/data .htm#plans.

Cohen, F., & Rogers, D. (1997). Effects of alcohol policy change. *Journal of Alcohol and Drug Education, 42,* 69–82.

D'Amico, E. J., Ellickson, P. L., Wagner, E. F., Turrisi, R., Fromme, K., Ghosh-Dastidar, B., et al. (2005). Developmental considerations for substance use interventions from middle school through college. *Alcoholism: Clinical and Experimental Research, 29,* 474–483.

Dawson, D. A., Grant, B. F., Stinson, F. S., & Chou, P. S. (2004). Another look at heavy episodic drinking and alcohol use disorders among college and non-college youth. *Journal of Studies on Alcohol, 65,* 477–488.

DiBlaso, F. A. (1986). Drinking adolescents on the roads. *Journal of Youth and Adolescence, 15,* 173188.

Dielman, T. E. (1995). School-based research on the prevention of adolescent alcohol use and misuse: Methodological issues and advances. In G. M. Boyd, J. Howard, & R. A. Zucker (Eds.), *Alcohol problems among adolescents* (pp. 125–146). Hillsdale, NJ: Erlbaum.

Dishion, T. J., Kavanagh, K., & Reid, J. B. (1989). Childrearing vs. peer interventions in the reduction of risk for adolescent substance use and adjustment problems: A secondary prevention strategy. Paper presented at the Conference for the Advancement of Applied Behavior Therapy, Washington, D.C.

Duncan, T. E., Duncan, S. C., & Hops, H. (1994). The effects of family cohesiveness and peer encouragement on the development of adolescent alcohol use: A cohort-sequential approach to the analysis of longitudinal data. *Journal of Studies on Alcohol, 55,* 588–599.

Epstein, J. A., Botvin, G. J., Diaz, T., & Schinke, S. P. (1995). The role of social factors and individual characteristics in promoting alcohol use among inner-city minority youths. *Journal of Studies on Alcohol, 56,* 39–46.

Fine, M. J. (1989). *The second handbook on parent education: Contemporary Perspectives.* New York: Academic Press.

Galotti, K. M., & Mark, M. C. (1994). How do high school students structure an important life decision? A short-term longitudinal study of the college decision-making process. *Research in Higher Education, 35,* 589–607.

Goldman, M. S., Greenbaum, P. E., & Darkes, J. (1997). A confirmatory test of hierarchical expectancy structure and predictive power: Discriminant validation of the alcohol expectancy questionnaire. *Psychological Assessment, 9,* 145–157.

Graham, J. W., Marks, G., & Hansen, W. B. (1991). Social influence processes affecting adolescent substance use. *Journal of Applied Psychology, 76,* 291–298.

Grant, B. F. (1997). Prevalence and correlates of alcohol use and DSM-IV alcohol dependence in the United States. Results of the National Longitudinal Alcohol Epidemiologic Survey. *Journal of Studies on Alcohol, 58,* 464–473.

Guilamo-Ramos, V., Jaccard, J., Dittus, P., & Bouris, A. (2006). Parental expertise, trustworthiness, and accessibility: Parent-adolescent communication and adolescent risk behavior. *Journal of Marriage and Family, 68,* 1229–1246.

Haines, M., & Spear, S. F. (1996). Changing the perception of the norm: A strategy to decrease binge drinking among college students. *Journal of American College Health, 45,* 134–140.

Hansen, W. B., Graham, J. W., Sobel, J. L., Shelton, D. R., Flay, B. R., & Johnson, C. A. (1987). The consistency of peer and parent influences on tobacco, alcohol, and marijuana use among young adolescents. *Journal of Behavioral Medicine, 10,* 559–579.

Hawkins, J. D., Catalano, R. F., & Miller, J. Y. (1992). Risk and protective factors for alcohol and other drug problems in adolescence and early adulthood: Implications for substance abuse prevention. *Psychological Bulletin, 112,* 64–105.

Hingson, R., Berson, J., & Dowley, K. (1997). Interventions to reduce college student drinking and related health and social problems. In M. Plant, E. Single, & T. Stockwell (Eds.), *Alcohol: Minimizing the harm: What works?* (pp. 143–170). London: Free Association Books.

Hingson, R. W., Heeren, T., Zakocs, R. C., Kopstein, A., & Wechsler, H. (2002). Magnitude of alcohol-related mortality and morbidity among U.S. college students ages 18–24. *Journal of Studies on Alcohol, 63,* 136–144.

Hurlbut, S. C., & Sher, K. J. (1992). Assessing alcohol problems in college students. *Journal of American College Health, 41,* 49–58.

Jaccard, J., & Turrisi, R. (2003). *Interaction effects in multiple regression* (2nd ed.). Newbury Park, CA: Sage.

Johnson, C. A., Pentz, M. A., Weber, M. D., Dwyer, J. H., Baer, N., MacKinnon, D. P., et al. (1990). Relative effectiveness of comprehensive community programming for drug abuse prevention with high-risk and low-risk adolescents. *Journal of Consulting and Clinical Psychology, 58,* 447–456.

Johnson, C. F, & Fromme, K. (1994). An experimental test of affect, subjective craving, and alcohol outcome expectancies as motivators of young adult drinking. *Addictive Behaviors, 19,* 631–641.

Johnston, L. D., O'Malley, P. M., & Bachman, J. G. (1991). *Drug use among American high school seniors, college students, and young adults, 1975–1990* (DHHS Publication No. ADM 91–1813). Washington, D.C.: U.S. Government Printing Office.

Kandel, D. B., & Andrews, K. (1987). Processes of adolescent socialization by parents and peers. *International Journal of Addictions, 22,* 319–342.

Kashubeck, S., & Christensen, S. A. (1995). Parental alcohol use, family relationship quality, self-esteem, and depression in college students. *Journal of College Student Development, 36*, 431–443.

Lange, J. E., Clapp, J., Turrisi, R., Reavy, R., Jaccard, J., Johnson, M., et al. (2002). College binge drinking: What is it? Who does it? *Alcoholism: Clinical and Experimental Research, 26*, 723–730.

Langhinrichsen-Rohling, J., Larsen, A. E., & Jacobs, J. E. (1997). Retrospective reports of the family of origin environment and the transition to college. *Journal of College Student Development, 38*, 49–61.

Larimer, M. E., & Cronce, J. M. (2002). Identification, prevention, and treatment: A review of individual-focused strategies to reduce problematic alcohol consumption by college students. *Journal of Studies on Alcohol, 14* (Suppl.), 148–163.

Larimer, M. E., Irvine, D. L., Kilmer, J. R., & Marlatt, G. A. (1997). College drinking and the Greek system: Examining the role of perceived norms for high-risk behavior. *Journal of College Student Development 38*, 587–598.

Larimer, M. E., Turner, A. P., Anderson, B. K., Fader, J. S., Kilmer, J. R., Palmer, R. S., et al. (2001). Evaluating a brief alcohol intervention with fraternities. *Journal of Studies on Alcohol, 62*, 370–380.

Maggs, J. L. (1997). Alcohol use and binge drinking as goal-directed action during the transition to postsecondary education. In J. Schulenberg & J. L. Maggs (Eds.), *Health risks and developmental transitions during adolescence* (pp. 345–371). New York: Cambridge University Press.

Mallett, K. A., Lee, C. M., Neighbors, C., Larimer, M. E., & Turrisi, R. (2006). Do we learn from our mistakes? An examination of the impact of negative alcohol-related consequences on college students' drinking patterns and perceptions. *Journal of Studies on Alcohol, 67*, 269–276.

Marlatt, G. A., Baer, J. S., Kivlahan, D. R., Larimer, M. E., Quigley, L. A., Dimeff, L. A., et al. (1998). Screening and brief intervention for high-risk college student drinkers: Results from a two-year follow-up assessment. *Journal of Consulting and Clinical Psychology, 66*, 604–615.

Marlatt, G. A., Baer, J. S., & Larimer, M. (1995). Preventing alcohol abuse in college students: A harm-reduction approach. In G. M. Boyd, J. Howard, & R. A. Zucker (Eds.), *Alcohol problems among adolescents* (pp. 147–172). Hillsdale, NJ: Erlbaum.

McDermott, D. (1984). The relationship of parental drug use and parents' attitude concerning adolescent drug use to adolescent drug use. *Adolescence, 19*, 89–97.

McPherson, K. & McKnight, A. J. (1987). *An evaluation of a parent alcohol program, West Virginia University.* Performed under contract to the National Highway Traffic Safety Administration, Contract No. DTNH 22–86-C-05144.

Newman, I. M., Crawford, J. K., & Nellis, M. J. (1991). The role and function of drinking games in a university community. *Journal of American College Health, 39*, 171–175.

O'Hare, T., & Sherrer, M. V. (1999). Campus substance abuse policies in action: The role of resident hall staff. *Journal of Alcohol and Drug Education, 45*, 13–31.

O'Malley, P. M., & Johnston, L. D. (2002). Epidemiology of alcohol and other drug use among American college students. *Journal of Studies on Alcohol, 14* (Suppl.), 23–39.

Peterson, P. L., Hawkins, D. L., Abbott, R. D., & Catalano, R. F. (1995). Disentangling the effects of parental drinking, family management, and parental alcohol norms on current drinking by black and white adolescents. In G. M. Boyd, J. Howard, & R. A. Zucker (Eds.), *Alcohol problems among adolescents* (pp. 33–57). Hillsdale, NJ: Erlbaum.

Prentice, D. A., & Miller, D. T. (1993). Pluralistic ignorance and alcohol use on campus: Some consequences of misperceiving the social norm. *Journal of Personality and Social Psychology, 64*, 243–256.

Reifman, A., Barnes, G., Dintcheff, B. A., Farrell, M. P., & Uhteg, L. (1998). Parental and peer influences on the onset of heavier drinking among adolescents. *Journal of Studies on Alcohol, 59*, 311–317.

Rohrbach, L. A., Hodgson, C. S., Broder, B. I., Montgomery, S. B., Flay, B. R., Hansen, W. B., et al. (1995). Parental participation in drug abuse prevention: Results from the Midwestern prevention project. In G. M. Boyd, J. Howard, & R. A. Zucker (Eds.), *Alcohol problems among adolescents* (pp. 173–195). Hillsdale, NJ: Erlbaum.

Schall, M., Kemeny, A., & Maltzman, I. (1992). Factors associated with alcohol use in university students. *Journal of Studies on Alcohol, 53*, 122–136.

Scheier, L. M., & Botvin, G. J. (1997). Expectancies as mediators of the effects of social influences and alcohol knowledge on adolescent alcohol use: A prospective analysis. *Psychology of Addictive Behaviors, 11*, 48–64.

Schulenberg, J., O'Malley, P. M., Bachman, J. G., Wadsworth, K. N., & Johnston, L. D. (1996). Getting drunk and growing up: Trajectories of frequent binge drinking during the transition to young adulthood. *Journal of Studies on Alcohol, 57*, 289–304.

Sher, K. J., Walitzer, K. S., Wood, P. K., & Brent, E. E. (1991). Characteristics of children of alcoholics: Putative risk factors, substance use and abuse, and psychopathology. *Journal of Abnormal Psychology, 100*, 427–448.

Socha, T. J., & Stamp, G. H. (1995). *Parents, children, and communication.* Mahwah, NJ: Erlbaum.

Spoth, R., Greenberg, M., & Turrisi, R. (2008). Preventive interventions addressing underage drinking: State of the evidence and steps toward public health impact, *Pediatrics, 121* (Suppl.), S311–S336.

Stewart, S. H., Zeitlin, S. B., & Samoluk, S. B. (1996). Examination of a three-dimensional drinking motives questionnaire in a young adult university student sample. *Behaviour Research and Therapy, 34*, 61–71.

Turner, A. P., Larimer, M. E., & Sarason, I. G. (2000). Family risk factors for alcohol-related consequences and poor adjustment in fraternity and sorority members: Exploring the role of parent-child conflict. *Journal of Studies on Alcohol, 61*, 818–826.

Turrisi, R. (1999). Cognitive and attitudinal factors in the analysis of alternatives to binge drinking. *Journal of Applied Social Psychology, 29*, 1510–1533.

Turrisi, R., Jaccard, J., Taki, R., Dunnam, H., & Grimes, J. (2001). Examination of the short-term efficacy of a parent intervention to reduce college student drinking tendencies. *Psychology of Addictive Behaviors, 15*, 366–372.

Turrisi, R., Padilla, K., & Wiersma, K. (2000). College student drinking: An examination of theoretical models of drinking tendencies in freshman and upperclassmen. *Journal of Studies on Alcohol, 61*, 598–602.

Turrisi, R., Wiersma, K. A., & Hughes, K. K. (2000). Binge-drinking-related consequences in college students: Role of drinking beliefs and mother-teen communications. *Psychology of Addictive Behaviors, 14*, 342–355.

Vuchinich, R. E., & Tucker, J. A. (1988). Contributions from behavioral theories of choice to an analysis of alcohol abuse. *Journal of Abnormal Psychology, Special Issue: Models of Addiction, 97*, 181–195.

Wechsler, H., Davenport, A., Dowdall, G., Moeykens, B., & Castillo, S. (1994). Health and behavioral consequences of binge drinking in college: A national survey of students at 140 campuses. *Journal of the American Medical Association, 272*, 1672–1677.

Wechsler, H., Issac, N. E., Grodstein, F., & Sellers, D. (1994). Continuation and initiation of alcohol use from the first and second year of college. *Journal of Studies on Alcohol, 55*, 41–45.

Windle, M. (2000). Parental, sibling, and peer influences on adolescent substance use and alcohol problems. *Applied Developmental Science, 4*, 98–110.

Wood, M. D., Hevey, C. A., Laird, R. D., Stevenson, J. F., & Mitchell, R. E. (2000, June). *Prospective examination of relations between social influences and alcohol use among college students: Evidence for reciprocal influences.* Poster presented at the annual meeting of the Research Society on Alcoholism, June 24—29, 2000, Denver, CO.

Wood, M. D., Nagoshi, C., & Dennis, D. (1991). Alcohol norms and expectations as predictors of alcohol use and problems in a college sample. *Journal of Studies on Alcohol, 52*, 312–322.

Wood, M. D., Read, J. P, Mitchell, R. E., & Brand, N. H. (2004). Do parents still matter? Parent and peer influences on alcohol involvement among recent high school graduates. *Psychology of Addictive Behaviors, 18*, 19–30.

Wood, M. D., Read, J. P., Palfai, T. P., & Stevenson, J. F. (2001). Social influence processes and college student drinking: The mediational role of alcohol outcome expectations. *Journal of Studies on Alcohol, 62,* 32–43.

Wood, M. D., Sher, K. J., & Strathman, A. (1996). Alcohol outcome expectancies and alcohol use and problems. *Journal of Studies on Alcohol, 57,* 283–288.

[6]

From Research to Practice

Development and Scaling Up of ImPACT, a Parental Monitoring Intervention for African American Parents of Adolescents

JENNIFER S. GALBRAITH and BONITA STANTON

Scientists working in prevention fields are increasingly calling for the widespread use of evidenced-based interventions (EBIs) to stimulate and sustain behavior change. At the same time, funding agencies more and more are requiring the use of EBIs. Simultaneously, there is mounting evidence that intervening with parents is an effective approach to adolescent behavior change. This chapter will follow the development of one community-based, parental monitoring HIV-prevention intervention designed for parents of African American, low-income, urban youth from its earliest creation to efforts to scale up the program for national dissemination. It will describe both the original evaluation and a second evaluation that combined the parent intervention with an adolescent intervention that independently has shown to have evidence of efficacy. The chapter will also describe efforts to adapt the program for a new population and setting and preparation of the intervention for national diffusion. Finally, lessons learned from all phases of scaling up the parental monitoring intervention will be discussed.

Intervention Development

Fifteen to 30 percent of all HIV infections occur among persons younger than 25 years (Morris et al. 2006). Racial disparities that characterize the adult epidemic seem to emerge during adolescence, with young African American men and women disproportionately impacted by the HIV epidemic. The majority of young African Americans are infected through sexual contact (Centers for Disease Control and Prevention [CDC] 2009). African American adolescents are more likely to face challenges associated with risk for HIV infection, including early age of sexual initiation, multiple partners, higher rates of sexually transmitted infections (STIs), and poverty (CDC 2006). Poverty is associated with reduced access to high-quality health care and dropping out of school. Since most HIV education for youth is conducted in schools or in clinic settings, out-of-school youth and those who do not access health care are less likely to receive HIV-prevention messages. Culturally and developmentally effective community-based interventions are needed to address these high-risk youth if we hope to ensure the future of young African Americans.

One possible intervention approach to address the issue of HIV in the African American youth community is increasing parental monitoring. One of the most robust findings across the globe has been the inverse relationship between parental monitoring (including parent-adolescent communication and parental supervision) and adolescent sexual risk behavior. Children and adolescents who think that their parents usually know where and with whom they are and what they are doing are significantly less likely to be involved in risky behaviors, including drug use, truancy, and sexual risk behaviors (Rai et al. 2003; Romer et al. 1999; Steinberg, Dornbusch, & Brown 1992; Wight 2006). Research has consistently found that perceived increases in parental knowledge (and other characteristics of parental monitoring) are associated with reductions in adolescents' engagement in risk (Ary et al. 1999).

Parental monitoring appears to be protective across multiple ethnicities, nations, and cultures (Cheung, Liu, & Lee 2005; Piko, Fitzpatrick, & Wight 2005; Shek & Lee 2006; Steinberg, Dornbusch, & Brown 1992). Equally important, both parents and children want parents to talk with their children about sex (Schouten et al. 2007). Research has shown that youth who report high levels of perceived parental monitoring were less likely to report early initiation of sex (under 10 years of age) and reported lower rates of sexual initiation as they got older. Children who perceived both high rates of parental monitoring and communication concerning sexual risk were also less likely to have engaged in anal sex (Romer et al. 1999). Reports of positive communication about sexual risk with parents by sexually active youth were associated with both initiation of and consistent use of condoms (Romer et al. 1999).

Informed Parents and Children Together (ImPACT) is a community-based parental monitoring intervention originally developed for parents of African American urban children living in resource-depleted communities. During the mid-1990s, when ImPACT was developed, there was limited research on ethnic differences in parental monitoring practices; however, existing data suggested the approach was promising (Romer et al. 1999). Our research team began developing a parental monitoring video with an intensive ethnographic phase, including participant observation, community informants, several focus-group discussions, and individual interviews. Interview guides were grounded in the research conducted by Steinberg, Fletcher, and Darling (1994) regarding parental monitoring, and focused on parental concepts of risk involvement, risk prevention, and the meaning of monitoring, supervision, and communication within the context of parenting, and how it changes by age and gender of the child. We sought to explore the challenge confronting parents of adolescents as to how they could afford their children's increased independence and yet provide sufficient structure and guidance to assure their safety and well-being. We wanted to explore culturally appropriate mechanisms to encourage authoritative parenting (e.g., warm but firm with articulated guidelines and rules). Specifically, we wanted to create an intervention that would encourage parents to listen to and acknowledge the perspectives of their children while simultaneously reinforcing the importance of children understanding parental expectations and parents' need to monitor them. Questions also centered on the role of other nonrelative adults in monitoring and identifying perceived impediments to effective monitoring. The interviews and community informants also were queried on more practical implementation issues, such as the optimum setting and arrangements for meeting with parents to deliver the intervention (e.g., alone or in groups, in public meeting places or at home, etc.), and how to deliver the intervention so as to engage the parents in a style that would maximize their learning.

A major issue for community-based researchers interested in parenting issues has been accessing parents. This challenge is all the more critical to address if the desire is widespread dissemination of efficacious interventions into practice. There are a variety of venues to potentially reach parents, including workforce programs, clinic settings, schools, faith-based organizations, community-based organizations, and homes. Our previous attempts to get parents to attend face-to-face groups at a local community setting for a different violence-prevention intervention had been unsuccessful. Parents of adolescents had many competing responsibilities, including younger children, jobs, household maintenance, and other family members. Employment often was not during the traditional 9-to-5 hours, which made it difficult to find a time that met the needs of all of the various parents in the group. Although the program attempted to provide child care, it was not always possible. Ultimately, attendance rates at the violence-prevention program were quite low, even though the issue had been identified as a pressing need by many parents. Based on this experience and through discussions with individual and groups of parents, we elected to intervene with parents and their children in their homes at a mutually agreed-upon time with a short face-to-face video-based intervention. By designing the intervention so that it could be administered in the home, we hoped to achieve a broad reach with this intervention that might not be achievable if parents were required to participate in group sessions. We also wanted to reach parents of youth who may be at the highest risk, e.g., parents who may not be employed and whose children may not be in school or accessing health care services, as these parents and youth may be lost by school- and clinic-based interventions.

The final intervention was approximately 60 minutes and consisted of a 20-minute, culturally appropriate video-documentary (*Protect Your Child from AIDS*), a discussion with a health educator, two guided role-plays, a pamphlet, and a condom demonstration. The video was viewed by the health educator, parent(s), and child together and was followed by a health educator–led discussion focused on reinforcing messages from the video on monitoring, communication, and HIV prevention. The health educator led two supervised, guided role-plays in which they directed parent(s) and youth through a practice mock-communication about monitoring, communication, abstinence, sex, condoms, STIs and HIV. The interactive role-plays were based on a realistic vignette. The final segment of the intervention was a condom demonstration during which both the parent and child practiced correct condom use.

We decided to produce a video because we wanted a format that would last beyond the actual face-to-face intervention but did not require substantial reading as our experience in the community indicated that literacy rates among parents were variable. We conducted a survey and found that most households had the appropriate technology for video-viewing (at the time, a TV and VHS player) in their home. The documentary, which was designed to be entertaining as well as informative, emphasized the importance of talking openly and clearly about values and expectations as they relate to sexual practices. The video used a documentary format rather than a script or fictional scenes. It was filmed in low-income Baltimore communities similar to those where the target audience lived. The video highlighted that conversations should be age-appropriate and progress as the adolescent gets older. The follow-up discussion reinforced these messages and enabled both the parent and child to practice their newly acquired communication skills. A pamphlet and a copy of the video were left behind in hopes of continued reinforcement of the messages and potential diffusion of the intervention through sharing with family and friends. Although we had determined that most families owned the equipment necessary for video-viewing, the intervention teams carried portable video units to show the film if necessary.

Evaluation

ImPACT Alone

The ImPACT intervention was originally evaluated as a stand-alone intervention. The evaluation was conducted with 237 parent-child (aged 12 to 16) dyads living in Baltimore, Maryland. Dyads were randomized to either the ImPACT intervention or a control intervention of the same length that consisted of a video and workbook activities (*GOAL for IT*) focused on goal-setting for career and school. At baseline, in both the intervention and control groups, parents underestimated youth risk behavior. Following the intervention, there were no significant differences between youth self-reports and parent perceptions of youth activities among dyads randomized to the intervention group. Parent-adolescent communication about risk/protective behaviors improved over time in the intervention group. In contrast, post-intervention, parents randomized to the control group significantly underestimated their child's involvement in protective and four risk activities (e.g., weapon-carrying, staying out all night, consuming alcohol, and using marijuana). However, by itself, ImPACT did not reduce adolescent risk behaviors (Li, Stanton, Galbraith et al. 2002).

Focus on Kids + ImPACT

A few years prior to the development of ImPACT, our research team and community partners had developed, implemented, and evaluated an adolescent HIV-prevention intervention, Focus on Kids, which had been designed to delay sexual initiation among virgins and to increase condom use among sexually active youth. We were pleased that Focus on Kids had a significant effect on behaviors (as well as intentions and perceptions) six months post-intervention (Stanton et al. 1996), but like most adolescent risk-prevention programs, the effects waned over time and there was no intervention impact after 18 months post-intervention (Li, Stanton, Feigelman, & Galbraith 2002). Therefore, we wanted to explore mechanisms to sustain the behavior change resulting from Focus on Kids.

The parent intervention ImPACT was an obvious choice to test for two reasons. First, the strong impact of parental monitoring and communication in general on adolescent risk reduction was well established. Second, we were encouraged by the findings from the evaluation of ImPACT that the intervention appeared to increase adolescent and parental communication and perceptions of parental monitoring.

Therefore, a three-celled randomized, longitudinal, community-based trial was conducted among 817 youths located in 35 urban, low-income communities in Baltimore. Randomization occurred at the community level. Communities were randomized to receive the Focus on Kids intervention alone with an attention-control session for the parents which focused on goal-setting and finding a job, the Focus on Kids intervention and the ImPACT intervention, or Focus on Kids plus ImPACT plus booster sessions (Wu et al. 2003).

Youth risk behaviors were assessed by youth self-report. At 6 months post-intervention, youths in families that were assigned to Focus on Kids plus ImPACT reported significantly lower rates of sexual intercourse, sex without a condom, alcohol use, and cigarette use than youths in families that were assigned to the attention-control group (Wu et al. 2003). At 24 months post-intervention, youth whose parents received the parental monitoring intervention compared with youth who received only Focus on Kids were less likely to use marijuana or other illicit drugs (18.3% vs. 26.8%, and 1.4% vs. 5.6%, respectively, $p < .05$), and were more likely to ask sexual partners about past condom use (77.9% vs. 64.9%, $p < .05$) (Stanton et al. 2004). The results suggest that the addition of a brief parental communication and monitoring intervention offered additional protection from adolescent risk-behavior involvement up to 24 months post-intervention.

Adaptation of ImPACT for a New Population: Caribbean ImPACT

Focus on Kids had been adapted in 1998 for use in the Bahamas. The new program, Focus on Youth, was institutionalized in the school system and delivered to 6th grade youth. Focus group discussions among parents revealed a desire for more education about HIV. Parents wanted to be able to help youth make healthy decisions for their future. The Bahamian Focus on Youth staff thought that the ImPACT program would be helpful, but that modifications would be necessary to ensure that the intervention was contextually appropriate for the new target population. Feedback from the Bahamian community identified several necessary adaptations: the video-documentary should be remade in the Bahamas using a Bahamian family and youth professionals; delivery of the intervention would need to be done in small groups instead of one-on-one delivery in the homes; and delivery needed to be implemented with only parents (not parents and their youth). Fidelity with other components of the ImPACT intervention was maintained, including (a) the main points of the video (see below); (b) a role-play in which the parent was able to practice having a discussion with a child (played by another parent) about sex and risk and protective factors; and (c) a condom demonstration in which parents were taught proper condom use and given an opportunity to practice. The adapted parental monitoring intervention was named Caribbean Informed Parents and Youth Together (CImPACT).

The CImPACT was also tested through a three-celled randomized controlled trial, which included randomization to one of three conditions: the adapted Focus on Youth alone, Focus on Youth with the parental monitoring intervention CImPACT, or an attention-control group (Deveaux et al. 2007). Post-intervention, adolescents who participated in the Focus on Youth intervention had significantly increased knowledge, intentions, condom-use skills, protective perceptions, and intentions to engage in safer behaviors. While parents who received the monitoring intervention did demonstrate significantly improved condom-use skills compared to parents in the control group, there were no differences at six months follow-up among youth in knowledge or condom-use skills based on whether or not their parents had been assigned to receive the parental monitoring intervention (Deveaux et al. 2007). However, at later follow-up periods (through 36 months), condom-use skills, self-efficacy, and eventually reported protective behaviors were increased (Chen et al. 2008; Gong et al. 2009).

Moving from Research to Practice: National Dissemination of ImPACT

ImPACT's initial success in Baltimore and the Bahamas, showing significant increases in parental monitoring and decreases in risk behaviors in adolescents, led developers to consider the value of further dissemination in the United States. Increasingly, agencies are recognizing the importance of successfully evaluated interventions and have programs that aid in the dissemination of these interventions to prevent disease and injury and promote health among adolescents. Agencies have begun identifying interventions that have credible evidence of reducing health-risk behaviors among youth and adults and packaging them for national dissemination. In this section, we will describe one such program, the CDC's Division of HIV/AIDS Prevention's model, and the experience of the ImPACT program as it was packaged through this model.

The CDC has a three-phase process for identifying, packaging, and disseminating EBIs. The CDC's HIV/AIDS Prevention Research Synthesis (PRS) Project, through a rigorous ongoing efficacy-review process, identifies evidence-based, individual- or group-level behavioral interventions for persons at high risk of acquiring or transmitting HIV. These interventions have been rigorously evaluated and have demonstrated efficacy in reducing HIV/STI incidence or HIV-related risk behavior or in promoting safer behavior (CDC 2006; Lyles et al. 2006; Sogolow et al. 2000).

TABLE 6.1

Summary of Evaluation Studies of Focus on Kids, ImPACT, and ClmPACT

INTERVENTION(S) NAME	DATES	RESEARCH DESIGN DETAILS	FINDINGS	CITATION(S)
Focus on Kids	1992–1997	2-cell RCT n = 383 African American youth ages 9–15 randomization: at group level attention control group	Self-reported condom use rates were significantly higher among intervention than control youths (85% vs. 61%; p < .05) at 6-month follow-up. By 12 months, differences in rate of condom use were no longer significant. After a booster session series, there was a significant difference in condom use at 18-month post-intervention.	Stanton et al. (1996) and Li et al. (2002)
ImPACT	1996–1998	2-cell RCT n = 237 dyads of AA youth ages 12–16 and their parent or guardian randomization at dyad level attention control group	Parent and youth concordance of youth behavior was significantly improved among dyads randomized to the intervention group. Parent-adolescent communication about risk/protective behaviors improved over time in the intervention group.	Li et al. (2002) and Stanton et al. (2000)

(continued)

TABLE 6.1 (*continued*)

INTERVENTION(S) NAME	DATES	RESEARCH DESIGN DETAILS	FINDINGS	CITATION(S)
Focus on Kids + ImPACT	1999–2002	3-cell RCT n = 817 dyads of AA youth ages 12–16 and their parent or guardian randomization at community level attention control group	At 24 months, post-intervention youth whose parents received ImPACT compared with youth who received only Focus on Kids were less likely to use marijuana or other illicit drugs (18.3% vs. 26.8% and 1.4% vs. 5.6%, respectively, $p < .05$) and were more likely to ask sexual partners about past condom use (77.9% vs. 64.9%, $p < .05$).	Wu et al. (2003) and Stanton et al. (2004)
Focus on Youth + CImPACT	2004– present	3-cell RCT n = 1,282 Bahamian 6th grade students randomization at group level attention control group	Significantly higher condom-use skills, self-efficacy, and eventually (at 36 months post-intervention) reported protective behaviors were found between parent-youth dyads randomized to CImPACT compared to those in the control group.	Deveaux et al.

Once EBIs have been identified to have demonstrated efficacy, the CDC's Replicating Effective Programs (REP) translates them into everyday language and user-friendly packages (Eke et al. 2006). The Diffusion of Effective Behavioral Interventions (DEBI) also packages programs and brings HIV-prevention EBIs to community-based service providers and state and local health departments through dissemination (Collins et al. 2006). The overall goal of the DEBI program is to disseminate evidence-based HIV-prevention interventions into prevention practice. DEBI follows an eight-step process that includes planning, marketing, policy incentives, intervention packaging, training, capacity building, quality assurance, and evaluation (Collins et al. 2006). Information on both REP and DEBI can be located online at www.cdc.gov/hiv/topics/prev_prog/rep and www .effectiveinterventions.org.

ImPACT along with Focus on Kids (Stanton et al. 2004; Wu et al. 2003) were identified as an intervention with best evidence of effectiveness by the CDC's PRS Project (CDC 2006; Lyles et al. 2007). As a result, the CDC's Division of HIV/AIDS Prevention prepared Focus on Kids and Im-PACT for national dissemination via DEBI. The first step toward national dissemination was the formation of a team to package the Focus on Kids and ImPACT interventions. The team was composed of the original developers and experts in curriculum packaging, training, and national diffusion of effective interventions. Once the team was assembled, the next steps in preparing the intervention for national dissemination were assessing whether the video, which was now ten years old and had been developed in just one community, was appropriate for national dissemination and development of core elements (see below). It was determined that a new video should be developed to make sure it had current information and resonated with youth and parents in the new millennium across a variety of geographic locations. Development of a new video required identifying the key components specific to the video to ensure that the new video had the same fundamentals, or "core elements" (Kelly et al. 2000), that were thought to have made the original video effective.

Core Elements

In order to allow local practitioners to adapt DEBI interventions for the cultural context of their local communities without compromising the integrity of the program, all DEBI programs have identified core elements which practitioners must implement with fidelity. The CDC's Division of HIV/AIDS Prevention defines core elements as the required elements that embody the theory and internal logic of the intervention and are most likely to produce the intervention's main effects (Kelly et al. 2000; McKleroy et al. 2006). The developers used a three-step process suggested by Kelly et al. (2000) to identify the core elements, which required participants to (a) examine the behavioral science theory; (b) use the experience and feedback from participants and experienced program staff to decide what activities were most effective; and (c) derive insights from controlled experiments of the intervention.

These core elements were organized into four different areas: video development, content, pedagogy, and delivery. Video development core elements are elements that are necessary if individuals choose to make a new video. Content core elements are the essential elements being taught by the intervention that are believed to change risk behaviors and usually are derived from the theoretical basis of the intervention. Pedagogical core elements are the essential elements of how the intervention content is taught. Finally, delivery core elements are the essential characteristics of an intervention that relate to some of the logistics that set up a positive learning environment (Education, Training and Research Associates [ETR] & CDC, in press). Core elements must be kept intact (i.e., done with fidelity) when the intervention is being implemented or adapted to produce program outcomes similar to those demonstrated in the original research. If core elements are changed or eliminated, the EBI should be evaluated again to ensure that it remains efficacious.

The concept of core elements has some limitations. Complex and costly trials are necessary to determine empirically which components of an intervention are responsible for positive behavior change. Such research has not been conducted for ImPACT; nor has it been done for most evidence-based interventions (Kelly et al. 2000). Nonetheless, the developers were able to identify core elements based on the theoretical foundation and their extensive experience implementing the intervention. Moreover, since several evaluations of ImPACT and Focus on Youth have been conducted, it was possible to look at the content and implementation of both to look for clues about what elements might be critical for intervention's success. The presumed core elements of the ImPACT intervention and their rationale are described below. They have been broken up into the following catego-

TABLE 6.2
Core Elements of Focus on Kids and ImPACT

INTERVENTION	CORE ELEMENTS
Focus on Kids	1. Delivering intervention to youth in community-based settings
	2. Using two skilled facilitators to implement the youth group sessions
	3. Using "friendship groups" to strengthen peer support
	4. Using culturally appropriate interactive activities proven as effective learning strategies to help youth capture the important constructs in the theory
	5. Including a "family tree" to contextualize and personalize abstract concepts such as decision-making and risk assessment
	6. Enabling participants to learn and practice a decision-making model
	7. Training participants in assertive communication and refusal skills specifically related to negotiation of abstinence or safer sex behaviors
	8. Teaching youth proper condom-use skills
ImPACT	1. The film is a documentary using real people instead of actors.
	2. Several key messages about parental monitoring, communication, and HIV prevention need to be emphasized in the video.
	3. The video should have entertainment value (e.g., singing, music, dancing, humor), making it enjoyable to watch.
	4. Use a health educator and other professionals, whom the parents find credible.
	5. The video has narration that reinforces key messages; the narrator is an individual whom the parents find credible, e.g., speaks with an accent and uses language that resonates with parents.
	6. The video includes a condom demonstration that shows the correct method for putting on a condom.
	7. Deliver the intervention to individual parent-youth dyads in their home or a convenient community-based setting (e.g., CBO, church, recreation center, or school) at a time that fits the schedule of the parent/guardian.
	8. Use of a health educator or pair of health educators whom parents and adolescents find credible and are skilled at building rapport with parents and youths at the beginning of the session
	9. Ideally, ImPACT should be delivered prior to the child beginning the Focus on Youth intervention.

(continued)

TABLE 6.2 *(continued)*

INTERVENTION   CORE ELEMENTS

10. Use of documentary that shows the challenges and importance of parents monitoring and talking to their children ages
12–15 about sex, abstinence, STIs, HIV, and condoms
11. The health educator, parent, and child should watch the video
together.
12. The intervention allows parents an opportunity to practice
and improve their monitoring skills and parents and children
an opportunity to improve and practice communication skills.
13. Teach parent and child proper condom-use skills.
14. All parents receive an informational pamphlet on good
communication and how to talk to your kids; importance of
parental monitoring; facts on STIs and HIV, including
prevalence data among young African Americans; and steps
on how to use a condom.

ries of core elements: (a) remaking the video, (b) delivery, (c) pedagogy, and
(d) content.

CORE ELEMENTS FOR REMAKING THE VIDEO

Six core elements for remaking the video were identified.

Core Element Video–One: *The film is a documentary using real people in-stead of actors.*

Parents and youth in the video should represent a variety of geographic
and socioeconomic backgrounds, with an emphasis on those populations
at the greatest risk, such as parents and youth living in geographic areas
or communities that have high HIV prevalence (e.g., the South) and families disproportionately affected by poverty. The individuals in the documentary should be part of the target population and should discuss the
real challenges and successes of monitoring and communicating with
their children about abstinence, sex, HIV, STIs, and condoms. This au-
thenticity increases the response efficacy of parents watching (e.g., if they
can do it, I can do it). In addition, professionals (health educators, social
workers, and teachers) should be used to guide parents toward successful
communication.

Core Element Video–Two: *Several key messages about parental monitoring, communication, and HIV prevention need to be emphasized in the video.*

When making the video, the videographer should ask open-ended questions that allow the messages to emerge naturally from discussions with parents and youth. Further, professionals (e.g., health educators, social workers, or teachers) can be used to have mock learning sessions or to discuss key messages. Messages that do not occur naturally should be scripted and incorporated into the voice-over narration. Key messages included in the original video were the following:

1. It is important for parents to talk to their child about sex, STIs, and pregnancy. The best time to influence youth is before they start having sex. Parents need to find a good time to talk with their children and should not wait for youth to ask about sex. Parents must have these discussions prior to youth becoming sexual active as parents will not be with their children at this moment to guide them.

2. It is important to know with whom children are socializing, what they are doing, and where they are doing it. Many parents are unaware as to what activities their youth are involved. Parents should spend time with their children, know their friends, and know what their children are facing.

3. Although at first parents have a difficult time talking with their child about sensitive subjects like sex, it does get easier with time. The video shows that parents and youth often feel awkward about these discussions and has thus been designed to help parents feel prepared for this unease. It's okay for parents to tell children that they don't know the answer to a question and will find out the answer later. Parents and children are doing this successfully—it can be done!

4. If parents feel that they cannot talk to their child about sex, it is important that they find someone else to talk to them. It is important to find someone who shares the parents' values and has a good rapport with their youth so they respect that person and enjoy talking to him/her.

5. It is important for youth to know how they would respond if they are in a situation in which they might be pressured into having sex (and the pressure could be a positive—a boyfriend/girlfriend discussing how much he/she loves the youth).

6. Parents should talk to their kids about abstinence. Parents should counter the perception of many youth that everyone is having sex.

7. Parents should talk to their kids about proper condom use. Talking to youth about condoms and making sure they know how to use condoms is not the same thing as encouraging them to have sex.

8. Communication goes both ways. Parents should be approachable—a parent's reaction to a youth coming to talk to them can encourage or stop future conversations. It is important for parents to listen to their kids. Youth are often happy that parents discuss sex with them as it shows that they care.

9. Parents need to discuss with their child the serious consequences of risky sexual behavior. Although treatment is now available that allows people to live much longer with HIV, there are still many difficulties with being HIV-infected, including serious treatment side effects and stigma. Sex can interfere with achievements of a youth's goals. The decisions teens make when young impact their future.

10. Parents should allow children to grow toward independence but set guidelines that help them mature into responsible adolescents and young adults. Ultimately, youth must make their own decisions, but it is the parents' job to give them information and to prepare them as much as possible.

Core Element Video–Three: *The video should have entertainment value (e.g., singing, music, dancing, humor), making it enjoyable to watch.*

The method in which health messages are delivered can impact participants' processing both in amount and type (Parrott 1995). Participants must pay attention to health messages and understand the message for retention and for the message to influence behavior (McGuire 1985). Entertainment value was included in the original video through dance scenes of youth at a local underage club and through humorous scenes between parents and children discussing sex. For example, in the opening scene, a mother asks her daughter a personal question about sex. In response, the daughter looks shocked at the mother's question, begins to laugh, and gets up and walks toward the camera yelling "Cut, cut!" The entertainment is also educational, e.g., the dancing, which is very close and suggestive, allows parents to understand how youth may behave when parents are not around. The humorous scenes of parents and youth as they hesitatingly initiate discussions about sex and HIV allow parents watching the video to understand that it is normal to feel awkward, but with a bit of laughter they can negotiate conversations. Moreover, with time, the discussions will be easier.

Core Element Video–Four: *Use a health educator and other professionals, whom the parents find credible.*

The health educator should be skilled at building rapport with parents and youth. The health educator should also match the racial and ethnic group of the targeted population. Professionals (two social workers and two health educators) used in the original video were individuals who were experienced working with parents and youth. They were respectful to both parents and youth and listened to their concerns and questions. They were also able to use humor to put the parent and adolescent at ease.

All professionals used in the original video were African American. Research has demonstrated that African Americans prefer to receive care, and report receiving better care, from physicians of the same race (Cooper-Patrick et al. 1999; Saha, Arbelaez, & Cooper 2003; Saha et al. 2000). Communication between the health educator and parent-child dyad is a critical piece of the ImPACT intervention. Ethnically matched caregivers have been shown to have positive impacts on adherence and overall outcomes with youth and their families in multisystemic therapy (Halliday-Boykins, Schoenwald, & Letourneau 2005; Schoenwald, Halliday-Boykins, & Henggeler 2003). We had also learned through focus groups and individual interviews that the African American parents in our study felt that the White parents had different parenting styles and faced very different issues. It was thus important that health educators in the video be individuals to whom the parents could relate and whom the parents believed would understand the unique monitoring needs they faced.

Core Element Video–Five: *The video has narration that reinforces key messages; the narrator is an individual whom the parents find credible, e.g., speaks with an accent and uses language that resonates with parents.*

The narration provides additional information and emphasizes key messages brought to life by parents and youth in the video. Similar to the professionals described in core element four, the narrator was African American for the same reasons discussed above.

Core Element Video–Six: *The video includes a condom demonstration that shows the correct method for putting on a condom.*

The demonstration should include a scene in which parents practice the correct way to use a condom. A growing consensus speaks to the importance of skill development in condom use, which may be difficult to achieve in the absence of viewing and/or practicing with a real condom or when drawing a picture of the process (Stanton et al. 2006). In the video, health educators should first demonstrate appropriate condom-application using a penile model. After the demonstration, they should teach parents how to put on a condom, using either a penile model or their fingers. Some of the scenes in both of the videos are humorous; again, we believe that humor is important for helping parents and adolescents to pay attention, retain the health message, and reduce potential discomfort associated with discussing such sensitive information together.

Taken together, these six core elements were determined to be integral if agencies chose to develop a new documentary to better meet the needs of their target population.

Implementation of Core Elements

Aside from the core elements to develop a new video, additional core elements were developed for implementation of the intervention. The intervention was composed of the video, a facilitated discussion with a health educator, two guided role-plays, a condom demonstration, and an informational brochure. Eight core elements were identified for implementation of the intervention. The eight implementation core elements were broken into three separate categories: (a) delivery, (b) content, and (c) pedagogy.

DELIVERY CORE ELEMENTS

Three delivery core elements were identified as essential to establishing a favorable environment for intervention success.

Core Element One: *Deliver the intervention to individual parent-adolescent dyads in their home or in a convenient community-based setting (e.g., community-*

based organization, church, recreation center, or school) at a time that fits the schedule of the parent/guardian.

In the original Baltimore study, the individual focus allowed the intervention to be tailored to the specific needs of each parent and child. The one-on-one session with the health educator and parent-child dyad in the Baltimore study required everyone to be involved and allowed the discussion and role-play to be personalized for each dyad and their potentially unique concerns. The health educator facilitating this conversation helped many parents and children to work through the awkwardness to successfully accomplish their first conversation about sex.

In the original study, the parent/guardian was defined broadly as an adult with whom the youth spent more than 50% of their time. This individual was not necessarily a legal guardian or a blood relative (although most were). The individual was someone with whom the youth spent substantial time and who influenced the youth.

Finally, ImPACT was originally conducted in homes of the youth and their parent/guardian. The home site was chosen to increase parent participation since, as described earlier, our prior experience had shown that group-level interventions in community sites were not popular with parents.

Core Element Two: *Use of a health educator or pair of health educators whom parents and adolescents find credible and are skilled at building rapport with parents and youths at the beginning of the session.*

Health educators for the original intervention were chosen for their ability to be comfortable with the parents and youth. Health educators worked in pairs for safety reasons and were matched to compliment each other's strengths. Younger health educators, who might be able to build rapport with youth, were paired with older health educators, who might have more credibility with parents. Health educators from the community were paired with graduate students who were not familiar with the local community. Although the majority of our health educators were African American for the reasons discussed above, those who were of other racial or ethnic groups were paired with an African American educator. Using individuals with a diverse range of characteristics and skills allowed the project to maximize its ability to engage parents.

Health educators were also trained in techniques to quickly build rapport with parents. They were told to start the ImPACT session with small talk with the parents, e.g., have conversations about the weather or current events, or to compliment the parents on something in their house. Similarly, health educators were instructed to ask the youth a question about their lives, e.g., school, their summer activities, or their Focus on Kids groups. Health educators were encouraged to learn the names of parents and children to ensure conversations were interactive. They were also encouraged to use examples in their discussion, and remain flexible and responsive to the needs and concerns of the parents. Finally, they were conscious of time and tried to stay within the time frame that parents had been told to expect.

Core Element Three: *Ideally, ImPACT should be delivered prior to the child beginning the Focus on Youth intervention.*

ImPACT and Focus on Kids are packaged to be disseminated together since research has found this implementation strategy to be most efficacious at changing adolescent risk behavior. In the Baltimore study, ImPACT was conducted prior to Focus on Kids, which allowed parents and youth to begin a dialogue on the issues taught in Focus on Kids. Parent participation in ImPACT may have increased youth willingness to discuss with their parents what they subsequently learned in Focus on Kids. ImPACT might also have encouraged parents to ask their children about what they learned in Focus on Kids. Finally, parents may have been more likely to support and encourage youth participation in Focus on Kids since they had discussed the Focus on Kids program with a health educator during ImPACT.

PEDAGOGY CORE ELEMENTS

Three pedagogical core elements critical to how the intervention is taught were identified.

Core Element Four: *Use a documentary that shows the challenges and importance of parents monitoring and talking to their children ages 12–15 about sex, abstinence, STIs, HIV, and condoms* (see discussion above around core elements for remaking video for discussion of this core element).

Core Element Five: *The health educator, parent, and child should watch the video together.*

In the original study, the health educator watched the video with the parent and youth instead of leaving the parent and child alone to watch the video. This situation ensured that the parent and youth focused on the video and were not distracted by other things. This was especially important given that they were in their own home and could be easily distracted by other children, the phone, etc. Viewing the video together also allowed for greater discussion when the video was over. The health educator was familiar with the content and could engage the parent and youth in a conversation about its messages.

Core Element Six: *The intervention allows parents an opportunity to practice and improve their monitoring skills, and gives parents and children an opportunity to improve and practice communication skills.*

Two guided role-plays were included to meet this core element. The parent and child were given a realistic scenario about the parent finding out that the child was involved in a new friendship with someone with whom there might also be a sexual relationship. The parent was asked to role-play with the adolescent a conversation in which the parent tries to learn more about the relationship. Once the parent and youth finished the first role-play, the health educator complimented the parent on the strengths of the role-play and made additional suggestions about how the parent could have improved his/her monitoring and communication in the role-play. The health educator provided concrete suggestions to the parent, including (a) asking whether or not the parent was interested in exploring the nature of the relationship the child was having with this new person; (b) sharing the parent's expectations of the future with the child; (c) explaining why the parent was interested in understanding the relationship and why it was important for the parent to know this; and (d) clarifying that the parent has a right and responsibility to know where the child is, who the child is with, and what the child is doing. The health educator prompted the parent to share with the child that wanting to know this information showed that the parent cared. The health educator offered additional monitoring suggestions if these had not already emerged, including interacting with the child's friends and getting to know their friends' parents. The health educator played an important role in this respect and ensured that parents and youth engaged in the targeted skills and gave intensive feedback that was necessary to improve parent-child communication.

CONTENT CORE ELEMENTS

Two core elements were identified as being important content for the ImPACT intervention.

Core Element Seven: *Teach parent and child proper condom-use skills.*

Aside from requiring communication and negotiation skills, using condoms correctly was another skill the ImPACT intervention included to ensure youth made healthy sexual decisions. ImPACT was designed to foster positive attitudes and norms toward correct and consistent condom use among sexually active youth by providing appropriate instructions and demonstrations. Health educators demonstrated correct condom use on a penile model and then offered the parent and child an opportunity to practice correct condom use with the model. The health educator informed parents that studies have shown that talking to children about correct condom use is not the same thing as encouraging children to become sexually active.

Core Element Eight: *All parents receive an informational pamphlet on good communication and how to talk to their kids; the importance of parental monitoring; facts on STIs and HIV, including prevalent data among young African Americans; and steps on how to use a condom.*

At the end of the ImPACT session, the health educators guided parents through an informational pamphlet that reinforced everything that was discussed during the intervention, including tips on communication and monitoring, steps on correct condom use, and information about HIV/AIDS in the African American community. The parents were encouraged to keep the pamphlet and to refer back to it when needed.

These eight core elements were identified to allow agencies to implement ImPACT with fidelity. By adhering to both the video core elements and the implementation core elements, agencies have the best chance of having similar success in changing parental monitoring practices and youth risk behaviors as occurred in the original study.

The new version of the video and an enhanced parent workbook was developed in preparation for national dissemination by ETR through a cooperative agreement with the CDC. The new version was piloted with six community-based organizations that have already implemented the

Focus on Kids (renamed Focus on Youth) intervention. ETR evaluated the selected agencies' implementation of the new version of ImPACT to ensure that it was feasible and appropriate. ETR revised the intervention package and training materials on the basis of the pilot. The pilot sites also allowed ETR to develop a technical assistance manual based on the implementation experiences of the pilot agencies. The full new version was completed in August 2009.

Lessons Learned

As ImPACT was prepared for national dissemination, several challenges emerged. Challenges included the intervention format, the narrow initial target audience, and aspects of the method of delivery. Some of these challenges might have been avoided if national dissemination had been a consideration during development.

Although there was a strong rationale for the documentary-video as an effective mechanism for the intervention, there were many problems with the format when going to scale. The video was an entertaining method of modeling good communication and monitoring, demonstrating youths' perspectives for parents, and providing factual information in a short amount of time. However, the use of the video was challenging when modifying it for new or broader audiences. Cross-cultural appropriateness and transferability problems arose as the original video was developed for a specific population. As a result, the video's general value to other target audiences was limited. The video also quickly became outdated. Ultimately, it was decided that a new video had to be developed to ensure appropriateness, long-term effectiveness, and sustainability of the intervention at the national level. If these issues had been considered during the development phase of the intervention, it might have been possible to reduce some of the problems (i.e., filming the video with individuals from a variety of racial and ethnic backgrounds and from a greater diversity of geographic locations may have made it more applicable to new audiences). Further, ensuring that classic hair styling, clothing, and language were captured might have allowed it to endure and not become dated so quickly.

Concerns have also been expressed by potential adopting agencies about delivering the interventions through home-based visits. This time-and-resource-intensive delivery method might be problematic for community-based agencies with a limited budget and staff. Safety concerns have also been expressed. During the pilot phase of the packaged interventions, possible solutions that allow implementing agencies to balance their resource needs along with the intervention needs for a health educator to work one-on-one with parent and child in a convenient, private location will need to be explored.

Feasibility challenges may have been reduced if, during development, we had worked collaboratively with agencies similar to those that are likely to be future adopters of the intervention. Although we worked with community-based agencies such as recreation centers, housing developments, and churches in Baltimore, research staff, not agency staff, conducted the home visits. This method did not allow a feasibility assessment for future adoption by agencies. The growing field of community-based participatory research speaks to the importance of researchers and community-based agencies working collaboratively as full partners to develop sustainable programs in community sites (Shoultz et al. 2006).

Development of the core elements of the ImPACT intervention was done post hoc in preparation for national dissemination of ImPACT. Eke et al. (2006) discuss the importance of preparing for future dissemination of the intervention when it will be used by prevention providers. They discuss the importance of keeping good records that can help providers with pre-implementation, implementation, and maintenance of the EBI. Identification of core elements was one of the most challenging aspects of packaging the intervention to go to scale. Along with documenting core elements during the development process, identifying appropriate places for adaptations could occur during development as well.

Discussion and Summary

Our research in Baltimore and the Bahamas showed that parental monitoring interventions can be successful at improving parental monitoring and increasing protective behaviors in youth. As more parental monitoring interventions are developed and found to be efficacious in preventing disease and injuries and in promoting health among adolescents and young adults, these interventions will need to be scaled up to ensure effectiveness and positive impact. The lessons learned from the ImPACT program can provide insights to program developers creating parental monitoring interventions that can increase the chance of success in later scaling up their interventions. Packaging and planning for national dissemination of the ImPACT intervention was done post hoc. If national dissemination had been thought of as a final goal of the ImPACT intervention from the beginning, we may have made different choices. Developers of parental monitoring interventions should consider the needs of scaling up during the original development. These needs should be considered when making decisions around content, delivery, and pedagogy. Decisions and methods should also be carefully documented throughout the development and testing process. Increasingly, those working in technology transfer of HIV behavioral interventions encourage developers to think about packaging and going to scale during intervention development (Eke et al. 2006). Developers should give consideration to collecting documentation during intervention development on process monitoring, identification of core elements, technical assistance and/or training needs, and places for adaptation and updating of their intervention.

We have described the process we used to design, evaluate, and translate a parental monitoring intervention for different contexts and for national dissemination. In doing so, we share lessons learned for others developing parental monitoring interventions. Great progress has been made in the field of parental monitoring and communication. There are increasing numbers of interventions with evidence of efficacy, and there are processes in place to move these interventions from research to practice. At this time, it is necessary to improve the translation process. More research is needed to understand how we can improve the process. One potential improvement would be to begin thinking about scaling up interventions during the development and evaluation phase of the program. Improving national dissemination of efficacious parental monitoring interventions seems a natural next step for having an impact on advancing the health and well-being of adolescents.

References

Ary, D. V., Duncan, T. E., Duncan, S. C., & Hops, H. (1999). Adolescent problem behavior: The influence of parents and peers. *Behavioral Research Therapy, 37,* 217–230.

Centers for Disease Control and Prevention [CDC]. (2009). *HIV/AIDS surveillance report, 2007*. Vol. 19. Atlanta: U.S. Department of Health and Human Services, Centers for Disease Control and Prevention. Also available at www.cdc.gov/hiv/stats/hasrlink.htm.

Centers for Disease Control and Prevention [CDC]. (2006). *HIV/AIDS prevention research synthesis project*. Retrieved June 21, 2006, from www.cdc.gov/hiv/topics/ research/prs/index.htm.

Chen, X., Lunn, S., Deveaux, L., Li, X., Brathwaite, N., Cottrell, L., Stanton, B. (2008). A cluster randomized controlled trial of an adolescent HIV prevention program among Bahamian youth: Effect at 12 months post-intervention. *AIDS and Behavior* (epub), December 30, 2008.

Cheung, C. K., Liu, S. C., Lee, T. Y. (2005). Parents, teachers, and peers and early adolescent runaway in Hong Kong. *Adolescence, 40*, 403–424.

Collins, C., Harshbarger, C., Sawyer, R., & Hamdallah, M. (2006). The Diffusion of Effective Behavioral Interventions project: Development, implementation, and lessons learned. *AIDS Education and Prevention, 18* (Suppl. A), 5–20.

Cooper-Patrick, L., Gallo, J. J., Gonzales, J. J., Vu, H. T., Powel, N. R., Nelson, C., et al. (1999). Race, gender, and partnership in the patient-physician relationship. *Journal of the American Medical Association, 282*, 583–589.

Deveaux, L., Stanton, B., Lunn, S., Cottrell, L., Yu, S., Brathwaite, N., et al. (2007). Adolescent risk reduction in developing countries: An HIV prevention intervention with and without a parental monitoring component targeting sixth grade students in The Bahamas. *Archives of Pediatrics and Adolescent Medicine.*

Education, Training, and Research Associates and the CDC. (In press). Adaptation guidance for science-based Pregnancy, STD and HIV prevention education programs for adolescents. Scotts Valley, CA: ETR Associates.

Eke, A., Neumann, M., Wilkes, A., & Jones, P. (2006). Preparing effective behavioral interventions to be used by prevention providers: The role of researchers during HIV prevention trials. *AIDS Education and Prevention, 18* (Suppl. A), 44–58.

Gong, J., Stanton, B., Lunn, S., Deveaux, L., Li, X., Marshall, S., Brathwaite, N.V., Cottrell, L., Harris, C., Chen, X. (2009) Effects through 24 months of an HIV/AIDS prevention intervention program based on protection motivation theory among preadolescents in the Bahamas. *Pediatrics (May) 123(5)*, e917–28.

Halliday-Boykins, C. A., Schoenwald, S. K., & Letourneau, E. J. (2005). Caregiver-therapist ethnic similarity predicts youth outcomes from an empirically based treatment. *Journal of Consulting Clinical Psychology, 73*, 808–818.

Kelly, J. A., Heckman, T. G., Stevenson, L. Y., Williams, P. N., Ertl, T., Hays, R. B., et al. (2000). Transfer of research-based HIV prevention interventions to community service providers: Fidelity and adaptation. *AIDS Education and Prevention, 12* (Suppl. A), 87–98.

Li, X., Stanton, B., Feigelman, S., & Galbraith, J. (2002). Unprotected sex among African-American adolescents: A three-year study. *Journal of the National Medical Association, 94,* 789–796.

Li, X., Stanton, B., Galbraith, J., Burns, J., Cottrell, L., & Pack, R. (2002). Parental monitoring intervention: Practice makes perfect. *Journal of the National Medical Association, 94,* 364–370.

Lyles, C. M., Crepaz, N., Herbst, J. H., Kay, L. S., & the HIV/AIDS Prevention Research Synthesis Team. (2006). Evidence-based HIV behavioral prevention from the perspective of CDC's HIV/AIDS Prevention Research Synthesis (PRS) Team. *AIDS Education and Prevention, 18* (Suppl. A), 21–31.

Lyles, C. M., Kay, L. S., Crepaz, N., Herbst, J. H., Passin, W., Kim, A., et al. (2007). Best evidence interventions: Findings from a systematic review of HIV behavioral interventions for U.S. populations at high risk, 2000–2004. *American Journal of Public Health, 97,* 133–143.

McGuire, W. J. (1985). Attitudes and attitude change. In G. Lindzey & E. Aronson (Eds.), *Handbook of social psychology,* vol. 2. New York: Random House.

McKleroy, V., Galbraith, J., Cummings, B., Jones, P., Harshbarger, C., Collins, C., et al. (2006). Adapting evidence-based behavioral interventions for new settings and target populations. *AIDS Education and Prevention, 18* (Suppl. A), 59–73.

Morris, M., Handcock, M., Miller, W., Ford, C., Schmitz, J. L., Hobbs, M. M., et al. (2006). Prevalence of HIV infection among young adults in the United States: Results from the Add Health Study. *American Journal of Public Health, 96.* 1091–1097.

Parrott, R. L. (1995). Motivation to attend to health messages: Presentation of content and linguistic considerations. In E. Maibach & R. L. Parrott (Eds.), *Designing health messages* (pp. 7–23). Thousand Oaks, CA: Sage.

Piko, B. F., Fitzpatrick, K. M., & Wright, D. R. (2005). A risk and protective factors framework for understanding youth's externalizing problem behavior in two different cultural settings. *European Child and Adolescent Psychiatry, 14,* 95–103.

Rai, A. A., Stanton, B., Wu, Y., Li, X., Galbraith, J., Cottrell, L., et al. (2003). Relative influences of perceived parental monitoring and perceived peer involvement on adolescent risk behaviors: An analysis of six cross-sectional data sets. *Journal of Adolescent Health, 33,* 108–118.

Romer, D., Stanton, B., Galbraith, J., Feigelman, S., Black, M., Ricardo, I., et al. (1999). Parental monitoring and communications as influences on adolescent sexual behavior in high-risk urban settings. *Archives of Pediatrics and Adolescent Medicine, 153,* 1055–1062.

Saha, S., Arbelaez, J. J., & Cooper, L. A. (2003). Patient-physician relationships and racial disparities in the quality of health care. *American Journal of Public Health, 93,* 1713–1719.

Saha, S., Taggart, S. H., Komaromy, M., & Bindman, A. B. (2000). Do patients choose physicians of their own race? *Health Affairs, 19,* 76–83.

Schoenwald, S. K., Halliday-Boykins, C. A., & Henggeler, S. W. (2003). Client-level predictors of adherence to MST in community service settings. *Family Process, 42,* 345–359.

Schouten, B. C., Bas van den Putte, B., Pasmans, M., & Meeuwesen, L. (2007). Parent-adolescent communication about sexuality: The role of adolescents' beliefs, subjective norm, and perceived behavioral control. *Patient Education and Counseling, 66,* 75–83.

Shek, D. T. & Lee, T. Y. (2006). Perceived parental control processes in Chinese adolescents: Implications for positive youth development programs in Hong Kong. *International Journal of Adolescent Medicine and Health, 18,* 505–519.

Shoultz, J., Oneha, M. F., Magnussen, L., Hla, M. M., Brees-Saunders, Z., Cruz, M. D., et al. (2006). Finding solutions to challenges faced in community-based participatory research between academic and community organizations. *Journal of Interprofessional Care, 20.* 133–144.

Sogolow, E. D., Kay, L. S., Doll, L. S., Neumann, M. S., Mezoff, J. S., Eke, A. N., et al. (2000). Strengthening HIV prevention: Application of a research-to-practice framework. *AIDS Education and Prevention, 12* (Suppl. A), 21–34.

Stanton, B., Cole, M., Galbraith, J., Li, X., Pendleton, S., Cottrell, L., et al. (2004). A randomized trial of a parent intervention: Parents can make a difference in long-term adolescent risk behaviors, perceptions, and knowledge. *Archives of Pediatrics and Adolescent Medicine, 158,* 947–955.

Stanton, B., Harris, C., Cottrell, L., Li, X., Gibson, C., Guo, J., et al. (2006). Trial of an urban adolescent sexual risk-reduction intervention for rural youth: A promising but imperfect fit. *Journal of Adolescent Health, 38,* 55.e25–55.e36.

Stanton, B., Li, X., Ricardo, I., Galbraith, J., Feigelman, S., & Kaljee, L. (1996). A randomized controlled effectiveness trial of an AIDS prevention program for low-income African-American youths. *Archives of Pediatrics and Adolescent Medicine, 150,* 363–372.

Steinberg, L., Dornbusch, S. M., & Brown, B. B. (1992). Ethnic differences in adolescent achievement: An ecological perspective. *American Psychologist, 47,* 723–729.

Steinberg, L., Fletcher, A., & Darling, N. (1994). Parental monitoring and peer influence on adolescent substance use. *Pediatrics, 93,* 1060–1064.

Wight, D. (2006). Parental influences on young people's sexual behaviour: A longitudinal analysis. *Journal of Adolescence, 29,* 473–494.

Wu, Y., Stanton, B., Galbraith, J., Kaljee, L., Cottrell, L., Li, X., et al. (2003). Sustaining and broadening intervention impact: A longitudinal randomized trial of three adolescent risk reduction approaches. *Pediatrics, 111,* 32–38.

[7]

A Three-Process System of Parental Monitoring and Supervision

JAMES JACCARD, VINCENT GUILAMO-RAMOS,
ALIDA BOURIS, and PATRICIA DITTUS

The strategy of increasing the amount and quality of parental monitoring during early adolescence holds considerable promise for reducing adolescent risk behavior. Studies suggest that parental monitoring of adolescents lessens the likelihood of problem behaviors in early to middle adolescence (e.g., Barnes et al. 2000; Dishion & McMahon 1998; Fletcher, Darling, & Steinberg 1995; Patterson & Stouthamer-Loeber 1984). However, research also suggests that parents of high-risk youth often disengage from monitoring during middle adolescence (Dishon, Nelson, & Kavanagh 2003) and that monitoring among parents tends to decrease as adolescents progress from middle to late adolescence.

This chapter draws upon and extends parental monitoring and supervision constructs to place parental monitoring into a broader nomological network for the analysis of adolescent problem behaviors. We place the construct of monitoring in a three-process multivariate system that includes the following components: (a) *parental communication of expectations,* whereby parents convey to their children their expectations about what is appropriate behavior; (b) *parental monitoring,* whereby parents determine if their children are acting in accord with those expectations; and (c) *parental discipline/inducement,* whereby parents discipline adolescents who transgress relative to parental expectations and try to induce or gain adolescent cooperation to act in accord with expectations. This three-process system incorporates notions of monitoring as well as supervision, and lays a foundation for developing interventions to help parents monitor and supervise their children more effectively and to reduce the likelihood of adolescent problem behavior by suggesting effective parenting strategies for (a) conveying expectations, (b) monitoring compliance with those expectations, and (c) encouraging compliance with expectations through discipline and inducement/cooperation strategies.

Adolescent Risk Behavior and Parental Monitoring Constructs

Rather than focusing on parental monitoring in general terms, our theoretical approach requires that the researcher identify a specific behavioral domain to apply parental monitoring constructs to. This might be in the area of alcohol use, drug use, sexual risk-taking, or school performance, to name but a few examples. The idea is that how one thinks about and implements monitoring constructs can differ depending on the particular behavioral domain one is interested in. To illustrate the framework, we focus this chapter on adolescent sexual risk behavior as an exemplar.

Adolescent Sexual Behavior: The Transition from Middle School to High School

The middle school and early high school years are a crucial time for interventions aimed at reducing adolescent sexual risk behavior. The transition from middle school to high school is a watershed event for most children. Although considered a normative developmental transition, this transition can be difficult (Barone, Aguirre-Deandreis, & Trickett 1991; Seidman et al. 1996), especially for urban adolescents (Seidman & French 1997). First-year high school students often are thrust into an environment with fellow students who are as much as four years older, and many of whom have engaged in a plethora of risk activities. The school itself is usually larger and further from home than the middle school. In high school, many youth show a decline in academic performance that is reflected in the grades they bring home (Barone, Aguirre-Deandreis, & Trickett 1991; Seidman et al. 1996), as well as increased disengagement from the school system (Seidman et al.).

The transition to high school also presents adolescent girls and boys with increased opportunities for dyadic experiences (e.g., dating), and increased opportunities for sexual activity (Zimmer-Gembeck, Siebenbruner, & Collins 2004). For girls entering 9th grade, high school usually leads to sustained contact with older boys (e.g., 11th and 12th graders). Young girls who date older boys are more likely to transition to sexual experience (Cavanagh 2004; Van Oss Marín et al. 2000). The younger the age of first sexual intercourse, the greater the risk of future unwanted pregnancy and sexually transmitted infections (Moore et al. 2004), because those who begin having sex at young ages are exposed to risk for a longer time, are less likely to use contraception, tend to have more sexual partners, and may engage in alcohol or drug use prior to sexual intercourse (for a review of this literature, see Moore et al.). Such findings argue for the development of interventions that target adolescents during the crucial transition from middle school to high school. Such interventions can set the course for future adolescent development and can be critically important. Most research on parental monitoring and adolescent sexual risk-taking has focused on older adolescents in the later years of high school. However, the development dynamics of adolescence suggests that we need to focus on the middle school and early high school years as well.

Parental Monitoring Research on Sexual Risk Taking: Ad Hoc but Consistent Relationships

Many studies have linked parental monitoring constructs to adolescent sexual risk-taking. For example, Longmore, Manning, and Giordano (2001) used data from the National Survey of Families and Households to predict adolescent sexual risk-taking from parental monitoring assessed four years earlier. They found evidence that parental monitoring reduces sexual risk-taking and argued that parental monitoring during early adolescence lays a basic foundation for young people to make good behavioral choices outside of the purview of parents. Miller, Forehand, and Kotchick (1999) examined family structural variables (family income, parental education, and maternal marital status) and family process variables (maternal monitoring, mother-adolescent sexual communication, and maternal attitudes about adolescent sexual behavior) as predictors of adolescent sexual behavior in two ethnic minority populations. They found that family structure variables were only weakly related to adolescent sexual behavior, but that family process variables, including maternal monitoring, predicted sexual risk-taking.

Although research on parental monitoring and sexual risk-taking has made useful contributions, much of the research has approached monitoring constructs using somewhat simplified conceptual frameworks. Rigorous definitions of monitoring often are absent, and the juxtaposition of monitoring with other constructs in multivariate systems often has been ad hoc. Despite this, parental monitoring constructs have proven to be quite robust in predicting adolescent risk behavior more generally and sexual risk behavior in particular (e.g., Biglan et al. 1990; Cotton et al. 2004; Rai et al. 2003; Rodgers 1999). Clearly, parental monitoring constructs are relevant for understanding adolescent sexual risk behavior.

Past Research and Conceptual Background

This section lays the groundwork for our broader conceptual system by briefly reviewing literature on basic issues in traditional monitoring research. We begin with a discussion of different strategies that have been used to define and measure parental monitoring. Then we consider research on the sources and correlates of monitoring knowledge. Next, we consider moderators of the relationship between parental monitoring and adolescent risk behavior. Finally, we consider the stability of parental monitoring over time.

The Definition and Measurement of Parental Monitoring

Parental monitoring traditionally has been defined as the acquisition of knowledge about the activities, whereabouts, and companions of one's son or daughter (Brown et al. 1993; Dishion et al. 1991; Pettit et al. 2001). When defining monitoring, some theorists emphasize the role of parental *monitoring behaviors*, namely, those behaviors parents perform that lead them to acquire information about the activities, whereabouts, and companions of one's son or daughter. Other theorists, by contrast, emphasize the actual knowledge levels parents have about these activities, whereabouts, and companions (see, for example, Dishion & McMahon 1998; Kerr & Stattin 2000). We use the term *monitoring knowledge* to refer to the knowledge levels parents have about the activities, whereabouts, and companions of their adolescents and the term *monitoring behaviors* to refer to the activities parents engage in to acquire such knowledge. Thus, we believe it is important to distinguish between monitoring behaviors and monitoring knowledge.

Most research on monitoring knowledge has used measures in which either parents characterize how knowledgeable they are about the activities, whereabouts, and companions of their children or in which adolescents characterize how much knowledge the parent has about these matters. In both cases, actual knowledge is not measured but instead, *perceptions* of parental knowledge are assessed. When the parent does the reporting, the measure reflects knowledge levels as perceived by the parent. When the child does the reporting, the measure reflects knowledge levels as perceived by the adolescent. Distinct from these approaches have been strategies that attempt to measure actual parent knowledge rather than perceived knowledge. For example, Crouter and McHale (1993; see also Crouter, Harris, & Sussman 1995; Crouter et al. 1999) had adolescents report on their activities during a given day, and parents were asked in a separate interview if their adolescent had engaged in those activities on that day. Monitoring knowledge was defined in terms of the concordance of adolescent reports with parent reports.

In general, the correlation between parental characterizations of how knowledgeable they are about the activities, whereabouts, and companions of their child and adolescents' characterizations of such matters is modest, typically being about 0.25 (e.g., Pettit et al. 2001; Stattin & Kerr 2001). Similarly, correlations between measures of perceived parental monitoring knowledge and measures based on Crouter's approach tend to be modest, about 0.30 (Crouter et al. 1999). Despite such divergence, all three types of measures tend to be correlated with adolescent risk behavior.

Similar divergence has been found in other areas of developmental science, such as with reports of the amount of parent-teen communication that has transpired as reported by parents versus teens (see Guilamo-Ramos et al. 2007). Low correlations do not necessarily mean the measures are bad, as is typically inferred when lack of convergence is observed. Instead, the lack of correspondence probably reflects the fact that different psychological dynamics are operating for each "source" when forming judgments about knowledge levels. The kinds of factors that parents take into account when characterizing their own knowledge levels may be different from the kinds of factors that adolescents take into account when characterizing their parents' knowledge levels. Parent and adolescent perceptions, whether or not they are accurate or converge, are of theoretical interest in their own right. For example, if a mother is convinced that she knows where her son is and what he is doing, then the mother is not going to engage in behaviors to find out where the son is and what he is doing. The mother might be wrong in her perceptions, but it is her perceptions that guide her behavior. Similarly, if the son thinks the mother knows where he is and what he is doing, he may act differently than if he thinks the mother is ignorant of these facts. In this case, it is the adolescent's perception of maternal knowledge that is influencing the adolescent's behavior, not the actual maternal knowledge per se. So, lack of convergence between adolescent and parental characterizations of monitoring knowledge should not be taken as a reason to abandon such measures. They still reflect constructs that are of theoretical import. Having said that, measures of perceived knowledge clearly tap into something distinct from actual monitoring knowledge as measured by Crouter and McHale (1993), and all three constructs reflected by the different measures may be important to work with.

In terms of influences on adolescent risk behavior, a great deal of research suggests that what matters most in predicting risk behavior of adolescents are the interpretations and construals of the adolescents themselves. For example, adolescents' perceptions of how much their mothers disapprove of them engaging in sex are better predictors of their sexual behavior than mothers' self-reported attitudes about how much they disapprove of their adolescent engaging in sex (Dittus & Jaccard 2000). To be sure, sometimes parental construals or indices of accuracy of adolescent construals predict independent variance in adolescent risk behavior over and above adolescent construals. But the general trend is for adolescent perceptions of the world around them to predict how that adolescent behaves.

Lack of convergence of reports between parents and adolescents also might suggest that something is amiss in the broader parenting/monitoring system. For example, parents may have a set of behavioral expectations about how their adolescent should be behaving and, ideally, these expectations should be clearly communicated to adolescents to the point that adolescents can accurately report on what the parental expectations are. Lack of convergence in measured parental expectations as reported by parents and by adolescents might signify that something has gone amiss in the communication of expectations (rather than the invalidity of measures).

Sources and Correlates of Monitoring Knowledge

Parents of young children typically monitor their child by direct observation or through observations made by other adults (e.g., child care providers). As children grow older, they spend more time in contexts that do not involve direct observation by an adult figure (Laird et al. 1998). In such cases, the acquisition of parental monitoring knowledge relies on processes other than direct observation. These include (a) parental solicitation of information from the adolescent (Laird et al. 1994); (b) adolescent self-disclosure to parents (Crouter & Head 2002; Stattin & Kerr 2001); (c) parental observation of adolescent activities or states that imply or lead to the inference of the performance of risk behaviors (e.g., the adolescent coming home with the smell of tobacco on his or her clothes); (d) parental reliance on information about the adolescent's activities from a spouse; (e) parental reliance on information about the adolescent's activities from other sources (e.g., reports from neighbors) (Crouter et al. 1999); and (f) parental establishment of rules that facilitate the acquisition of monitoring knowledge (e.g., "you must phone in at 11 p.m."; Snyder & Patterson 1987).

Numerous variables have been shown to be associated with reports of monitoring knowledge. One robust correlate is the quality of the parent-child relationship (Ary et al. 1999; Kerns et al. 2001; Laird et al. 2003; Sampson & Laub 1994). This probably reflects a greater willingness on the part of the adolescent to self-disclose to parents they feel close to. Several demographic factors have been found to be associated with monitoring knowledge, such as child gender and age: Parents tend to know more about females than males and about younger as opposed to older adolescents (Crouter et al. 1999; Li, Feigelman, & Stanton 2000). Crouter and coworkers (1999) found that mothers as compared to fathers tended to be more knowledgeable about daughters and that fathers, as compared to mothers, tended to be more knowledgeable about sons. Gender-role attitudes also have been implicated as predictors of monitoring knowledge (Bumpus, Crouter, & McHale 2001).

Parents tend to know more about their second-born child as opposed to their first-born child (Crouter et al. 1999). Parental education levels also have been found to be related to monitoring knowledge, especially for fathers (Crouter et al. 1999). Pettit and coworkers (2001) found that mothers in single-parent families said they were less knowledgeable of child activities than mothers in two-parent households, even when socioeconomic status was held constant. Several studies have found that poverty is associated with lower levels of monitoring knowledge (e.g., Pettit et al. 2001). Employment histories of both adolescents and parents have been implicated in monitoring knowledge. Manning (1990) found that the more hours adolescents worked, the less likely adolescents were to be required by parents to let them know where they are. Shanahan and colleagues (1996) reported that the more money adolescents earned on the job, the less mothers reported monitoring them. Crouter and coworkers (1999) found no differences in monitoring knowledge as a function of maternal work hours. Crouter and McHale (1993) found that father's monitoring knowledge was more likely to decrease when mother's work hours were cut back at certain times of the year. Bumpus, Crouter, and McHale (1999) found that high paternal work demands and low marital quality predicted lower levels of monitoring knowledge.

In addition, Pagani and colleagues (1998) found that family transitions were associated with monitoring knowledge. Specifically, monitoring knowledge was lower for parents of adolescent boys whose custodial parents experienced remarriage during adolescence. This was especially true when the remarriage happened when the boy was 12 to 14 years of age (see also Mekos, Hetherington, & Reiss 1996). Finally, adolescent beliefs in the legitimacy of parental control efforts have been found to be associated with monitoring knowledge (Laird et al. 2003; Smetana & Daddis 2002). The more legitimate adolescents perceive control behaviors to be, the higher the levels of monitoring knowledge.

In sum, studies of the correlates of parental monitoring knowledge have implicated social, psychological, and demographic variables in the acquisition of such knowledge. The studies have found considerable variability in monitoring knowledge, and this variability is systematically related to a wide range of factors.

Moderators of Monitoring and Adolescent Risk Behavior:
A Robust Relationship

In general, the commonly observed association between parental monitoring behavior and knowledge and adolescent risk behavior has been robust, manifesting itself across a wide range of situations, family characteristics, and risk activities. Despite this, some moderator variables have been identified. Huebner and Howell (2003) observed an interaction between monitoring knowledge and the amount of parent-adolescent communication in predicting adolescent sexual activity. Specifically, they found that sexual risk-taking was elevated only for the group characterized by low monitoring and low communication. Donenberg and colleagues (2002) found that parental monitoring was more strongly associated with sexual risk-taking in troubled girls than troubled boys. Jacobson and Crockett (2000) found that gender and grade level of the child moderated the relationship between parental monitoring and adolescent delinquency, with the effect size of parental monitoring increasing across grade levels for boys, and decreasing across grade levels for girls. In addition, maternal employment moderated the relationship between monitoring and sexual behavior: For both boys and girls, monitoring was a significant predictor of sexual activity among adolescents whose mothers worked full time. The effects of monitoring also may depend on the initial levels of problem activities. Adolescents who are well behaved initially seem not to need monitoring as much as adolescents who engage in risk activities at an early stage of adolescence (e.g., Laird et al. 2003; Pettit et al. 1999).

Stability of Monitoring: Monitoring Decreases as Adolescents Get Older

A fairly consistent finding in the literature is that monitoring knowledge tends to decrease as adolescents get older (e.g., Patterson & Stouthamer-Loeber 1984; Stoolmiller 1994). It is thus ironic that as adolescents are placed in settings that increase the likelihood of risk behavior, parental monitoring seems to decrease. Despite this trend in mean trajectories, variability in monitoring trajectories over time also exists (Laird et al. 2003). It is thus important to identify and characterize factors that impact monitoring trajectories. Relatively little research has addressed this issue in early adolescence. Several studies suggest that manifestation of problem behaviors over time may impact monitoring as much as monitoring impacts problem behaviors, i.e., that the link is bidirectional (e.g., Jang & Smith 1997; Laird et al. 2003).

It is clear based on the above cursory review that social scientists have acquired considerable knowledge about parental monitoring constructs. But there is still much to be learned. We believe that parental monitoring research will benefit by placing such constructs into a broader conceptual framework that will allow linkages between traditional monitoring concepts and parenting behaviors that are closely related to them. We now turn to a description of such a framework.

A Three-Process System of Parental Monitoring and Supervision

Whereas past research has conceptualized monitoring primarily as the knowledge that parents have of their child's activities, whereabouts, and companions, we approach monitoring in the context of a more general system of parental influence. Our framework for effective parental monitoring and supervision contains three core processes. First, parents must establish behavioral standards for their adolescents and clearly convey those standards to adolescents to ensure that their adolescents know and understand what is expected of them. In the case of sexual activity, one such behavioral expectation may be that the adolescent should not engage in sexual intercourse. Other standards/expectations might include avoidance of mixed-gender parties without adult supervision, not allowing social outings on school nights, and not allowing the adolescent to date older adolescents. We refer to such standards as *parental behavioral expectations*.

Consistent with our focus on specific behavioral domains, the behavioral expectations a parent has will vary depending on the domain of interest. In the current example, we are interested in adolescent behaviors in the dating and sexual domain that the parent thinks the adolescent should or should not perform. In any given system of behavioral expectations, there will be *superordinate behavioral expectations* focused on global risk behaviors (e.g., the adolescent should not engage in sexual intercourse), as well as *subordinate behavioral expectations* focused on behaviors that increase or decrease the likelihood that the superordinate behavioral expectation will be met (e.g., the adolescent should not date older adolescents). Theorists need to elaborate and consider both the superordinate and subordinate behavioral expectations of parents.

Second, parents must monitor their adolescents to ensure they are acting in accord with behavioral expectations. We refer to this as *parental behavioral monitoring* and it reflects both information-gathering and inferences that lead the parent to make an overall judgment about whether the adolescent is performing the behaviors s/he is expected to perform and avoiding those that are prohibited. *Parental monitoring knowledge* refers to whether parents are accurate in their assessments of their adolescent's behavior.

The third process is *parental behavioral inducement and enforcement*. This refers to both the actions (e.g., incentives, punishments, and rewards) parents take to encourage their adolescent to comply with behavioral expectations, and the discipline strategies parents use when adolescents transgress from behavioral expectations, so as to prevent further transgressions.

We now highlight some distinctive features of the above framework and elaborate on the three processes, conceptually.

Behavior-Specific Versus Global Monitoring

Our three-process model differs from traditional monitoring research in important ways. One difference is that traditional measures of monitoring knowledge focus on knowledge about global constructs, namely the general activities, whereabouts, and companions of the adolescent. Such measures are not tied to a specific risk behavior but rather the same measures are used no matter what the risk domain. For example, the classic measure used by Steinberg and coworkers (1994) asks adolescents, "How much do your parents REALLY know about . . . (a) who your friends are, (b) where you go at night, (c) how you spend your money, (d) what you do with your free time, and (e) where you are most afternoons after school?" Note that this measure does not focus on sexual risk-taking or behaviors that increase risks of engaging in sexual intercourse, such as knowing if one's daughter is dating older adolescents and if she is attending unsupervised parties. The measure is global, whereas our framework focuses on specific behaviors related to sexual risk-taking and elaborates parental expectations and parental monitoring with respect to those specific behaviors.

Although global measures of monitoring have their place, a large body of literature in personality and social psychology suggests that focusing on predictors that are more directly tied to a behavioral criterion will be more fruitful and powerful. For example, research on locus of control has found that measures of specific types of locus of control (e.g., contraceptive locus of control) predict behavior (using contraceptives) better than global measures of locus of control. Similarly, research suggests that attitudes that are specific to the behavioral criterion predict behavior better than global attitudes (Ajzen & Fishbein 1977, 1981). The same will probably hold true for monitoring constructs.

Parental Behavioral Expectations

A first step in applying our framework is to identify relevant superordinate and subordinate behavioral expectations in the behavioral domain of interest.

PARENTAL DISAPPROVAL OF SEXUAL INTERCOURSE

One obvious superordinate behavioral expectation in the sexual domain is that the adolescent should not engage in vaginal sexual intercourse. Although it is commonly assumed that nearly all parents hold such an expectation for their adolescents, research has indicated this may not be the case. For example, in a national sample of 7th and 8th grade students that we conducted, parents were asked if they would approve or disapprove of their adolescent having sexual intercourse at this time in his or her life. Although 77% of the parents strongly disapproved of their child engaging in sexual intercourse, 23% did not express such disapproval, suggesting that a small but significant minority of parents do not seem to have strong feelings about whether their adolescent children engage in intercourse. Interestingly, several studies have shown that adolescents who perceive their parents as less disapproving of sexual intercourse are more likely to engage in sexual intercourse (e.g., Dittus & Jaccard 2000).

Not only should parents have behavioral expectations consistent with the avoidance of sexual activity if their child is to not engage in the behavior, but these perceptions must be clearly conveyed to and accurately perceived by adolescents. Our prior research suggests that many adolescents misperceive the degree of parental disapproval regarding their engagement in sexual intercourse. In one study of a national sample of adolescents and mothers, the correlation between maternal reports of disapproval and adolescent perceptions of that disapproval was only 0.26 (Dittus & Jaccard 2000). Analyses of correlates of misperception revealed adolescents were more likely to underestimate maternal disapproval of them engaging in sexual intercourse if (a) the mother expressed approval of the use of birth control (suggesting that adolescents may have difficulty dealing with "mixed" messages), (b) the adolescent had already engaged in sexual intercourse (suggesting the operation of dissonance reduction and post-behavior rationalization), and (c) the adolescent perceived his or her mother as being less involved in his or her life.

PARENTAL DISAPPROVAL OF ACTIVITIES SURROUNDING SEXUAL INTERCOURSE

Research generally has not addressed the issue of identifying which subordinate behavioral expectations are relevant for discouraging adolescent sexual activity. Through qualitative research with a group of Latino and African American mothers and their adolescents, Dittus and colleagues (2007) identified the following subordinate behaviors around which behavioral expectations might be formed (the behaviors are phrased here as "items" for mothers with respect to their daughters in a direction that would encourage sexual activity, so the expectations would be about not allowing these behaviors): (a) "My daughter can stay out as late as she wants on weekend nights"; (b) "I allow my daughter to have boys over to the house when no adult is at home"; (c) "I let my daughter go out socially on school nights"; (d) "I let my daughter go to unsupervised parties where there will be both boys and girls"; (e) "I let my daughter hang out with older girls (one or two grades older than her)"; (f) "I allow my daughter to go out on dates with boys"; (g) "I allow my daughter to go out on dates with boys who are older than her"; and (h) "I allow my daughter to hang out with friends I do not approve of." Borawski and coworkers (2003) examined the predictive utility of items rated by adolescents such as "I am allowed to stay out past curfew as long as I call home first," "I am allowed to have friends over when my parents are not home, as long as I tell my parents beforehand," "I am allowed to have opposite-sex friends in my bedroom," and "There is a place in my house where I am allowed to hang out with my friends where my parents won't bother us." A composite measure of these items was correlated with several indices of sexual risk-taking.

In any given behavioral domain, one can probably identify a dozen or so behaviors that parents can have behavioral expectations about (both superordinate and subordinate) that should be relevant to the adolescent risk behavior of interest. A first step in developing an effective intervention is to identify what these behaviors are based on previous research and formative, qualitative research. Once isolated, research can obtain measures of the expectations that parents have with respect to each behaviors.

Some behavioral expectations may be more important in reducing the likelihood of the general risk activity (engaging in unprotected sexual intercourse) than others. Another important goal of research should be to identify behavioral expectancies that have the largest structural coefficients for determining future sexual activity, thereby identifying behavioral expectations that are most important to focus interventions on.

A FRAMEWORK FOR STUDYING BEHAVIORAL EXPECTATIONS

Figure 7.1 presents a general path diagram that can guide analyses of behavioral expectations. The two most important conceptual categories in this figure are the box containing the different parental behavioral expectations and the box containing the adolescent perceptions of those expectations. The path going from the former to the latter reflects the idea that adolescent perceptions of parental behavioral expectations are influenced by the behavioral expectations that parents actually have. Ideally, this would be the only determinant of adolescent perceptions of parental behavioral expectations. Unfortunately, this is not always the case. The challenge for the researcher is to identify what these other determinants are so that they can be addressed in intervention efforts. The variables can take the form of moderators (path d in figure 7.1) or factors other than parental expectancies that impact adolescent perceptions (paths e through g). As an example of a moderator variable, one might find that the more parents talk about a behavioral expectation with their children, the stronger will be the correspondence between the parental expectation and adolescent perceptions of the expectation. For influences on adolescent perceptions other than parental expectations, it might be that adolescents who have already engaged in sexual intercourse or who intend to engage in sexual intercourse will underestimate parental opposition to them engaging in sexual intercourse, as the adolescents rationalize their current beliefs based on their past

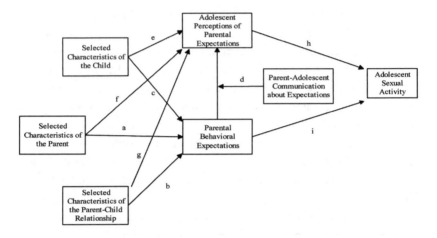

Figure 7.1   Parental expectations as mediators of adolescent sexual activity

behavior. Or it might be the case that children of parents who have talked
with them about the importance of using birth control if they engage in
sex will underestimate parental opposition to them engaging in sex because of the "mixed message" that such discussions might convey.

Figure 7.1 also shows that one should expect individual differences in
parental behavioral expectations (see paths a, b, and c). For example, parents might be more strict in the sexual and dating domains for girls than
for boys, and they may be more strict for younger as opposed to older adolescents. Religious parents might be stricter than nonreligious parents,
and parents also might be stricter with children who have disobeyed them
in the past. Parents also might be less strict when they have a good relationship with their children. Another important focus of research should
be on documenting and understanding individual and contextual differences in behavioral expectations that parents hold.

Finally, figure 7.1 includes the possibility that actual parental expectations will predict sexual activity over and above adolescent perceptions of
those expectations (path i in figure 7.1). As noted, past research suggests
that adolescent perceptions of expectations have priority, but some studies
have found that parental expectations predict independent of adolescent
perceptions (e.g., Dittus & Jaccard 2000).

Figure 7.1 is a "snapshot" at a single point in time. It is, of course, important to document how parental behavioral expectancies change over

time, such as through the analysis of "trajectories" in expectancies through growth-curve-like models. We suspect that the trajectories will tend to show a decline in behavioral expectations over time for sexual behavior, as parents become more accepting of intimacy as adolescents get older. One can study not only trajectories for parent characterizations of their behavioral expectations but also the trajectories of adolescent perceptions of those expectations as well. Finally, one can determine if the trajectories for one variable (e.g., parental expectations) are associated with trajectories for another variable (e.g., adolescent perceptions of parental expectations, sexual activity).

A careful analysis of the behavioral expectations that parents have and adolescent perceptions of those expectations will not only be informative, but it also sets the stage for the analysis of monitoring and the processes by which parents "come to know" if their children are behaving in accord with their expectations (i.e., monitoring knowledge).

Parental Monitoring

Once behavioral expectations have been established and conveyed to adolescents, parents must monitor their adolescent's behavior to determine whether the adolescent is acting in accord with those expectations. Of particular interest are the strategies parents use to gain knowledge of their child's activities with respect to the target expectations and how successful these strategies are in leading the parent to make accurate inferences.

Following the qualitative work of Crouter and colleagues (1995, 1999), for each behavior/expectation of interest, we recommend asking parents to indicate the source of their knowledge (i.e., how they know that the adolescent is conforming to or transgressing from the behavioral expectation). We suggest using qualitative methods to identify the different strategies parents report and then using these strategies as well as those identified by Crouter and coworkers (1999) in more quantitatively oriented research to identify the best predictors of monitoring knowledge. Individual differences in monitoring knowledge can be evaluated, using variables similar to those identified in previous research as reviewed above. Note, however, that past research has tended to focus on global *perceived* monitoring knowledge rather than actual monitoring knowledge about specific activities tied to sexual risk-taking.

ADOLESCENT SELF-DISCLOSURE

We believe that a key source of parental monitoring knowledge is adolescent self-disclosure, both voluntary and in response to parental solicitations for information. Accordingly, an important task for the theorist is to identify factors that influence an adolescent's willingness to disclose information and respond positively to parent solicitations.

Research we have conducted suggests that adolescents are more likely to communicate with and self-disclose to their parents if they think their parents (a) can be trusted (i.e. that their parents are looking out for their best interests and are honest with them), (b) have useful advice to offer (i.e., have expertise), and (c) are accessible (Guilamo-Ramos et al. 2006). A review of the literature on communication styles suggests eight dimensions of communication styles of parents that also might impact adolescent willingness to self-disclose and communicate with their parent. These are (a) avoiding and/or dealing with conflict (Canary & Spitzberg 1987); (b) use of parental self-disclosure (Jourard 1971; Wheeless & Grotz 1976); (c) parental display of empathy and understanding (Redmond 1985; Wiemann 1977); (d) parental supportiveness (Bochner & Kelly 1995; Duran 1983); (e) staying calm and relaxed during conversations (Booth-Butterfield & Kelly 1986; Duran 1983); (f) being responsive (Cegala 1981; Norton & Pettigrew 1979); (g) exhibiting effective interaction management skills, such as listening respectfully and not interrupting (Clark & Delia 1979; Ruben 1977); and (h) being direct (Rose 1975; Steffan, Greenwald, & Langmeyer 1979). Thus, adolescents will be more likely to self-disclose if they trust their parents, believe their parents give good advice, think their parents are accessible, and if their parents communicate in ways that are consistent with positive "scores" on the eight communication style dimensions.

PARENTAL-IMPLICIT THEORIES OF SEXUAL ACTIVITY

Independent of adolescent self-disclosure, parents also have implicit theories about the type of adolescent who engages in sexual intercourse (or who engages in the subordinate behavior around which the expectation is focused). Parents may use these theories to make inferences about whether their child is acting in accord with behavioral expectations. Through qualitative research, researchers can identify what parents tend to think are the personality characteristics and attributes of the kind of adolescent who engages in sexual intercourse as well as the "cues" that would suggest an expectation transgression. The idea is that parental attributions of sexual activity on the part of their child will be influenced by the extent to which they think their child has attributes or exhibits behaviors that map onto these "implicit theories of adolescent sexual activity."

Whereas traditional monitoring theories have focused on adolescent self-disclosure and a host of other monitoring behaviors parents engage in (as reviewed earlier), few theories incorporate the notion of parental-implicit theories as a means for parents making inferences about transgressions. We believe that this will be a fruitful pursuit for future research.

Parental Enforcement and Inducements

If a child fails to act in accord with parental expectations and the parent becomes aware of this transgression, then disciplinary actions may be taken to address the transgression and to minimize its happening again. Of interest are the kinds of discipline strategies that parents use to address such transgressions and whether some strategies are more effective than others at preventing the recurrence of future transgression. Parents also may use a variety of strategies to motivate the adolescent to comply with expectancies *before* a transgression occurs. Such inducements can take the form of threats, rewards, or the structuring of the environment so as to encourage compliance with expectations.

DISCIPLINE STRATEGIES

There is a substantial literature on general parental discipline strategies, but few studies focus on discipline strategies used in a specific behavioral domain for a specific behavioral expectation. Hoffman (1963, 1970; Hoffman & Saltzstein 1967) described three common forms of parental discipline: power assertion, love withdrawal, and induction. Power assertion involves the use of physical punishment, force, threat, and/or the removal of privileges or material possessions. Love withdrawal involves ignoring or isolating the child, refusing to speak to the child, and/or explicitly stating a dislike for the child. Induction involves the use of reasoning, the communication of clear standards of behavior, and/or an emphasis on intentions, feelings, and reparation. Each of the strategies has been linked to risk behavior, but in complex and sometimes inconsistent ways (e.g., Ge et al. 1996; Shaw & Scott 1991). In general, research with younger children suggests that parental use of induction, when contrasted with the use of power assertion or love withdrawal, is associated with favorable outcomes, including heightened empathy and prosocial behavior (Eisenberg et al. 1992; Hoffman & Saltzstein 1967; Krevans & Gibbs 1996); lower levels of antisocial behavior (Hart, DeWolf, & Burts 1992; Maccoby & Martin 1983); more mature moral judgment (Nevius 1977; Olejnik 1980); and greater popularity among peers (Dekovic & Janssens 1992; Dishion 1990). In addition, induction is more likely than power assertion or love withdrawal to encourage the development of an internalized motive to follow parent-imposed rules and regulations in the parent's absence (Dix & Grusec 1983; Hoffman 1970; Maccoby 1992; Maccoby & Martin 1983).

To study the disciplinary techniques used by parents of adolescents as applied to transgressions of specific behavioral expectations in a specific behavioral domain, we suggest that researchers first conduct qualitative research to explore the disciplinary strategies parents use or would use when behavioral transgressions related to a specific behavioral expectation occur. In doing so, we recommend using unstructured exploratory questions, perhaps followed by questions guided by the Hoffman framework. Based on this, researchers can develop quantitative measures that assess (a) if parents endorse the use of a given discipline strategy for a given transgression and (b) the extent to which they have used the strategy in the past. Researchers can then document if use of a given discipline style predicts the occurrence of future behavioral transgressions to help identify discipline techniques that are most effective in preventing transgressions. Additionally, both parent and adolescent reports of parental use of disciplinary tactics should be pursued to assess concordance between the two and to determine whether degree of concordance is associated with adolescent compliance.

INDUCEMENT

Inducement strategies are parental techniques that encourage compliance with behavioral expectations and that do not rely on punishment or disciplining as discussed in the previous paragraph. An indirect form of inducement is simply to have a good relationship with the adolescent; adolescents with higher levels of relationship satisfaction will tend to be more compliant, everything else being equal. Studies on children's conceptualizations of adult authority also suggest that children's evaluations of the legitimacy and fairness of an authority figure's demands impacts their compliance with those demands (Laupa & Turiel 1986; Tisak 1986; Tisak & Tisak 1990). Thus, adolescent perceptions of the fairness and legitimacy of the behavioral expectation is an important variable to measure and relate to behavioral transgressions. If such legitimacy and fairness factors are found to be important, then an intervention strategy might be to help parents discuss the legitimacy of their expectations with their adolescent children.

IMPLEMENTATION INTENTIONS

Yet another strategy that parents can use to encourage compliance derives from research on implementation intentions (Gollwitzer, Fujita, & Oettingen 2004). This approach assumes that adolescents are motivated to comply with the expectation of the parents, but then finds oneself in a situation where it is difficult to do so or where they may be tempted to transgress. For example, an adolescent might be pressured by peers to attend a party where no adult supervision is present. Parents can help adolescents anticipate such "high risk" situations where they might transgress, and then provide adolescents with action plans (practical strategies for avoiding the transgression) to use in such situations, i.e., they can help the adolescent implement their intentions.

ADDITIONAL INFLUENCES

There obviously are a wide range of additional factors that can influence adolescent compliance deriving from a host of individual differences and contextual influences. We encourage researchers to think about such influences in the context of the specific behavioral domains they are working within.

As with the other processes, it is important to study the above dynamics from a developmental perspective to document trajectories in the use of different discipline, inducement, and implementation intention strategies.

Conclusions

This chapter has suggested that we take a somewhat broader view of parental monitoring constructs and think about them in the context of a three-process system of monitoring and supervision associated with parents conveying behavioral expectations, parents monitoring if those expectations are adhered to, and parents disciplining/inducing adolescents to act in accord with expectations. Our framework differs from traditional monitoring research in that it focuses on behavior-specific monitoring rather than global monitoring constructs that are independent of the behavioral domain of interest. We also underscore the importance of a developmental focus. The three-process system permits analyses of concomitant trajectories for the risk behavior of interest, parental behavioral expectations, parental monitoring behaviors, parental monitoring knowledge, parental discipline, and parental inducements as adolescents transition from middle school to high school. Such research can yield important insights into the developmental dynamics of these phenomena.

Coupled with the recommended qualitative research, application of our framework should provide useful information for the design of parent-based interventions aimed at reducing sexual risk-taking in children by increasing the quality of parental monitoring and supervision. Such research should allow social scientists to (a) identify which subordinate behavioral expectations are most strongly associated with reductions in sexual risk-taking and which expectations tend to be inaccurately perceived by adolescents, (b) specify mechanisms that lead to inaccurate perceptions of behavioral expectations on the part of adolescents, (c) identify strategies parents use to monitor adolescents to determine if they are acting in accord with the behavioral expectancies and assess which strategies lead to the most accurate inferences, (d) identify the implicit theories that parents use in making attributions of their children's behaviors related to sexual activity, (e) specify parent communication variables most likely to encourage and facilitate adolescent self-disclosure and positive responses to parental solicitations for information, and (f) identify strategies for encouraging adolescent behavioral compliance and effective discipline strategies when adolescents transgress. Such research should lay a foundation for the development of effective parent-focused interventions aimed at improving the quality of parental monitoring and supervision.

References

Ajzen, I., & Fishbein, M. (1977). Attitude-behavior relations: A theoretical analysis and review of empirical research. *Psychological Bulletin, 84,* 888–918.

Ajzen, I., & Fishbein, M. (1981). *Understanding attitudes and predicting social behavior.* Englewood Cliffs, NJ: Prentice Hall.

Ary, D. V., Duncan, T. E., Biglan, A., Metzler, C. W., Noell, J. W., & Smolkowski, K. (1999). Development of adolescent problem behavior. *Journal of Abnormal Child Psychology, 27,* 141–150.

Barnes, G. M., Reifman, A. S., Farrell, M. P., & Dintcheff, B. A. (2000). The effects of parenting on the development of adolescent alcohol misuse: A six wave latent growth model. *Journal of Marriage and Family, 62,* 175–186.

Barone, C., Aguirre-Deandreis, A. I., Trickett, E. J. (1991). Means-ends problem-solving skills, life stress, and social support as mediators of adjustment in the normative transition to high school. *American Journal of Community Psychology, 19,* 207–225.

Biglan, A., Metzler, C., Wirt, R., Ary, D., Noell, J., Ochs, L., et al. (1990). Social and behavioral factors associated with high risk sexual behavior among adolescents. *Journal of Behavioral Medicine, 13,* 245–261.

Bochner, A. P., & Kelly, C. W. (1995). Interpersonal competence: Rationale philosophy, and implementation of a conceptual framework. *Speech Teacher, 28,* 279–301.

Booth-Butterfield, S., & Kelly C. W. (1986). The Communication Anxiety Inventory: Validation of state and context-communication apprehension. *Communication Quarterly, 34,* 194–205.

Borawski, E., Levers-Ladis, L., Lovegreen, L., & Trapl, E. (2003). Parental monitoring, negotiated unsupervised time, and parental trust: The role of perceived parenting practices in adolescent health risk behaviors. *Journal of Adolescent Health, 33,* 60–70.

Brown, B. B., Mounts, N., Lamborn, S. D., & Steinberg, L. (1993). Parenting practices and peer group affiliation in adolescence. *Child Development, 64,* 467–482.

Bumpus, M., Crouter, A., & McHale, S. (1999). Work demands of dual-earner couples Implications for parents' knowledge about children's daily activities in middle childhood. *Journal of Marriage and Family, 61,* 465–475.

Bumpus, M. F., Crouter, A. C., & McHale, S. M. (2001). Parental autonomy granting in adolescence: Exploring gender differences in context. *Developmental Psychology, 37,* 163–173.

Canary, D. J., & Spitzberg, B. H. (1987). Appropriateness and effectiveness perceptions of conflict strategies. *Human Communication Research, 14,* 93–108.

Cavanagh, S. E. (2004). The sexual debut of girls in early adolescence: The intersection of race, pubertal timing, and friendship group characteristics. *Journal of Research of Adolescence, 14,* 285–312.

Cegala, D. J. (1981). Interaction involvement: A cognitive dimension of communicative competence. *Communication Education, 30,* 109–121.

Clark, R. A., & Delia, J. G. (1979). Topic and rhetorical competence. *Quarterly Journal of Speech, 55,* 187–206.

Cotton, S., Mills, L., Succop, P., Biro, F., & Rosenthal, S. (2004). Adolescent girls' perceptions of the timing of their sexual initiation: "Too young" or "just right"? *Journal of Adolescent Health, 34,* 453–458.

Crouter, A. C., & Head, M. R. (2002). Parental monitoring and knowledge of children. In M. Bornstein (Ed.), *Handbook of parenting, 2nd ed., vol. 3: Becoming and being a parent* (pp. 461–483). Mahwah, NJ: Erbaum.

Crouter, A. C., Harris, M., & Susman, A. (1995). Parenting during middle childhood. In M. Bornstein (Ed.), *Handbook of parenting,* vol. 1 (pp. 65–89). Mahwah, NJ: Erlbaum.

Crouter, A. C., Helms-Erikson, H., Updegraff, K., & McHale, S. M. (1999). Conditions underlying parents' knowledge about children's daily lives in middle childhood: Between and within-family comparisons. *Child Development, 70,* 246–259.

Crouter, A. C., & McHale, S. M. (1993). Temporal rhythms of family life: Seasonal variation in the relation between parental work and family processes. *Developmental Psychology, 29,* 198–205.

Dekovic, M., & Janssens, J. M. A.M. (1992). Parents' child-rearing style and children's sociometric status. *Developmental Psychology, 28,* 925–932.

Dishion, T. J. (1990). The family ecology of boys' peer relations in middle childhood. *Child Development, 61,* 874–892.

Dishion, T. J., & McMahon, R. J. (1998). Parental monitoring and the prevention of child and adolescent problem behavior: A conceptual and empirical formulation. *Clinical Child and Family Psychology Review, 1,* 61–75.

Dishion, T. J., Nelson, S. E., & Kavanagh, K. (2003). The Family Check-Up for high-risk adolescents: Motivating parenting monitoring and reducing problem behavior. In J. E. Lochman & R. Salekin (Eds.), Behavior oriented interventions for children with aggressive behavior and/or conduct problems [Special Issue]. *Behavior Therapy, 34,* 553–571.

Dishion, T. J., Patterson, G. R., Stoolmiller, M., & Skinner, M. L. (1991). Family, school, and behavioral antecedents to early adolescent involvement with antisocial peers. *Developmental Psychology, 27,* 172–180.

Dittus, P., & Jaccard, J. (2000). The relationship of adolescent perceptions of maternal disapproval of sex and of the mother-adolescent relationship to sexual outcomes. *Journal of Adolescent Health, 26,* 268–278.

Dittus, P., Jaccard, J., Guilamo-Ramos, V., & Bouris, A. (2007). Perceptions of general and situation-specific parental monitoring and associations with adolescent sexual risk behavior. Unpublished manuscript.

Dix, T., & Grusec, J. E. (1983). Parental influence techniques: An attributional analysis. *Child Development, 54,* 645–652.

Donenberg, G., Wilson, H., Emerson, E., & Bryant, F. (2002). Holding the line with a watchful eye: The impact of perceived parental monitoring on risky sexual behavior among adolescents in psychiatric care. *AIDS Education and Prevention, 14,* 138–157.

Duran, R. L. (1983). Communicative adaptability: A measure of social communicative competence. *Communication Quarterly, 31,* 320–326.

Eisenberg, N., Fabes, R. A., Carlo, G., Troyer, D., Speer, A. L., Karbon, M., et al. (1992). The relations of maternal practices and characteristics to children's vicarious responsiveness. *Child Development, 63,* 583–602.

Fletcher, A. C., Darling, N., & Steinberg, L. (1995). Parental monitoring and peer influences on adolescent substance use. In J. McCord (Ed.), *Coercion and punishment in long-term perspectives* (pp. 259–271). New York: Cambridge University Press.

Ge, X., Best, K. M., Conger, R. D. & Simons, R. L. (1996). Parenting behaviors and the occurrence and co-occurrence of adolescent depressive symptoms and conduct problems. *Developmental Psychology, 32,* 717–731.

Gollwitzer, P., Fujita, K., & Oettingen, G. (2004). Planning and the implementation of goals. In K. Vohs & R. Baumeister (Eds.), *Handbook of self-regulation: Research, theory, and applications* (pp. 211–228). New York: Guilford Press.

Guilamo-Ramos, V., Jaccard, J., Dittus, P., & Bouris, A. (2006). Parental expertise, trustworthiness, and accessibility: Parent-adolescent communication and adolescent risk behavior. *Journal of Marriage and Family, 68,* 1229–1246.

Guilamo-Ramos, V., Jaccard, J., Dittus, P., Bouris, A., Holloway, I., & Casillas, E. (2007). Adolescent expectancies, parent-adolescent communication, and intentions to have sexual intercourse in inner city, middle school youth. *Annals of Behavioral Medicine, 34,* 56–66.

Hart, C. H., DeWolf, D. M., & Burts, D. C. (1992). Linkages among preschoolers' playground behavior, outcome expectations, and parental disciplinary strategies. *Early Education and Development, 3,* 265–283.

Hoffman, M. L. (1963). Parent discipline and the child's consideration for others. *Child Development, 34,* 573–588.

Hoffman, M. L. (1970). Moral development. In P. H. Mussen (Ed.), *Carmichael's manual of child psychology,* vol. 2 (pp. 261–360). New York: Wiley.

Hoffman, M. L., & Saltzstein, H. D. (1967). Parent discipline and the child's moral development. *Journal of Personality and Social Psychology, 5,* 45–57.

Huebner, A. J., & Howell, L. W. (2003). Examining the relationship between adolescent sexual risk-taking and perceptions of monitoring, communication, and parenting styles. *Journal of Adolescent Health, 33,* 71–78.

Jacobson, K. C., & Crockett, L. J. (2000). Parental monitoring and adolescent adjustment: An ecological perspective. *Journal of Research on Adolescence, 10,* 65–97.

Jang, S. J., & Smith, C. A. (1997). A test of reciprocal causal relationships among parental supervision, affective ties, and delinquency. *Journal of Research in Crime and Delinquency, 34,* 307–336.

Jourard, S. M. (1971). Self disclosure: An experimental analysis of the transparent self. New York: Wiley-Interscience.

Kerns, K., Aspelmeier, J., Gentzler, A., & Grabill, C. (2001). Parent-child attachment and monitoring in middle childhood. *Journal of Family Psychology, 15,* 69–81.

Kerr, M., & Stattin, H. (2000). What parents know, how they know it, and several forms of adolescent adjustment: Further support for a reinterpretation of monitoring. *Developmental Psychology, 36,* 366–380.

Krevans, J., & Gibbs, J. C. (1996). Parents' use of inductive discipline: Relations to children's empathy and prosocial behavior. *Child Development, 67,* 3263–3277.

Laird, R. D., Pettit, G. S., Bates, J. E., & Dodge, K. A. (2003). Parents' monitoring relevant knowledge and adolescents' delinquent behavior: Evidence of correlated developmental changes and reciprocal influence. *Child development, 74,* 752–768.

Laird, R. Pettit, G., Dodge, K., & Bates, J. (1998). The social ecology of school age child care. *Journal of Applied Developmental Psychology, 19,* 341–360.

Laird, R. D., Pettit, G., Mize, J., Brown, E., & Linsey, E. (1994). Mother-child conversations about peers: Contributions to competence. *Family Relations, 43,* 425–432.

Laupa, M., & Turiel, E. (1986). Children's conceptions of adult and peer authority. *Child Development, 57,* 405–412.

Li, X., Feigelman, S., & Stanton, B. (2000). Perceived parental monitoring and health risk behaviors among urban low-income African-American children and adolescents. *Journal of Adolescent Health, 27,* 43–48.

Longmore, M., Manning, W., & Giordano, P. (2001). Preadolescent parenting strategies and teens' dating and sexual initiation: A longitudinal analysis. *Journal of Marriage and Family, 63,* 322–335.

Maccoby, E. E. (1992). The role of parents in the socialization of children: An historical overview. *Developmental Psychology, 28,* 1006–1017.

Maccoby, E. E., & Martin, J. A. (1983). Socialization in the context of the family: Parent-child interaction. In P. H. Mussen (Series Ed.) & E. M. Hetherington

(Vol. Ed.), *Handbook of child psychology: Socialization, personality, and social development*, vol. 4 (pp. 1–102). New York: Wiley.

Manning, W. D. (1990). Parenting employed teenagers. *Youth and Society, 22,* 184–200.

Mekos, D., Hetherington, E., & Reiss, D. (1996). Sibling differences in problem behavior and parental treatment in non-divorced and remarried families. *Child Development, 67,* 2148–2165.

Miller, K., Forehand, R., & Kotchick, B. (1999). Adolescent sexual behavior in two ethnic minority samples: The role of family variables. *Journal of Marriage and Family, 61,* 85–98.

Moore, K., Miller, B., Sugland, B., Morrison, D., Glei, D., & Blumenthal, C. (2004). *Adolescent sex, contraception, and childbearing: A review of recent research.* Washington, D.C.: Child Trends.

Nevius, J. R. (1977). Level of moral judgment as a function of inductive discipline. *Journal of Social Psychology, 103,* 155–156.

Norton, R. W., & Pettegrew, L. S. (1979). Attentiveness as a style of communication: A structural analysis. *Communication Monographs, 46,* 13–26.

Olejnik, A. B. (1980). Adults' moral reasoning with children. *Child Development, 51,* 1285–1288.

Pagani, L., Tremblay, R., Vitaro, F., Kerr, M., & McDuff, P. (1998). The impact of family transition on the development of delinquency in adolescent boys: A 9-year longitudinal study. *Journal of Child Psychology and Psychiatry, 39,* 489–499.

Patterson, G. R., & Stouthamer-Loeber, M. (1984). The correlation of family management practices and delinquency. *Child Development, 55,* 1299–1307.

Pettit, G. S., Laird, R. D., Dodge, K. A., Bates, J. E., & Criss, M. M. (2001). Antecedents and behavior-problem outcomes of parental monitoring and psychological control in early adolescence. *Child Development, 72,* 583–598.

Rai, A. A., Stanton, B., Wu, Y., Li, X., Galbraith, J., Cottrell, L., et al. (2003). Relative influences of perceived parental monitoring and perceived peer involvement on adolescent risk behaviors: An analysis of six cross-sectional data sets. *Journal of Adolescent Health, 33,* 108–118.

Redmond, M. V. (1985). The relationship between perceived communication competence and perceived empathy. *Communication Monographs, 52,* 377–382.

Rodgers, K. B. (1999). Parenting processes related to sexual risk-taking behaviors of adolescent males and females. *Journal of Marriage and Family, 61,* 99–109.

Rose, S. D. (1975). In pursuit of social competence. *Social Work, 20,* 33–39.

Ruben, B. D. (1977). Guidelines for cross-cultural communication effectiveness. *Group and Organization Studies, 2,* 470–479.

Sampson, R., & Laub, L. (1994). Urban poverty and the family context of delinquency: A new look at structure and process in a classic study. *Child Development, 65,* 523–540.

Seidman, E., Aber., J. L., Allen, L., & French, S. E. (1996). The impact of the transition to high school on the self-system and perceived social context of poor urban youth. *American Journal of Community Psychology, 24,* 489–515.

Seidman, E., & French, S. E. (1997). Normative school transitions among urban adolescents: When, where, and how to intervene. In H. J. Walberg, O. Reyes, & R. P. Weissberg (Eds.), *Children and youth: Interdisciplinary perspectives.* Thousand Oaks, CA: Sage.

Shanahan M. J., Elder, G. H., Burchinal, M., & Conger, R. D. (1996). Adolescent paid labor and relationships with parents: Early work-family linkages, *Child Development, 67,* 2183–2200.

Shaw, J., & Scott, W. A. (1991). Influence of parent discipline style on delinquent behavior: The mediating role of control orientation. *Australian Journal of Psychology 43,* 61–67.

Smetana, J., & Daddis, C. (2002). Domain specific antecedents of parental psychological control and monitoring: The role of parenting beliefs and practices. *Child Development, 73,* 563–580.

Snyder, J., & Patterson, G. (1987). Family interaction and delinquent behavior. In H. C. Quay (Ed.), *Handbook of juvenile delinquency* (pp. 216–243). New York: Wiley.

Steffan, J. J., Greenwald, D. P., & Langmeyer, D. (1979). A factor analytic study of social competence in women. *Social Behavior and Personality, 7,* 17–27.

Steinberg, L., Lamborn, S. D., Darling, N., Mounts, N. A., & Dornbusch, S. M, (1994). Over-time changes in adjustment and competence among adolescents from authoritative, authoritarian, indulgent, and neglectful families. *Child Development, 63,* 754–770

Stoolmiller, M. (1994). Antisocial behavior, delinquent peer association, and unsupervised wandering for boys: Growth and change from childhood to early adolescence. *Multivariate Behavioral Research, 29,* 263–288.

Tisak, M. S. (1986). Children's conceptions of parental authority. *Child Development, 57,* 166–176.

Tisak, M. S., & Tisak. J. (1990). Children's conceptions of parental authority, friendship, and sibling relations. *Merrill-Palmer Quarterly, 36,* 347–368.

Van Oss Marín, B., Coyle, K. K., Gómez, C. A., Carvajal, S. C., & Kirby, D. B. (2000). Older boyfriends and girlfriends increase risk of sexual initiation in young adolescents. *Journal of Adolescent Health, 27,* 409–418.

Weimann, J. M. (1977). Explication and test of a model of communication competence. *Human Communication Research, 3,* 195–213.

Wheeless, L. R., & Grotz, J. (1976). Conceptualization and measurement of reported self-disclosure. *Human Communication Research, 2*, 338–346.

Zimmer-Gembeck, M. J., Siebenbruner, J., & Collins, W. A. (2004). A prospective study of intraindividual and peer influences on adolescents' heterosexual romantic and sexual behavior. *Archives of Sexual Behavior, 33*, 381–394.

Part II

Expert Perspectives on Parental Monitoring

In this portion of the book, we adopt a more informal approach to gaining insights into parental monitoring. We (Guilamo-Ramos, Jaccard, and Dittus) posed seven questions to a senior author of every chapter in part I and asked all of them to answer the same questions, albeit in an informal way, based on their expert knowledge and their sense of the field more generally. In this section, we present each question and then share the answers of the experts. This is followed by a commentary by us on the answers that were given to that particular question. The idea is to free the experts from the typical constraints in writing about a specific topic in a chapter and to encourage broader reflection on the field from different points of view. Some authors elected not to answer some questions because they felt the knowledge base too inadequate to offer informed answers. The seven questions are:

1. *Definition of Monitoring:* What is monitoring and how does monitoring differ from control?
2. *Measuring Monitoring:* What is the best way to measure monitoring and how do you explain the discrepancies between reports of adolescents and parents about the monitoring of adolescents by parents? Do such discrepancies mean the measures are not valid?

3. *Factors Influencing Parental Monitoring:* What do you think are the three most important factors that influence the extent to which a parent monitors his or her adolescent's behavior? Elaborate on each one as to why it is important.

4. *Factors Influencing Adolescent Compliance:* Some monitoring behaviors require adolescent compliance and others do not. What are the best ways to get adolescents to comply with parental requests related to monitoring (such as, "call me if you go somewhere else"; "be home by midnight").

5. *Parental Monitoring as an Influence of Adolescent Risk Behavior:* Some studies find that parental monitoring is related to adolescent risk behavior whereas other studies do not. Why? Setting aside possible methodological problems, what are the moderators of the influence of parental monitoring on risk behaviors? In what cases or instances will monitoring not have an impact on adolescent risk behavior as opposed to cases or instances where it will?

6. *Designing Interventions to Impact Monitoring:* What advice would you give on how to best design an intervention that is practical, that has the potential to reach large numbers of families *and* that will make parental monitoring more effective? That is, what are the most important factors to take into account in designing such an intervention?

7. *Future Directions:* What future research or research questions do you think are most important for the field to conduct/address?

Questions, Responses, and Commentary

Question 1. *Definition of Monitoring:* What is monitoring and how does monitoring differ from control?

BELLE: We believe that "monitoring" is an active verb and should be used to refer to initiatives parents take to learn about and keep track of their children. Parents are "monitoring" when they telephone home from the workplace to check that their children are at home and are accomplishing the homework or chores they are supposed to be doing. Parents are monitoring when they examine physical evidence for information about their children's behavior, such as the mother we interviewed who examined the arrangement of furniture in the house to learn if her son had invited friends over, or the mother who felt the back of the television set to learn if her child had violated family rules by watching television in the after-school hours. Parents are also monitoring when they question other individuals about their children's behaviors or whereabouts, and when they talk with the children themselves in order to learn about the children's behaviors, experiences, and emotional lives.

In contrast, "control" refers to actions parents take to restrict or direct their children's behavior. Monitoring can be part of a control strategy, since children who realize their parents are checking up on them may be less inclined to violate family rules about behavior. Parents can also control children's behavior without monitoring through forbidding certain actions or making such actions difficult or impossible through the denial of funds, transportation, or other resources the child would need to engage in the actions. Monitoring can occur without the intention of controlling the child, as when parents ask about the child's experiences that day at school in order to learn more about the child's interpersonal experiences, successes, problems, and moods. Such knowledge could, of course, be used to control the child's future behavior, but it could also be used to enrich the parent-child relationship and to enable the parent to provide more effective support to the child.

DISHION: In 1997 a group of us researchers met to discuss the concept of parental monitoring. We discussed a variety of issues related to this complex concept, many of which have been recently discussed in the scientific literature. One of the main issues is the role of parent-child communication in general and the adolescent's disclosure, in particular. Clearly, parental monitoring is facilitated with open and trusting parent-child relationships and disclosure of activities.

However in our discussion, we purposely highlighted the parents' behaviors and not the child's as being critical for the monitoring process. Today, we still feel that defining parental monitoring involves two assumptions: (a) that the parent-child relationship is at a developmental stage where it is inherently hierarchical and parents serve a leadership function with their child; (b) that the parental monitoring process is effortful and involves active parenting behaviors that are responsive to the child's characteristics but also to the environment. Thus, the concept of "control" is implied in the parental monitoring construct, but the term is, unfortunately, vague.

The following features, originally articulated by Dishion and McMahon (1998), remain central to the definition of parent monitoring.

Parental monitoring is a complex set of skills that vary over the course of development. The function of parental monitoring is to facilitate parents' awareness of the child's activities, including with whom, where, and what they were doing. It also involves an active effort on the parent's part to structure activities that promote positive development in health and decrease the likelihood of unsafe events or activities or unhealthy behaviors.

Thus, we suggest using the term *adult leadership* rather than control. Clearly, there are many activities and events in a child's life that parents cannot control. Moreover, there are a variety of strategies that parents use to exercise influence over their child's development with respect to structuring environments that promote healthy outcomes. These certainly vary by cultural and community context.

LAIRD: I make a distinction between the processes of becoming and remaining aware of an adolescent's activities and the rules or guidance that a parent may or may not provide as part of the interaction. I think of monitoring as part of the awareness process and control as establishing and enforcing behavior standards. I find Hayes, Hudson, and Matthews's (2003) model of the monitoring process to be helpful. The first phase of their five-phase model is called *pre-free time monitoring* and gives parents an opportunity to provide clear rules and expectations for the adolescent's behavior when unsupervised. The second phase is the *adolescent's behavior when unsupervised* while the third phase, labeled *post-free time monitoring*, provides parents an opportunity to determine how, where, and with whom adolescents have spent their free time. The fourth phase, termed *parent response*, provides parents an opportunity to respond if their adolescents violated rules or expectations, and the fifth phase, *adolescent response*, considers the adolescent's response to the parents' behavior. In my interpretation of the Hayes and colleagues' (2003) framework, control is most relevant to the first and fourth phases when parents impose rules (phase 1) and respond to rule violations (phase 4). The activities in the third phase most closely resemble what I think of as monitoring behavior, but parents also may engage in monitoring behavior in phase 1 as they assess the appropriateness of the adolescent's plans. I think the model is particularly useful because it depicts monitoring as a process and demonstrates how monitoring and control are tightly integrated.

Both monitoring and control may facilitate parents' efforts to manage the behavior of their adolescent. For example, many parents in our study report that they always ask if the parents will be home when their adolescent asks to go to a friend's house. Many parents also report that they have a rule prohibiting their child from spending time at friends' homes when the friend's parents are not home. Presumably, the parents are monitoring by asking a question that will allow them to control their child's behavior by providing or declining permission to go to the friend's house. However, in other circumstances, parents may choose to monitor situations or behaviors without exerting control. For example, a parent may have concerns about their adolescent's new romantic partner. The parent may make a concentrated effort to find out as much as possible about the partner and attempt to be informed regarding all contacts between their adolescent and the partner. However, the parent also may choose to not actively prevent or discourage the relationship. I realize that it is possible to argue that monitoring and control are always linked by arguing that a parent who allows the relationship to continue is still exerting control, but I believe that it is conceptually cleaner to think of control as requiring some action by the parent. I think that many parents monitor but find little need to exert control, whereas other parents may monitor because they feel that their adolescents need to be regularly controlled.

Part of the conceptualization challenge results from the fact that monitoring and controlling behaviors can differ widely in scope. Consider the examples above. In one case a parent is monitoring an adolescent's romantic relationship, whereas in another the parent is monitoring the adolescent's planned activity over the next few hours. Likewise, controlling behaviors can vary widely in scope—in this case from prohibiting contact with a romantic partner (see Shakespeare for the potential ramifications) to prohibiting hanging out at a friend's house because the parent is not at home. In smaller, more mundane interactions monitoring and control may be closely linked and difficult to distinguish. However, when the issues are larger and more serious, I think monitoring activities may be more pronounced and control activities more deliberate.

STANTON: Monitoring is the process concerned with providing the atmosphere in which the child knows that the parent both cares about what he/she is doing and either has a pretty good idea as to what is going on or has pretty good access to that information such that the child would know that this information could be obtained by the parent. The purpose of the partnership and the knowledge gained therefrom is to establish between the child and parent rules and expectations on both of their parts as to what is acceptable behavior—including acceptable monitoring behavior. The purpose of the monitoring knowledge is to keep the child within mutually agreed-upon boundaries of safety—that will broaden as the child ages and demonstrates responsibility. Control, by contrast, is one-sided and may or may not have anything to do with a child's safety. Even if it is established for that purpose, it does not allow for the growth that monitoring allows.

STATTIN: To monitor is to take active steps to find out about a youth's whereabouts, activities, and associations when he or she is away from direct parental supervision. The active steps could be requiring youths to get permission before going out or to tell where they are going and whom they will be with. They could also be asking questions of various people who might have information about where youths go, what they do, and whom they associate with away from home. These people might include youths themselves, their friends, their friends' parents, neighbors, siblings, or others. Parents who are not monitoring are not taking any steps to find out what their adolescents are doing when they are away from home.

There are many different types of control. It is difficult to say how monitoring differs from all of them.

TURRISI: As teens transition into college, parental monitoring is characterized primarily by communication via telephone calls, emails, instant messaging, campus visits, and home visits. Each of these methods of monitoring helps the parent to determine whether or not their teen's behavior is within the previously established boundaries. Almost all of the teen's time in college will be spent without parent supervision. Importantly, monitoring is not limited to simply checking in with teens regarding their intentions for any given evening, event, etc., but it also extends to following up with teens to see whether or not things went as planned. Ultimately, monitoring allows parents to be actively involved while also fostering independence among teens as they gain more freedoms throughout this developmental period.

Whereas monitoring allows parents to communicate with their teens, and determine whether or not they are adhering to established guidelines and making safe choices, control implies regulating teens' behavior. Because many parents pay for their teens to attend and live at college, they may exercise financial control as a means of regulating behavior. Ultimately, exercising control, as opposed to monitoring, can lead teens to feeling rebellious or overly dependent as they are not given the freedom to express their views and make their own choices.

COMMENTARY

The definitions offered by the theorists vary in scope and the constructs they invoke, but almost all of them emphasize that monitoring is focused on parental activities that allow the parent to gain awareness about the activities, whereabouts, and companions of their adolescent child. Some of the definitions go on to emphasize constructs like parental initiatives, skill sets, promoting development, creating atmospheres and partnerships, and determining if children have acted within boundaries, but the heart of most all the characterizations is how parents go about the business of finding out about what their children are doing, where and with whom. The variants around this "core essence" often reflect the broader theoretical orientations of the scientist, as the definition becomes nuanced to the theory within which the scientist works. But the common core of the different definitions also is evident.

It is interesting that when referring to monitoring some of the scientists invoke behaviors, some invoke creating atmospheres and partnerships, some invoke processes, and some invoke notions of skill sets. Thus, we see contextualism being brought to bear, systems approaches, features of the dyadic relationship, and perspectives that encourage us to think of the skills that are involved. This reflects the diverse ways in which monitoring has been thought about as its "core essence" is elaborated upon.

In the framework we presented in chapter 7, monitoring pertains not to general knowledge about the activities, whereabouts, and companions of one's child. Rather, it focuses on parental awareness of the extent to which an adolescent has violated or adhered to a specific behavioral expectation of the parent. The expectation can include who the child should be interacting with or where the child should be, but the focus is on, nevertheless, a behavioral expectation. The processes that a parent invokes to make an inference about a behavioral transgression constitute monitoring, and these processes include not only traditional parental monitoring behaviors but also implicit attribution theories of parents that they invoke to determine if a transgression has occurred. We also distinguished between the perception of a transgression on the part of a parent, the adolescent's perception of the parent's knowledge of a transgression, and whether an actual transgression has occurred.

The scientists also were in reasonable agreement in distinguishing between control and monitoring. It is one thing to be aware of what your child is doing and it is quite another to try to control what your child does. Monitoring focuses on what parents do to gain awareness. Control is closer to the concept of supervision, where the parent tries to influence the behavior of the adolescent.

Question 2. *Measuring Monitoring:* **What is the best way to measure monitoring and how do you explain the discrepancies between reports of adolescents and parents about the monitoring of adolescents by parents? Do such discrepancies mean the measures are not valid?**

BELLE: We do not conceptualize monitoring as a continuous variable for which one seeks a quantitative score. Parents monitor different aspects of their children's lives, for different purposes, and in different ways. Some parents keep close track of child behavior, but make little attempt to learn about their children's emotional lives. Other parents focus on their children's moods and thoughts as well as their behaviors. Some parents are able to rely on their children's voluntary self-disclosure, and become quite well informed about their children's lives without engaging in much active monitoring. Other parents make many monitoring attempts, but are rebuffed or misled by their children. Monitoring is a process, one that is dependent on parents, children, and the evolving parent-child relationship, and monitoring can fluctuate over time. Qualitative assessments of parental monitoring are helpful in capturing some of these complexities.

Family life is experienced differently by different family members, and this has been a recurrent theme in modern family research. It would be quite surprising, in fact, if parents and their children experienced and reported identical visions of family life. As Stacey (1991) has noted,

> Any unitary family history imposes arbitrary order upon the multiple, and often contradictory, subjectivities of the individuals whose diverse narratives it attempts to distill. It masks, thereby, those telling discrepancies between the His and Her marriages, as well as the Yours and

Mine parent, child, sibling, and extended kin relationships that all families contain (p. 183).

Such discrepancies emerged when Larson and Richards (1994) equipped mothers, fathers, and adolescents with electronic pagers that would signal them simultaneously several times a day over the course of a week. Family members were then to respond to standardized questionnaires concerning their activities, thoughts, and emotions just before the beep. Family members showed a low rate of agreement even in describing whether they were "with" another family member when they were beeped. On half the occasions that a mother or teenager described herself as with the other, the second person did not agree. Nor were spouses always in accord on this most basic observation. Such findings led Larson and Richards to argue that within families "interpretation of the most basic events may be contested" (p.viii) and to title their book about the emotional experiences of individuals in families, *Divergent Realities*.

Discrepancies between the reports of parents and their children do not mean that measures are invalid. They do mean, however, that measures cannot be taken at face value. Adolescents are often motivated to believe themselves freer of parental control and supervision than they, in fact, are. Parents often wish to believe themselves to be more engaged with their children and more knowledgeable about their children's lives than they, in fact, are. Reports from both parents and children should be evaluated with some skepticism, keeping in mind the motivations that can influence reports. Agreement between parents and children is an encouraging sign that reports of parental monitoring reflect the actual situation rather well.

DISHION: We have found that the best measures of parental monitoring are direct observation. In early childhood, we used a home visitor impression of parental involvement that we see as a measure of parental monitoring. This measure can be derived from the home assessment of families with home visitors rating parents as tracking and involved in the toddlers' activities. Thus, in early childhood, the core component of monitoring is readily observable.

We have found considerable success in a videotaped parent-child interaction task on parental monitoring for childhood and adolescence. This task involves a query to the child to describe a time he or she was with friends not in the company of an adult. Their task is to describe what they were doing, who they were with, and where they were. We ask parents to not interrupt in the child's discussion until the child is finished and then to ask questions regarding anything they deem appropriate.

We rate the direct observation task on a variety of dimensions, including the child's apparent disclosure, truthfulness, and the parent-child communication process, as well as whether or not the child appears to have significant time with friends unsupervised by adults. This measure has shown to be sensitive to change with respect to parent intervention and to predict substance use and other problematic outcomes.

We have also had success with a very simple and brief telephone interview which asks simply the following, "How many hours in the last day were you with friends, unsupervised by an adult?" The number of hours children spent unsupervised with friends was found to predict growth in problem behavior from ages 12 to 15. It was also found that the number of hours increased during this developmental phase. Moreover, the parent and child reports on the number of hours correlated quite highly at all phases of development (Dishion, Bullock, & Kiesner 2008).

Although we have used parent and youth reports, we find that these are generally less useful. One problem with both parent and youth reports is seen on a five-point scale, with "5" being highly monitored and "1" being not monitored at all. Both reporters tend to report high levels of monitoring (mean level equals 4 and above). There is actually a ceiling effect on reports of parental monitoring. In addition, we have found that parent reports tend to be less reliable vis-à-vis internal consistency and require more items than what is usually represented in questionnaires on monitoring. Kiesner and colleagues (under review) found only moderate correlations between parent and youth reports of the Stattin and Kerr dimensions of monitoring. Thus, these measures do reflect perceptions of monitoring but also undoubtedly are saturated with reporting bias and social desirability. In one analysis using a multi-trait, multi-method approach to measuring various parenting constructs, we found that parent and youth reports were those indicators that loaded the highest on method variation (Dishion, Burraston, & Li 2002).

LAIRD: I can think of three general approaches to measuring monitoring. We could measure the activities or actions of parents, typically in the form of what kind of questions they ask and how often they ask them. We could measure the structures that parents or adolescents put in place to keep parents aware of the adolescents' whereabouts and activities such as curfews, rules, or phone calls to check in with parents. Or we could (and often have) measure(d) how aware or knowledgeable parents are regarding their adolescents' whereabouts and activities. All three approaches have limitations, and discrepancies in parent and adolescent reports probably have different meaning across the approaches.

Discrepancies between parents' and adolescents' reports likely result from many sources. Of course adolescents and parents have different points of view and are likely to interpret the same behavior or interaction in different ways. However, it is also likely that parents and adolescents have limited knowledge of one another's behaviors, motivations, and intentions. For example, parents typically report that they are more aware of the adolescent's behavior than does the adolescent. But, in my opinion, neither report can be considered more accurate than the other. The parents have access to their knowledge but limited access to the adolescent's behavior while adolescents know about their own behavior but have limited access to their parents' knowledge. We would be foolish to think that adolescents do not try to hide things from their parents (and most likely the researchers as well). In informal conversations, parents often tell me that they intentionally conceal their monitoring behaviors and the information they learn. Parents tell me that they do so, in part, to avoid overresponding to little things that may cost them access to information should anything more important come along. Neither parents nor adolescents have full access to the information required to judge how much parents really know. Nonetheless, I am not arguing that these reports are invalid—in fact, they are often quite predictive. Rather, I am arguing that parent and adolescent reports reflect unique perspectives. Furthermore, it is possible that these perspectives function differently as protective mechanisms. Adolescents' beliefs that their parents are aware may curtail misbehavior whereas parents' beliefs that they are knowledgeable may reflect the parents' interest and intention to monitor adolescent behavior.

I think parents who are able to monitor most successfully are genuinely interested in their adolescents' lives. These parents are able to engage their adolescents in conversation and maintain an interest and connection with the adolescent's friends and activities. When asked about monitoring behaviors, the adolescents may or may not report that their parents ask a lot of questions or always need to know where they are going and what they are doing, although the adolescents are likely to report that the parents know a lot about their friends and activities. My point is that if the monitoring behaviors are seamlessly integrated into the broader context of caring and responsive parenting, the monitoring behaviors may be more difficult for both outsiders and insiders to recognize. However, when parents are making explicit attempts to monitor because of a perceived need, I would expect that parents and adolescents would be able to describe those activities.

STANTON: Monitoring is a process—and like most processes its measurements will be somewhat subjective and defined by the outcome of interest. Rather than invalidating the concept or the measures, the discrepancies between youth and parents can provide important additional information.

STATTIN: The best way to measure monitoring is to operationalize the actions parents might take to monitor. Parental monitoring should be measured as parental behaviors—i.e., parents' actions that are attempts to find out about their adolescents' whereabouts and behaviors. We are aware of very few measures of these kinds of behaviors, and for those we know about, the discrepancies between parents' and adolescents' reports are no more than one would expect for measures from two different informants.

TURRISI: We have focused on measuring three different constructs: monitoring activity, teen self-disclosure, and parental knowledge. First, we measure parental monitoring activity by asking parents, "How often do you ask your teen where they are going at night?" We also ask teens, "How often do your parents ask you where you are going at night?" Our teen self-disclosure measures are, "How often do you tell your parents where you go at night?" and "How often do you tell your parents what you do after school?" Finally, parental knowledge is assessed by asking teens questions like, "How often do your parents really know where you are at night?" or "How often do your parents really know where you are after school?"

As researchers and as parents, we know that simply asking where your teen is at night is not all there is to a parent's job of monitoring. Even with the most active monitoring tendencies there are serious limits to how much parents can actually know when teens are living away at college without honest and open communications. Successful parental monitoring involves engaging in positive parenting practices that serve to build trust and positive communication avenues with teens, as well as engaging in monitoring activity. Evidence from studies that have found an inverse relationship between positive parenting practices and teen drinking outcomes supports this notion.

Sometimes lost in the conversations about whether parental monitoring items are valid is the notion of how motivated teens are to engage in high-risk behaviors. Most teens will attempt to withhold information from their parents if they perceive that their own actions will result in being interrogated, not being trusted, and receiving economic and behavioral sanctions from their parents, not to mention also not being able to engage in the behavior (e.g., drinking alcohol). For example, take the situation where parents engage in the habit of asking their teens where they are going at night, but their teens are highly motivated to drink heavily. More often than not, these teens will deliberately conceal their true intentions and behaviors from their parents. In this case there would be a discrepancy between parental monitoring activity as measured by asking parents how often do you ask your teens where they are going at night and actual knowledge as measured by asking teens how often do your parents really know where you are at night, even though both measures are valid indices of what they are trying to assess. In contrast, in a situation where parents engage in the habit of asking their teens where they are going at night, and teens are not highly motivated to drink heavily, teens will be less likely to conceal their true intentions and behaviors from their parents. In this situation there will be no discrepancy between monitoring activity and actual knowledge, even though both measures are no more valid than in the previous example. So the discrepancy between monitoring activity and actual knowledge may have less to do with the validity of the parental monitoring items and more to do with the conceptualization of the motivation of teens to engage in the high-risk behavior and the parent-teen relationship.

COMMENTARY

The measurement of monitoring produced several different but interesting perspectives. Belle is uncomfortable with attempts to derive a quantitative index of monitoring and prefers to think of it in qualitative terms. She fully expects parental and adolescent characterizations of monitoring to diverge because "family life is experienced differently by different family members." She advocates the position, echoed by several of the scientists, that discrepancies between the reports of parents and their children do not mean that measures are invalid but rather that they cannot be taken at face value.

Dishion prefers a measurement strategy he calls direct observation, which is essentially where a trained observer visits a home, makes observations, and then makes inferences about the amount of monitoring that is taking place. As with all measurement strategies, this approach must deal with the inherent limitations of the method, which in this case include rater reliability, behavior being affected by the presence of observers, and the representativeness of the events being observed to everyday behavior. Dishion and his colleagues have addressed these issues head-on in his broader research program. Dishion supplements his direct observations with simple self-reports from parents and children, but finds limitations to this approach due to base-rate problems, social desirability, and reporting bias. The challenge for direct observation approaches is how to use them practically in large sample size scenarios, such as national surveys.

Laird highlights not only the above points concerning the challenges of self-reports and the expected lack of convergence between parent and adolescent reports but also emphasizes some of the different facets of monitoring that can be measured that might give insights into the amount and nature of monitoring, such as the kinds of questions parents ask their children and how often they ask them, the structures that parents or adolescents put in place to keep parents aware of the adolescents' whereabouts and activities such as curfews, rules, or phone calls to check in with parents, in addition to how aware or knowledgeable parents are regarding their adolescents' whereabouts and activities. Turrisi also adopts this multi-facet perspective, emphasizing questions about how often parents ask their teen where the teen is going at night and after school, as reported by both the parent and the adolescent. He also targets indices of adolescent self-disclosure and adolescent reports of parental awareness.

Stattin, as well as others, emphasize the need to focus on parental behaviors and activities.

From a classic measurement perspective, researchers need to first identify the constructs or latent variables that they desire to assess. This is determined by one's theoretical approach to monitoring. Is "monitoring" best represented by a single latent variable or is it multi-faceted, requiring multiple latent variables. Most of the scientists seem to agree that it is multi-faceted and that it requires multiple latent variables. At a minimum, the scientists agree, with some exceptions, that one latent variable would focus on monitoring as characterized by the parent and the other would focus on monitoring as characterized by the adolescent. These latent variables might be correlated, but not necessarily highly. Dishion's favored approach is direct observation, but keep in mind that such direct observations are used to infer a person's standing on an underlying latent construct, namely that of monitoring. Direct observations are just another approach, different from self-reports, to obtaining an indicator of the latent construct. Belle's analysis suggests the interesting possibility that perhaps the latent variables should not be construed as quantitative, but instead as being qualitative in character.

The scientists show divergence that is driven by their particular theoretical orientations in what they highlight are the different types of facets on which researchers should focus. Some facets emphasize different contexts, some emphasize different reporters, some emphasize different strategies parents use to acquire knowledge, some emphasize perceived versus actual knowledge and so on.

It is noteworthy to us the richness with which the scientists discuss the construct of monitoring on the one hand, yet the rather simple way it is traditionally operationalized in so much of monitoring research. There are a few items that have become the "traditional" or "standard" measure of monitoring in the literature, but these seem so simplistic when juxtaposed against the research and discussions reported in this book. We believe the field would benefit greatly from solid, carefully thought-out psychometric studies of core monitoring constructs which address issues of conceptual definitions, reliability, arbitrary metrics, convergent validity, discriminant validity, construct validity, and method variance for a wide range of diverse populations (both developmentally, contextually, and demographically), all while preserving the richness the monitoring constructs deserve. We also are sympathetic to Belle's suggestion that we consider eschewing traditional measurement approaches and think about approaching the matter from a more qualitative, process-oriented framework. We are reminded of the noteworthy contributions of Mary Ainsworth and her qualitative approach to the assessment of attachment as evidence that these kinds of approaches can bear fruit.

Question 3. *Factors Influencing Parent Monitoring:* **What do you think are the three most important factors that influence the extent to which a parent monitors his or her adolescent's behavior? Elaborate on each one as to why it is important.**

BELLE: Parental monitoring is constrained profoundly by parents' work responsibilities, which are particularly heavy in this country. Adults in the

United States work longer hours than do adults in any of the other industrialized nations, and increasing numbers work afternoon and evening shifts when children are not in school. Parents who must work long hours, those who have afternoon and evening work schedules, and those whose workplace rules limit telephone calls and visits home cannot monitor their children as consistently as other parents who do not face these constraints. Single parents, who are solely responsible for income-provision as well as for child care, face daunting obstacles in attempting to monitor their children successfully. Low-income parents are disadvantaged when attempting to arrange for others to monitor their children, as they cannot easily afford after-school programs or babysitters. In earlier generations grandparents often cared for or monitored children while parents worked, but today grandparents are typically employed themselves and unable to be with their grandchildren while the parents are away at work.

Effective parental monitoring may decline when parents themselves are stressed, depressed, or demoralized. As one of our parents said, "I've been working so hard. I'd never encourage anyone to have a child alone. I just don't have the energy to deal with things. Sometimes I come home from work, tired and worn out, and I walk into the house and see he hasn't done anything—I come into my room and close the door. I'm feeling angry and depressed and [my son] knows enough just to stay away." Effective parental monitoring may decline when parents simply do not have the energy to carry through on their intentions to monitor.

Children's emotional and sometimes physical withdrawal from parents, often at the onset of adolescence, makes parental monitoring extremely difficult. Parents report that they are not able to spend as much time with their children as they once did, and that even when they are together they find it more difficult to "read" their children, to understand their emotional states, or to learn about their lives. Parents and children get out of the habit of doing things together, largely because adolescents resist such togetherness. Conversations diminish in frequency and in intimacy. Parents are kept away from their children's inner lives.

DISHION: We see the three following factors most influential on whether a parent monitors the child. First is the extent that the parent is in a leadership role with the child. In our intervention work, we find that many parents have communication processes with their child or adolescent that are positive, yet not parental. That is, when youth report unsafe or unhealthy behaviors, the parents remain inactive or perhaps even laugh or join in.

The willingness of a parent to redirect a wayward child and deal with the challenges of conflict and stress in exerting leadership during pivotal times is a key factor influencing parental monitoring. We find that parents of high-risk children understandably "give up" in early adolescence.

Thus, the second most important factor influencing parental monitoring is the high-risk behavior of the youth. Stoolmiller (1994) published a seldom-cited paper on child wandering as a predictor of future problem behavior. In essence, some children pull themselves away from parental supervision and either do not disclose their activities or lie about them. They become essentially very difficult to monitor. Many parents, faced with a difficult challenge, give up. Intertwined with this factor is the child's premature autonomy (Dishion, Nelson & Bullock 2004).

The third most important factor is the parent's informal social ties. In Native American culture, there was a system in place for uncles, aunts, and other members of the tribe to informally track children. There was no way that a child could engage in problem behavior and have the adults in that system not be aware and react accordingly. However, in the current Western cultural context, family, autonomy, and independence are the cultural norm. Therefore, the nuclear family is more responsible for engaging in activities that assure that the children are monitored and attended to. The extent that families are engaged in a network of informal social ties dramatically increases the likelihood that parents will be supported for their monitoring efforts and that their child will be likely to disclose activities that the parent will eventually be aware of; this makes it easier to track the child's whereabouts and activities. The significant barrier to parental monitoring is social and/or community isolation.

LAIRD: I think the three most important factors are parents' beliefs and expectations, the history and quality of the parent-adolescent relationship, and the adolescents' cooperation. Parents' beliefs and expectations determine the rules and behavioral standards the parents expect and wish to enforce. Beliefs and expectations can also determine whether parents feel a need to actively monitor their children's behavior, activities, and companions. For example, a parent who believes that most adolescents behave reasonably well and that his or her adolescent is a good kid who makes good decisions might be less likely to engage in deliberate monitoring behavior compared to a parent who believes that trouble is just around the corner and that it is his or her job to protect the adolescent. I also would expect beliefs and expectations to be tailored to the family's living situation, the community in which the family resides, and the child's personality and behavioral history. Some neighborhoods and communities feel much safer than others. In my current study, some of the adolescents tell us that they are not allowed to leave their home or apartment without an adult. Other adolescents tell us they are allowed to roam their neighborhood. I think these differences are more likely to reflect parents' beliefs and expectations than differences in their ability or interest in monitoring their adolescents' behavior.

I believe the history and quality of the parent-adolescent relationship have a great influence on the level and quality of the day-to-day monitoring activities. When strong parent-child relationships are well established, I would expect parents to have greater access to the adolescent's life and for parents' monitoring behaviors to be considered a sign of caring rather than intrusion by the adolescent. Conversely, when the parent-adolescent relationship is weak, I would expect parents to face more difficulty in obtaining information from the adolescent and I would also expect parents to be less motivated to actively monitor the adolescent's behavior.

Finally, I think Stattin and Kerr did us a great service by emphasizing the influence of adolescents' cooperation in the monitoring process. When adolescents actively resist monitoring efforts, or habitually fail to cooperate and respond to parents' attempts to monitor, I would expect parents to reduce their monitoring attempts. For example, if asking where the adolescent is going is likely to initiate parent-adolescent conflict, I would expect that most parents would be less inclined to ask.

STANTON: First, we should convey to parents an understanding of what monitoring is and what it is not. Second, we should increase a parent's confidence in his or her ability to monitor. Third, we should increase a parent's confidence that monitoring is important.

TURRISI: As teens transition into college, the most important factors influencing sustained parental monitoring become parental perceptions about how important it is to sustain monitoring activity even though the teens no longer live at home, an awareness of different communication channels, and perceptions of self-efficacy.

Perception of Importance. The first area of influence concerns the underlying assumptions parents hold regarding the importance of monitoring their teens at this late stage of development. Parents who think it's important to check in with their teens and believe it will lead to positive outcomes as their teen transitions through adolescence are more likely to en-gage in that behavior. Conversely, parents who feel that monitoring their adolescent is unnecessary are going to be less likely to monitor. In recruiting parents for our studies related to alcohol use and parent-teen communication, a common response from some parents is that they don't feel the need to participate in a study about alcohol use or communicating with their teen because their teens don't drink and/or they already have a great relationship. As previously noted, their response runs counter to epidemiological data that show that by the time teens graduate from high school the majority have already tried alcohol and that almost a third are drinking five or more drinks per occasion on a weekly basis. One challenge we face with prevention efforts is to find the best way to change the underlying assumptions parents hold so they are more likely to engage in sustained monitoring activity in their teens' first years of college when high-risk drinking and alcohol-related consequences are at their peak.

Awareness. Parents differ in their awareness of communication channels they use to monitor their teens after they leave for college and on the importance of sustained monitoring. Some utilize many different approaches (e.g., telephone calls, emails, instant messaging, campus visits, and home visits) whereas others use only one or two. Although we have very little scientific evidence as to which or how many different channels work best, we do know that there is an inverse relationship between sustained monitoring activity and high-risk drinking. One of the most cited papers on the relationship between parents and teens in the area of alcohol consumption that found low empirical support for parental involvement (e.g., Hawkins, Catalano, & Miller 1992) was published prior to the everyday use of cell phones, text messages, emails, and instant messaging. Our focus group data suggest that parents engage in more frequent communications with their college-aged teens than in previous years and use communication channels that did not exist 10 to 15 years ago. These channels permit greater opportunities for involvement and sustained monitoring activity.

Self-Efficacy. Lastly, parents not only need to perceive monitoring as important and to be aware of the different opportunities by using different channels, they also need to feel that they can be effective if they put in the effort. Some parents may perceive monitoring as an effective approach at lowering their teen's risk, but feel that they don't have the skills to communicate, which is the primary method of monitoring at this stage. This is where we believe that our research program has been successful. We provide parents with informational materials that assist in improving communications with teens in general and about specific topics where communication may be more difficult (i.e., alcohol). In turn, we have observed significant increases in positive communication practices and parental monitoring activities, and subsequent reductions in teen high-risk drinking and alcohol-related consequences.

COMMENTARY

When asked to provide the three most important factors that influence the extent to which a parent monitors, most of the scientists could not contain themselves and described more than three. Some framed their answers in terms of factors that would interfere with monitoring and others framed their answers in terms of factors that would promote monitoring. Here is a simple listing of the constructs the scientists emphasized: work responsibilities, low income, single parenthood, parental stress, parental depression, parental demoralization, child emotional withdrawal, high-risk behaviors on the part of youth, parents taking on a leadership role with their child, positive communication between parent and child, informal social ties and support networks, positive parent-child relationships in general (that promote self-disclosure and allow for active involvement of a parent in a child's life), adolescent cooperation, parents' confidence in their monitoring abilities, how safe a neighborhood is perceived as being (with higher perceived safety leading to less monitoring), how responsible the adolescent is perceived as being (with more responsible adolescents requiring lesser monitoring), how parents define monitoring, the parent's perceived importance of monitoring, and parental awareness of communication channels available to them.

There was little overlap in the factors that the scientists mentioned, with the exception of parental self-efficacy about monitoring and parent-child communication. Some of the variables mentioned had a more "micro" flavor to them (beliefs, attitudes, motivations) and others had a more "macro" flavor (demographic or contextual). Some emphasized individual variables (focused on either the parent or the child), while others emphasized dyadic variables (such as the nature of the relationship and dyadic communication). This suggests to us the need to build conceptual frameworks for understanding monitoring that integrate micro-analytic and macro-analytic perspectives and that consider individual characteristics and backgrounds as well as dyadic interactions and dynamics among the participating individuals. At the micro level, there are powerful theories that focus on individual decision making, including Fishbein and Ajzen's theory of planned behavior (1975), Bandura's social learning theory (1975), and self-regulation models that could be brought to bear. At the macro level, there are numerous contextual theories that emphasize peer contexts, family contexts, school contexts, neighborhood contexts, media contexts, religious contexts, policy/government contexts, and cultural contexts that could be brought to bear. There also is considerable research on dyadic interactions and relationships that could be used to good effect. The lack of convergence in what the scientists identified as being most important drives home to us the need for a larger integrative framework.

Question 4. *Factors Influencing Adolescent Compliance:* **Some monitoring behaviors require adolescent compliance and others do not. What are the best ways to get adolescents to comply with parental requests related to monitoring (such as, "call me if you go somewhere else"; "be home by midnight").**

BELLE: Ultimately, adolescent compliance with parental monitoring attempts depends on the nature of the ongoing parent-child relationship as well as on the developmental status of the adolescent. Young people who feel close to their parents and wish to please them are much more likely to comply with parental monitoring attempts than are those who feel more distant or hostile. Young people who are engaged in differentiating themselves from parents will certainly be less inclined to comply with parental monitoring attempts than will young people who are not struggling to achieve independence and a separate sense of self. In our work, adolescent girls have often seemed more ready than adolescent boys to cooperate with parental monitoring requests and, in fact, more likely to "self-monitor" or internalize parental values. And of course young people who are already violating parental rules and expectations are less likely to comply with parental monitoring attempts than those who are following parental guidelines.

The very best way to get adolescents to comply with parental monitoring requests is to build and maintain a close, supportive, and trust-building relationship with the adolescent. Parents can also turn to strategies of surveillance, threats, and punishment to increase their adolescent children's likelihood of complying with monitoring requests. Such a strategy may be the only viable one if the adolescent is in the throes of rebellion from parental authority, does not have a close relationship to the parents, and is involved with peers who engage in forbidden behavior. However, such a strategy runs the risk of producing psychological reactance in the adolescent who finds his or her freedom threatened, leading to disapproved behavior as a method of asserting the adolescent's contested freedom.

DISHION: There are two stages to the compliance problem. Many parents anticipate the adolescent struggle by working hard to find a niche in which their child can engage in activities that involve other prosocial youth and/or parents. Examples include sports, musical events, church groups, and other adult-supervised activities. Given the success of establishing these activity niches, there is not a great distance between what the parent is requesting and what the child wants to do.

However, as children move up the risk continuum, there is a gap between the child's interests and the parent's monitoring request. When this occurs, it is very important for parents to have a well-articulated set of expectations that can be easily tracked for compliance. For example, we have often suggested that parents of high-risk youth use the 24-hour rule. No request may be made to spend the night at a child's friend's house unless the parent has 24-hour notice and can check in with the child's friend's parents to establish mutual expectations. The 24-hour rule is a proactive structuring technique that parents can use to assure that their children do not get into unmonitored contexts in which they cannot track the child's activities. Another example that is especially applicable to youth that are higher risk is checking up on activities such as attending school, completing homework, and grades. School life is a ubiquitous feature of children and adolescents, and it is an arena where parents can get independent sources of information. Child compliance is induced by parents' monitoring of the truthfulness of their child's responses vis-à-vis independent reports. Encouragement can be provided for compliance, and limit-setting can be established when children have been deceptive or noncompliant.

Also, for children engaging in high-risk behaviors, we firmly suggest that they follow what we call SANE guidelines for limit-setting. There are four principles to limit-setting that encourage compliance and discourage children's deception and/or noncompliance. These are articulated in our book on adolescent problem behavior (Dishion & Kavanagh 2003). Briefly, they are as follows. S—Small consequences are better than large consequences. Parents tend to overreact when children engage in problem behavior, and that feeds a cycle of coercion and, often, avoidance, withdrawal, and deception on the child's end. Small consequences are better than large consequences, in that they empower the parents to stay involved and are not overly punitive. A—Avoid punishing the parent. This principle encourages parents to use consequences that do not significantly undermine their own happiness and well-being. For example, a parent restricting a child for two months could be as punishing to the parent as to the child. Similarly, a consequence of driving the child to school and picking him up every day could be very difficult on a single parent's life. Thus, we encourage consequences that do not involve punishing the parent. N— Nonabusive to the child goes without saying. In our approach, we discourage not only physical punishment in general, but any aversive punishment that is potentially abusive to children or adolescents. E—Effective consequences are consistent consequences. This is a summary principle that actually involves all three of the guidelines described above, in that small consequences are more easily followed through; not punishing the parent promotes the parent's consistency in setting limits, and nonabusive consequences are consequences that can be used regularly. These are factors that have been found repeatedly in a variety of interventions to encourage a parent's leadership in establishing compliance and discouraging noncompliance.

LAIRD: I can think of two primary factors that might influence adolescent compliance. The first factor is, again, the quality of the parent-adolescent relationship. I think adolescents are more likely to comply and cooperate if monitoring behaviors are interpreted as a sign of love and interest rather than as intrusive and controlling. The second factor influencing compliance is the consequences of compliance versus noncompliance. Simply put, if adolescents are better able to get what they want by complying than by noncompliance, they should be more likely to comply. For example, if an adolescent believes her parents are more likely to let her go out with her friends next weekend if she returns home on time this weekend, then she should be motivated to return on time this weekend. Conversely, if an adolescent believes he will be more successful by deceiving his parents than by telling them the truth about his plans, he would be more inclined to deceive them.

I am proposing that, to some extent, compliance can be managed by the parents. When parents respond strongly or harshly to minor violations, they run the risk of undermining future compliance and cooperation. However, many parents are also aware that minor violations can grow larger over time if they are not addressed early. I like that Hayes, Hudson, and Matthews's (2003) model of monitoring does not stop with the parents' enforcement, but that the importance of the adolescents' response is also explicitly acknowledged.

STANTON: First, explain to the adolescent why the request is being made. Second, explore alternatives which might yield the same measure of comfort for the parent but be more acceptable for the youth. Third, make sure the adolescent knows the agreement is a partnership—even if a bit one-sided!

TURRISI: When teens leave home for college, parental monitoring takes on completely different forms and requires the cooperation of teens. Active parental solicitation does not guarantee that teens will comply and participate in open communication. Probably the most important elements for parents to work on are developing positive parent-teen relationships and effecting teens' motivations not to engage in high-risk behaviors. As mentioned earlier, most teens will attempt to withhold information from their parents if they perceive that their own actions will result in being interrogated, not being trusted, and sanctions from their parents.

As part of our research, we have developed a parent handbook specifically for the transition to college designed to facilitate and develop positive communication and effect motivations not to engage in high-risk drinking. According to our approach, parents exposed to our interventions are more likely to have specific communications about alcohol with their teens which will in turn ultimately reduce drinking behaviors and alcohol-related negative consequences. The parent is the "source" of a "message" and the child is the "recipient" of that message. Research suggests that two factors are especially relevant when parents communicate with their teens: (a) the perceived expertise of the source (e.g., gives good advice) and (b) the perceived trustworthiness of the source (e.g., looking out for the teen's best interest) (Guilamo-Ramos et al. 2006). A third source variable that is very important is that the parent must be seen as available and accessible. If the parent is seen as being too busy and generally unavailable, then the adolescent will not seek out the parent's advice. Another crucial set of variables comes from communication theory and focuses on the manner in which the message is communicated. Our research emphasizes the following relevant dimensions: (a) showing empathy and understanding, (b) using self-disclosure, (c) staying calm and relaxed, (d) being direct, (e) being responsive, (f) being supportive, (g) avoiding and/or dealing with conflict, and (h) conveying one's logic and feelings in a clear and understandable way. If parents can be helped to develop communication styles that maximize these dimensions, which are exactly what our parent materials are designed to do, then their discussions with teens will be that much more effective and teens will be more likely to comply with parental requests to self-disclose about their behaviors.

COMMENTARY

When the scientists were asked for the best ways to gain adolescent compliance and cooperation in the monitoring process, there was considerable convergence on two factors. The first factor emphasized building a quality relationship between parent and adolescent with the idea that young people who feel close to their parents and who wish to please them will be more likely to comply. The second factor emphasized the nature and administration of consequences for transgressions. The underlying themes here were to avoid overreacting by structuring consequences that are too severe and the importance of being clear and consistent in one's administration of consequences. Additionally, explaining the rationale for monitoring/disciplining was mentioned, as was building a relationship that engenders trust, accessibility, and perceived expertise.

The above ideas are consistent with a large body of research on parental discipline strategies in developmental science. However, it is one thing to tell a parent that he or she should "have a good relationship with his or her adolescent" and it is quite another thing for the parent to go about the business of establishing one. To us, the challenge for monitoring researchers is to develop specific strategies and action plans that parents can implement to help them build high-quality relationships with their children. It is not enough, for example, to tell a parent "communicate with your child about sex." Rather, we need to provide practical advice on what to say, when to say it, how to say it, where to say it, and how often to say it, among other things. How do you get conversations started? How do you react when you hear something you don't want to hear? What do you do when your child starts asking you questions you are uncomfortable with? In some respects, social science theories operate at the level of abstract variables and provide us with useful knowledge about which abstract variables are important to address. But life is concrete and plays itself out at a more specific level than what much of social science focuses on.

Thus, we call on monitoring researchers to go beyond general exhortations for parents to "build a good relationship with your child" or to "administer appropriately sized consequences consistently" and to develop practical, implementable guidelines to help parents do so. This type of practical research is not rewarded in professional journals that emphasize theory development. But any scientist who has designed a monitoring intervention (and many of the contributors to this volume have done so) has undoubtedly experienced the disconnect between what is in the scientific literature and a parent's need for clear, practical, implementable advice on how to monitor. The field is in need of this type of knowledge.

Question 5. *Parental Monitoring as an Influence of Adolescent Risk Behavior:* **Some studies find that parental monitoring is related to adolescent risk behavior whereas other studies do not. Why? Setting aside possible methodological problems, what are the moderators of the influence of parental monitoring on risk behaviors? In what cases or instances will monitoring not have an impact on adolescent risk behavior as opposed to cases or instances where it will?**

BELLE: Causal connections between parental monitoring behavior and adolescent risk behavior run in both directions, with complex feedback loops possible. Parents who monitor their children effectively can hope to see a reduction in the children's risk behavior, while parents who are heavy-handed in their monitoring, or who ignore the child's emotional life while focusing entirely on a set of disapproved behaviors, may actually increase their children's risk behavior. Conversely, adolescent risk behavior may lead parents to intensify their monitoring or may have the opposite effect, by leading to parental demoralization and a slackening of parental monitoring.

Monitoring is most likely to have a benign effect on adolescent risk behavior when it encompasses the whole child, not merely the child's disapproved behaviors, and when it serves to strengthen the overall parent-child relationship. Parents who use their monitoring to learn what their child is experiencing and how their child is faring will be in a better position to provide needed supportive and/or corrective actions than parents who focus relentlessly on preventing disallowed behavior, while ignoring other aspects of the child's lived experience.

DISHION: The majority of findings that do not show a connection between parental monitoring and adolescent risk behavior are those where there has been poor measurement. Often, scales measuring parental monitoring involve five or six self-report items. Internal consistency is relatively low. We found that, simply by increasing the item pool, one can dramatically improve the validity of the parenting constructs (Dishion, Burraston, & Li 2002). There is also emerging literature indicating that parental monitoring may be most important in highest-risk settings. Wilson (1980) first found that parental supervision was most predictive of delinquent behavior in highest-risk London neighborhoods. In general, some of our studies may be conducted in settings that are either relatively low risk or that the particular approach to parental monitoring is culturally inappropriate. We assume that cultural contexts that emphasize communal features should require a different set of monitoring behaviors than those emphasizing autonomy. The cultural relativity of parental monitoring practices needs further exploration as suggested below under future directions.

LAIRD: Clearly, measurement issues are important, but setting those aside, I would propose that two factors are influential. First, I think the large portion of the protective power of monitoring resides in the parent-adolescent relationship. If researchers assess monitoring behaviors (e.g., asking questions, requiring certain information) without assessing the quality of the parent-adolescent relationship, it is likely that the meaning of the monitoring behaviors, as well as adolescents' compliance, will vary dramatically across families. I believe that assessments of perceived knowledge are more consistently associated with risk behaviors than measures of more specific monitoring behaviors, in part, because knowledge reflects the outcome of the process rather than the starting point.

Second, I think that serious consideration should be given to monitoring as a protective factor, and by that I mean that monitoring may be most effective at reducing risk behavior when adolescents are facing an explicit risk. I have to believe that most adolescents are behaving appropriately most of the time and that they would be doing so whether or not their behavior was being monitored. However, on those occasions when adolescents have the opportunity to misbehave, whether or not their behavior is being monitored may be much more influential. Thus, when the opportunity for misbehavior is low, monitoring is not likely to have much of an effect, but when the opportunity is high, monitoring is likely to distinguish those who engage in misbehavior from those who do not.

STANTON: I really am not aware of many studies that find no relationship.

STATTIN: If setting aside possible methodological problems means ignoring the fact that monitoring has not been validly operationalized in many studies, we do not think it is meaningful to do so. We are aware of only a few studies that have validly measured parents' monitoring actions, and they do not find robust relations to adolescent risk behaviors.

TURRISI: The inconsistencies found in the literature at earlier phases of adolescent development do not seem to generalize to college years. The published studies on college students consistently report inverse relationships between parental monitoring and high-risk drinking tendencies (e.g., Barnes 1990; Wood et al. 2004). That being said, there are a number of potential theoretical moderators that might serve to strengthen or weaken the relationship between parental monitoring and high-risk behaviors at this phase of development at both the level of the parent and teen. In our research program, we encourage parents to check in with their teenage sons and daughters while at college about drinking. The check-ins can occur during phone conversations, emails, instant messaging, text messages, and campus visits or home visits. The theoretical model guiding our research on parental influence on college teens' high-risk drinking suggests that parental checking-in about alcohol will be more effective to the extent that the parents engage in behaviors and communication styles that elicit a positive response on the part of their teen. These behavioral tendencies are intended to improve the quality of the relationship between the parent and the teen and thus increase the quality for other interactions, one of these being parental checking-in or monitoring. All things being equal, a high-quality relationship should also improve the level of teen responsiveness to their parents' check-ins. Teens will perceive their parents as being interested and involved in their lives as opposed to their parents prying into their privacy. Finally, as parents engage in practices that improve the quality of the relationship and the teens become more responsive to their parents, this should increase parents' perceptions of self-efficacy—that they can effectively monitor their teens and communicate about high-risk behaviors. Thus, the quality of the parent-teen relationship, the responsiveness of the teen to parenting tendencies, and parents' self-efficacy could all potentially serve as moderators.

COMMENTARY

When we asked the scientists to reflect on moderators of the relationship between parental monitoring and adolescent risk behavior without resorting to methodological sources, many had a difficult time setting methodological matters aside. There clearly is displeasure with the measurement strategies used in studies, and there also is agreement that if one is in a low base-rate scenario in terms of the risk behavior, monitoring constructs are not going to predict much (indeed, this would be true of any construct). So this is a clear message to the field: Get your measurement house in order and tighten up your studies methodologically.

Monitoring was thought to be more effective when it takes a holistic perspective and when it is done in the context of a positive parent-child relationship. As with other questions, several scientists mentioned the importance of the quality of the relationship between parent and child. Monitoring was thought to be less effective if the monitoring is pursued in cultural contexts where it is not seen as being culturally appropriate to monitor. Monitoring was also thought to be more effective when parents engage in behaviors and communications styles that elicit positive responses on the part of their adolescent.

From our perspective, the field might benefit from thinking more about the boundary conditions of monitoring constructs and then elaborating on how to overcome those boundaries. When will monitoring fail? Even if a parent does the best of monitoring practices and knows the whereabouts, activities, and companions of her child, under what conditions and circumstances and for whom will this not be enough? Then, is there a way we can make it work in such cases? Or from the reverse perspective, suppose a parent does everything wrong in terms of monitoring? He or she has no clue what his/her child is doing, who his/her child is doing it with, or where his/her child is. Under what conditions and circumstances and for whom will this not matter, because the child still turns out fine? What are the implications of this for monitoring theory?

Question 6. *Designing Interventions to Impact Monitoring:* **What advice would you give on how to best design an intervention that is practical, that has the potential to reach large numbers of families, *and* that will make parental monitoring more effective? That is, what are the most important factors to take into account in designing such an intervention?**

BELLE: Interventions must take into account the real-life limitations on parents' abilities to monitor their children. Not all families start at the same place, and not all strategies will be effective in all families. Parents who are away at work many of the hours their children are out of school have fewer monitoring options than those who are home, particularly if their jobs forbid their telephoning or visiting the child during work hours. Single parents and low-income parents have fewer resources (of time and of money) with which to facilitate effective monitoring. Beginning as we do with a concern about these practical limitations on effective parental monitoring, we would like to see workplace interventions that provide assistance to parents and families otherwise at high risk for inadequate monitoring of children. Since many employed parents are distracted with worries about their children during the hours children are out of school but parents are not at home, we would like to see creative interventions to provide opportunities for such parents to check in with their children. Sometimes this might mean a simple suspension of rules against workplace telephone calls. In other cases, it might mean providing parents with cell phones they can use from the workplace to reach their children. If such small modifications of work life can improve parent-child communication and facilitate successful parental monitoring, this would be a strong argument to make such family-friendly practices possible at all workplaces. Companies that pioneer such strategies should also reap the rewards of favorable publicity in the community as well as a less distracted, more productive workforce.

DISHION: We have two examples of interventions that have impacted parental monitoring. One, published in a prominent pediatric journal by Stanton and colleagues (2004), involved a brief intervention focusing on parental monitoring within a public school context. This intervention resulted in improvements in adolescent risk behavior. The second was published by our group (Dishion, Nelson, & Kavanagh 2004). This randomized trial revealed that encouraging parental monitoring was a mediator in adolescent changes in drug use. Improvements in parental monitoring predicted reductions in adolescent drug use from age 11 to 14.

Our intervention activity reveals to us that parental monitoring is highly malleable. As we suggest in our earlier work on the definition of parental monitoring, some parents simply are not aware of the importance of the construct (Dishion & McMahon 1998). Thus, a motivational interviewing strategy for providing parents feedback about their child's lack of supervision is often perceived as helpful and new information to many parents. Given the pervasive influence of media and the resulting ambiguity in norms, parents can often benefit on feedback regarding their own normative expectations. We have found that parents are very receptive to interventions that support parental monitoring practices.

One of the critical features, however, of providing intervention services for parents is to provide them tools for effective responses to problem behavior should it occur. As stated above, one reason parents avoid monitoring is a lack of confidence regarding how to respond in the event that they should find out information that requires a reaction. Thus, we support parents on communication skills, listening skills, and positive reinforcement strategies to improve their functioning in the leadership role in their families. Without the support, many parents will find themselves in over their heads when they attempt to monitor. Thus, a tiered approach to supporting parents that assesses their parenting skills in addition to their monitoring practices is helpful. Some parents require a modicum of support, and others require more intensive support, which is why we have developed a tailored model for parenting interventions (Dishion & Stormshak 2007).

LAIRD: I would expect that for an intervention to be most effective, monitoring would need to be addressed in the context of an intervention focused on the parent-adolescent relationship. In my opinion, the parents-adolescent relationship is extremely relevant to both the parents' monitoring activities and to adolescents' compliance. Therefore, I believe that the most effective interventions would need to address the complexities of monitoring and control while maintaining and strengthening the parent-adolescent relationship. I also think participants would benefit from discussions of monitoring in relation to adolescent autonomy and independence and from hearing how other parents approach these issues. Parents may benefit from understanding the developmental issues faced by adolescents, and this may help them to understand why their good intentions are resented and resisted.

In essence, I think that many parents may benefit from an open discussion of the complexity of the decisions they are likely to face. For example, what is the best response when an adolescent comes home late from a party because he or she had given rides to other kids who were drinking alcohol? How can the parent simultaneously acknowledge the mature and responsible elements of the evening while appropriately addressing the risky elements? Likewise, how can a parent respond to the adolescent who willingly tells of his or her involvement in unacceptable behavior without cutting off future disclosure or condoning the misbehavior? Finally, how can a parent best respond to noncompliance with monitoring attempts or conflict initiated by monitoring behavior in a way that meets the parents' monitoring goals without irreparably damaging the parent-adolescent relationship? It is likely that many parents have struggled with these complex issues. I believe that giving parents a set of questions to ask without addressing the ramifications of those questions may do more harm than good.

STANTON: As noted above, teaching them what monitoring is and is not—and giving them practical examples and practice.

TURRISI: We are presently conducting a universally focused intervention funded by the National Institute on Alcohol Abuse and Alcoholism designed to impact monitoring and positive communication between parents and incoming college freshmen. Particularly, this intervention attempts to enhance parental monitoring and conversations with teens based on the premise that sustained parental behavior produces more desirable outcomes than transitory efforts. Our current program provides parents with materials developed and empirically tested in our previous research that detail the problem of college drinking and best-practices for communication, and then encourages parents to talk with and monitor their teens.

The conversations parents are to have with their teens will take place in one of three conditions:

1. Prior-to-college matriculation (PCM) during the transition period between high school and college. This would follow the time period between high school and college which represents a teachable window where parent-teen communications may have the benefit of conveying parental concern about teens' welfare and establishing or reinforcing parental norms about drinking since campus drinking norms have not yet been established.

2. Prior-to-college matriculation and then throughout the fall semester, resulting from booster parent "check-ins" (PCMB). Under this condition, continued conversations from summer through fall would permit parents to evaluate whether their summer conversations had the impact of making teens more unfavorable toward drinking and drinking-related activities and then respond in kind by reinforcing the protective behaviors and discouraging any transgressions.

3. After-college matriculation during the fall of the first semester at college (ACM). Many teens have direct experiences (blackouts, fights, unwanted sexual experiences) and indirect experiences (e.g., babysitting someone who was sick after drinking too much) for the first time during their freshman year in college. Thus, the delivery of specific parent-driven communications may have a greater impact because students might relate better now and be more open to parent communications about alcohol (as opposed to pre-matriculation communication which might be "preachy").

Although there have been reports of post-matriculation parent involvement, no systematic theory-driven research has explored whether there is a critical period for implementing parent interventions with college students and, if so, what the best time or best approach (phone vs. home visits vs. campus visits) for those intervention efforts might be. In addition to exploring the timing of the intervention on positive teen outcomes, this study is attempting to explore the idea of dosage and sustainability through the use of parent booster materials in the PCMB condition. Parents in the PCMB condition will receive a booster package during the first week of the fall semester for phone calls, home visits, and campus visits. The central themes of the booster check-ins are (a) for parents to continue to communicate about alcohol during the semester (and beyond); (b) to evaluate how well their summer conversations about alcohol were received; and (c) to respond to their teen in these conversations with the goal of reinforcing the positive elements of their teen's behavior and discouraging high-risk behavior without creating barriers and closing communication channels.

In sum, this is an intervention that we believe takes a positive step toward helping parents of college-aged children communicate and monitor to dramatically reduce risk and negative consequences associated with college alcohol use.

COMMENTARY

When asked about advice for designing effective monitoring interventions, we obtained a range of answers. Some scientists emphasized the importance of taking into account context, such as developing workplace interventions that can provide assistance to parents and families who would be at high risk for inadequate monitoring of children. Other scientists emphasized the importance of addressing constructs that have already been discussed in answers to previous questions, such as discussing with parents the importance of the monitoring, and addressing communication skills, listening skills, and positive reinforcement strategies to improve parental functioning in the leadership role in their families. Dishion suggested the potential for motivational interviewing strategies, where information is tailored to individuals and where the interviewing process is used to reveal to parents their motivations and obstacles to effective monitoring. Several scientists emphasized the concept of intervention tailoring, with the idea that some parents require a modicum of support, and others require more intensive support, all of which can be qualitatively different from one individual to the next.

For an earlier question, we noted the importance of the need for practical information for parents, and this theme was evident in several answers to the current question. For example, Laird asked such questions as "what is the best response when an adolescent comes home late from a party because he or she had given rides to other kids who were drinking alcohol? How can the parent simultaneously acknowledge the mature and responsible elements of the evening while appropriately addressing the risky elements? Likewise, how can a parent respond to the adolescent who willingly tells of his/her involvement in unacceptable behavior without cutting off future disclosure or condoning the misbehavior?" Laird's queries underscore the need for practical translations of research principles.

Several scientists stressed again the importance of addressing not just monitoring but the parent-adolescent relationship more generally. There also was an emphasis on the importance of sustained parental behavior, not just transitory efforts at monitoring.

The challenge for interventionists is to develop effective interventions that are brief, efficient, cost-effective, sustainable, and that can reach large segments of the population. This is a tall order and requires both a strong theoretical point of view and a strong practical point of view.

Question 7. *Future Directions:* **What future research or research questions do you think are most important for the field to conduct/address?**

BELLE: We believe it is important to study the factors that promote voluntary child self-disclosure, as this is probably the most important source of parental knowledge about young people. Longitudinal research could be used to try to tease apart ways in which the roots of such self-disclosure can be found in early parenting practices, the child's temperament, or aspects of the parent-child relationship.

It would also be important to try to gain a better understanding of parental philosophies of monitoring. How do parents think about their own monitoring behavior? Why do they choose certain strategies and not others? Why try to discover information about some things and not others? Do parents perceive external impediments to their successful monitoring?

Similarly, how are adolescents thinking about their parents' efforts to monitor, in the context of the ongoing parent-child relationship? How do adolescents understand their own willingness or unwillingness to self-disclose to parents? Gaining such an interior view of both parent and child perspectives might make it possible to design more effective interventions in the future.

DISHION: There are two major future directions that we would suggest at this time. Consistent with our own chapter in this volume, we think that the nuances of parenting in general and monitoring in particular need further exploration with respect to culture and community contexts. For example, in our chapter we found very little evidence to link deviant peers and problem behavior in India compared to Montreal (Quebec) and Padua (Italy). This is an interesting anomaly from the standard literature. We realize in analyzing these data that a vast majority of the "cross-cultural research" is conducted in Western countries. We think it is important to understand the strategies used in non-Western countries that are effective in promoting child and adolescent development. The last great work on this question was the Whiting and Edwards study (1988), which focused more on experiences that promoted children's prosocial development. In this study, it was found that daily chores and routines related to family survival were the most facilitative of prosocial development around the world. We think it would be worthwhile to step out of the box of Western culture and consider how parents of other cultural traditions monitor their children. Approaching this cross-cultural work on a strength-based perspective rather than a deficit-hunting strategy would enrich theory considerably.

In the long run, parental monitoring is an exercise in self-regulation. It involves the parent's ability to engage in the effortful process of tracking the child's activities and whereabouts and focusing less attention on themselves. As cohorts emerge that are more self-centered, they may have more difficulty engaging in key parenting practices that involve their own self-regulation. Thus, it may be helpful to examine facets of parents' self-regulation that (a) serve as barriers for parental monitoring as in parents' own romantic relationships, psychopathology, and/or drug use, and (b) can be modified in interventions that promote parents' active efforts to track and serve as leaders in their child's development.

LAIRD: As this volume reveals, research on monitoring could branch off into many different directions. Personally, I believe there is a need for a much better understanding of how the monitoring process operates in the day-to-day life of families. Likewise, I think we need to better understand how monitoring emerges developmentally in families. How is monitoring influenced by prior interactional patterns? Are there key experiences or developmental tasks that transform monitoring?

I also think we need to think more about why monitoring appears to be a protective factor. Why is monitoring effective? Monitoring may be effective because it is a proxy for adolescent compliance or for parents' interest and commitment to the adolescent. Alternatively, monitoring may be effective because it provides parents the opportunities to respond and correct misbehavior. At this point, we can argue, speculate, and present data that may favor one process over the other, but we know too little about how families experience monitoring on a day-to-day basis to draw firm conclusions.

STANTON: Unquestionably how do we best "teach" parental monitoring.

STATTIN: Most important, in our opinion, is to reexamine with new empirical studies the widely held conclusions about monitoring, which in most studies have been based on measures of questionable validity. Science requires openness, and in this case researchers must be open to the possibility that the conclusions might change.

TURRISI: As research is just beginning to highlight the importance of parental monitoring among high school students transitioning to college, there are many basic questions that have not yet been addressed. One such issue is that of sustained monitoring. The research presented in our chapter shows that sustained parental monitoring from high school through students' fall semester of their freshman year of college is related to less positive beliefs about alcohol as well as lowered consumption among students. However, we do not know exactly how long parents should continue to monitor their sons and daughters. For example, freshman college students are particularly vulnerable to experiencing alcohol-related incidents, so does parental monitoring continue to benefit students beyond their freshman year, once students have had a chance to acclimate to their environment? Or is there a point in time when it is no longer necessary for parents to monitor their students' behavior?

In addition to examining how long parents should continue to monitor their adolescents, future research needs to address the level at which the monitoring occurs. Specifically, as teens transition from high school to college, what level, or dosage, of monitoring is associated with the most positive outcomes? Our past research shows that when asked to communicate with their teens about alcohol prior to leaving for college (given a handbook about alcohol to provide knowledge about the topic as well as enhance communication skills), most parents were willing to talk, which later led to less drinking and alcohol-related problems among these teens. Interestingly, when conducting focus groups with some of the parents in our studies after their teens transitioned to college, we were curious to learn whether the conversations about alcohol evolved once their teens were living away from home. When we asked parents questions about this we received blank looks and silence. This sent us a message that most parents thought a one-time conversation with their teen was sufficient. If we are going to encourage parents to continue monitoring, future research should address the levels at which this is to occur.

In addressing the extent to which monitoring should be sustained among late adolescents, as well as to what level it should occur, it is also important to examine how parental monitoring should be tailored (if at all) depending on characteristics of the adolescents themselves, as well as their environment once outside their parents' homes. For example, is a higher dosage of parental monitoring beneficial for teens more at risk of experiencing alcohol-related harm once in college (e.g., student athletes, fraternity/sorority members, and students with depressed mood)? Similarly, what about teens attending schools in high-risk environments where drinking traditions are embedded in the culture? At universities where heavy episodic drinking is normative at least two to three days each week (which is the case at many colleges and universities throughout the United States), the level of monitoring that is sufficient for adolescents in environments that are of average risk may not work as well due to the increased environmental pressures.

As we gain more insight as to what levels of parental monitoring are associated with the best adolescent outcomes, as well as how that might change based on the characteristics of the adolescent and his or her environment, the next step is to understand the best ways to enhance parent motivations to engage in monitoring behaviors. Our experience tells us that when given the appropriate tools, many parents are willing to communicate with their teens; however, not all parents buy into the idea that talking makes a difference. Despite the research that shows talking about alcohol leads to less drinking and related consequences, some parents in our studies expressed that talking and checking in with their teens wasn't necessary as they had been living with their teens long enough to convey their values and expectations regarding alcohol use. Clearly some parents don't see monitoring as necessary and are in turn less likely to engage in that behavior with their teen. The challenge lies in finding the most effective ways to change the underlying assumption held by some parents that the need to monitor their teens is no longer necessary as teens mature through adolescence. Future research studies and interventions should be targeted at enhancing parent motivations to communicate with and monitor their teens to the extent it is found to be beneficial and lead to positive outcomes among adolescents.

COMMENTARY

As demonstrated by the diverse contributions to this volume, there were a number of suggestions for directions for future research on parental monitoring. Not surprisingly, several scientists stated that it was important to study factors that promote voluntary child self-disclosure, as this is probably the most important source of parental knowledge about young people. Given that the state of knowledge on voluntary child disclosure is still growing, contributors noted that longitudinal research would be particularly helpful, as it could identify early parenting practices, child temperament, or aspects of the parent-child relationship that promote voluntary self-disclosure. Additionally, longitudinal studies would help researchers to understand the dynamics of self-disclosure as children progress from childhood to adolescence and into early adulthood.

Some scientists also thought that future research should focus on obtaining a better understanding of parental and adolescent philosophies of monitoring. Instead of scientists imposing their conceptualizations of monitoring onto parents and children, what happens if we take a more emergent theory approach and probe in more depth the monitoring philosophies of parents and children?

With respect to interventions, contributors offered a number of priorities. First, there was strong support for research that could identify how to best "teach" parental monitoring to parents. Second, consensus also emerged around identifying effective mechanisms to enhance parents' motivations to monitor their children. Although many parents are willing to communicate with their teens, especially when given the tools to do so, not all parents appear to buy into the idea that talking makes a difference. A number of scientists also discussed the importance of identifying thresholds or dosage effects for parental monitoring. Although monitoring has been found to be a protective factor, little is known about what levels of parental monitoring are associated with the best adolescent outcomes. Related to this point, if an optimal level of parental monitoring is identified, is it the same for all parents or do optimal levels change based on the characteristics of the parent, characteristics of the adolescent, and their shared and independent environments?

Additionally, several contributors felt that interventions will be improved when research identifies why monitoring is an effective protective factor. Although monitoring may be a proxy for adolescent compliance or for parents' interest and commitment to adolescents, it also may be effective because it provides parents opportunities to respond and correct misbehavior. At this point, researchers know too little about how families experience monitoring on a day-to-day basis to draw firm conclusions. Multiple contributors believed that there is a need for a much better understanding of how the monitoring process operates in the day-to-day life of families, including how monitoring is influenced by prior familial interactional patterns.

Research indicates that quality and quantity of parental monitoring changes as children grow and develop. Given this, a number of authors believed it was important for future research to elucidate the developmental dynamics of parental monitoring. How does monitoring emerge developmentally in families? Are there key experiences or developmental tasks that transform monitoring? These are some of the developmentally oriented questions that were deemed important.

To date, the field does not know exactly how long parents should continue to monitor their sons and daughters. Does parental monitoring continue to benefit students beyond their freshman year, once students have had a chance to acclimate to their environment? Or is there a point in time when it is no longer necessary for parents to monitor their children's behavior?

Additional points of emphasis included the importance of taking into account the cultural context of monitoring and the self-regulatory nature of monitoring.

Concluding Comments

In sum, we have addressed the most pressing issues related to the parental monitoring of adolescents. Our approach has been twofold. We start with a set of core questions that emerged from the CDC-sponsored meeting in 2004. The questions were put forth to each of the scientists that contributed chapters to part I of this volume. This is followed with a commentary by the editors of the volume synthesizing the individual responses from each of the contributing scientists. Our intent was to identify opportunities for future research and applied parental monitoring strategies that can be disseminated to parents of teens. Several interesting themes suggestive of the importance of the role of parental monitoring of adolescents are highlighted.

The volume offers both researchers and practitioners concrete suggestions that should be considered if effective parental monitoring interventions are to be developed and implemented. Specifically, researchers, practitioners, and parents should take note of the meaning of *monitoring*. In general, we define monitoring as the parental activities that allow parents to gain greater levels of awareness about the activities and peers of their adolescent children. This is an active process that should take into account the specific behaviors that are of interest. Parents are advised to target their monitoring efforts to specific behaviors that they wish to prevent as opposed to more general monitoring knowledge.

In terms of the measurement of monitoring, differing strategies are identified in this volume. When sample sizes are small or when the focus is a parent attempting to monitor his or her individual child, direct observation may be most promising. However, as described, we know this may not be possible when one seeks to gather information from larger numbers of youths. In these instances, self-reports may be used. However, depending upon who provides the self-report, there may be differences in the extent of involvement in the targeted behavior of the level of monitoring. We seek to encourage researchers and parents to think critically about how they gather data related to parental monitoring. Differences in self-reports contingent upon who provides the data may be meaningful and reflective of the unique perspectives of distinct family members. Numerous reasons for differences in the extent of parental monitoring have been offered. Some of these reasons were more macro (e.g., work schedules) and some more micro (e.g., beliefs). The list of diverse factors that potentially influence the extent of parental monitoring is useful from the point of view that larger theoretical frameworks are needed. In order to integrate these factors into one framework, they need to be identified. This volume has done so. Future work should critically consider how these factors come together to best influence parental monitoring. Chapter 7 of this volume attempts to provide such a framework.

Despite the lack of consensus regarding those factors most influential in terms of the extent of parental monitoring, two factors warrant further discussion. Parent-adolescent communication and parental monitoring self-efficacy were widely identified by the experts who contributed to this volume. Future efforts to develop and implement research-based monitoring interventions should carefully consider the role of these two constructs in preventing or reducing adolescent problem behavior. Likewise, we explored the issue of compliance with parental expectations of monitoring. Here two constructs were identified: (a) the relationship between the adolescent and the parent, and (b) the administration of consequences for transgressions from parental behavioral expectations. This volume emphasizes the dominant finding in the extant literature that supports the protective role of a strong parent-adolescent relationship. In short, parental monitoring is most effective within the context of a strong parent-adolescent relationship. Additionally, overreacting to adolescent transgressions in regard to parental rules or behavioral expectations is ill-advised. The contributing experts generally felt it more prudent to be clear and consistent in one's use of discipline. Lastly, in designing an ideal intervention or parental monitoring strategy, we believe it most effective to develop monitoring interventions that are brief, practical, and cost-efficient.

In conclusion, this volume offers researchers, practitioners, and parents essential tools for thinking about methods for best monitoring their adolescent children. We believe we have addressed some of the most pressing issues in the field and offer readers innovative new directions for considering methods for keeping adolescents safe and healthy through improvements to how parents monitor their teen children.

Applied Issues in the Development of Parental Monitoring Interventions

Parental monitoring of adolescents remains one of the most efficacious parenting practices for preventing adolescent problem behaviors. Throughout this text, the authors of the chapters have addressed contemporary issues for researchers and practitioners interested in developing evidenced-based monitoring interventions. Part II takes what we have learned from earlier chapters and applies them to intervention design. Our intent is to highlight core issues and to suggest strategies that will be useful to practitioners and researchers interested in developing family-based monitoring interventions that target the prevention or reduction of adolescent risk behavior. In doing so, we draw upon examples from our own research, the *Linking Lives Health Education Program* (Guilamo-Ramos, Jaccard, & Dittus 2003), a parent-based intervention to prevent or reduce tobacco use and sexual behavior among middle school–aged youth. Our discussion begins with a brief overview of three core issues that we believe are important for developing effective parental monitoring interventions. This discussion is followed by a case example from *Linking Lives*, where we illustrate how these core issues were addressed.

The importance of a strong theoretical basis of monitoring. One of the core themes highlighted by all of the contributors to this volume is the importance of using strong theories of parental monitoring. For example, theory helps us to define and measure parental monitoring, to make and test hypotheses about the relationship between parental monitoring and adolescent risk behavior, and to identify the mechanisms to strengthen parents' monitoring efforts. In short, theory is integral for both research and practice, as without theory we cannot obtain new insight into parental monitoring, develop effective interventions, or provide parents with evidence-based recommendations on how to effectively monitor their adolescent children.

In the present volume, the contributors to chapters 1, 2, 4, and 7 all underscore the importance of theory when studying parental monitoring. In keeping with the findings of these authors, researchers and practitioners are encouraged to view parental monitoring as a multi-faceted and dynamic parenting strategy that (a) has cultural dimensions, (b) is embedded in a dynamic parent-adolescent relationship, and (c) extends beyond parental knowledge to encompass other parental behaviors, as well as adolescent behaviors (see chapters 2, 3, 5, and 7). For example, the framework in chapter 7 highlighted a number of other parenting constructs that are central for effective parental monitoring, such as the transmission of clear expectations regarding adolescent behavior, parental follow-up to assess if expected norms are being adhered to, and the discipline strategies that parents apply if adolescents do not adhere to parental expectations. Although early research most often defined parental monitoring as knowledge that parents have about their child's friends, activities, and whereabouts, the work in the present volume shows that parental monitoring interventions cannot rely on theories that are limited solely to parental knowledge of their children's whereabouts and friends. The multivariate context in which such monitoring variables has been placed is far richer (and more demanding) than this. Researchers and practitioners interested in developing parent-based monitoring interventions should use strong theories of parental monitoring that reflect the extant knowledge in the scientific literature.

Developing parent-based interventions that respect the constraints of real-world settings. A second core issue addresses the problem of developing a parent-based intervention that can be readily applied in real-world settings. To date, the majority of parent-based interventions require parents to attend multiple sessions over an extended period of time. For example, a parent might be asked to attend ten separate sessions, with each session lasting from one to four hours, depending on the intervention. From a research perspective, having a parent attend multiple sessions is desirable because increasing a parent's exposure, or dosage, to an intervention is thought to increase the likelihood of behavior change. This is because multiple intervention sessions enable program developers to reinforce intervention content over time and to provide parents with additional opportunities to practice intervention content or skills under the supervision of a trained facilitator. However, parents are busy and do not have the time to attend multiple intervention sessions. Indeed, research on parental participation in family-based interventions has documented parental recruitment rates ranging from 8% to 70% (e.g., Bronstein et al. 1998; Dumka et al. 1997). Intervention research has tended to segregate issues of intervention efficacy from intervention feasibility and sustainability. But how much value is an efficacious intervention that few parents or adolescents will participate in or which is impossible to implement faithfully in the face of diminished resources?

Parents need interventions that are practical and feasible. Unfortunately, designing interventions that do not fit easily into the daily routines and responsibilities of parents is a common error in applied intervention research. Relatively little research has systematically investigated parents' preferences regarding intervention design and delivery. This is troublesome as it means that many parent-focused interventions are designed in ways that are unlikely to foster high levels of parent participation and retention. From an applied perspective, we recommend that family-based interventions be designed in a way that takes advantage of the naturalistic behaviors and opportunities that are a part of a parent's everyday life or behavioral repertoire. For example, Turrisi and colleagues (chapter 5) identified viable mechanisms for parents to monitor their children across the transition from high school to college. Similarly, Galbraith and Stanton (chapter 6) highlighted the importance of real-world settings when seeking to disseminate interventions to a broader population. These issues are critical when developing monitoring interventions to fit into the daily activities and routines of families that are likely to be successful and sustainable.

One strategy for developing such an intervention would be to limit the number of sessions that parents are required to attend. Instead of asking parents to attend ten sessions, try two sessions, or three sessions at maximum. In addition to limiting the number of intervention sessions, alternative mechanisms for delivering intervention content should be explored. Specifically, the use of DVDs, videos, and written materials that parents can take home and use as reference materials are concrete examples of ways to deliver monitoring interventions without requiring multiple, in-person sessions. Giving parents homework assignments to complete, including short booster follow-up phone calls, and using Web-based accessible information also can reduce the burden of multiple, in-person sessions. These types of materials are ideal for two reasons. First, they lend themselves to use at times and in locations that are flexible to parental needs. Second, they contain intervention content that is delivered and/or reinforced each time a parent refers to or uses the intervention materials. In addition, interventions can be delivered via other mediums, such as email or text messages. Program developers are encouraged to think carefully and creatively about how best to reach families in ways that are likely to be impactful and easily integrated into family life.

Another option is to deliver monitoring interventions to parents in workplace settings or during times when they may be accompanying their child to required appointments. For example, most adolescents have annual physical exams that are required as part of the school registration process and are likely to visit a health clinic for their exam. During these times, a parent may be sitting in the waiting room while their adolescent is examined by a health care provider. This "waiting period" is an opportune moment to engage parents in a meaningful activity such as the delivery of a monitoring intervention—it takes advantage of a regular part of a family's routine and does not place an undue time burden on parents. Relying on familiar institutions for delivering interventions also may increase the likelihood of successfully engaging parents. For example, in addition to taking advantage of "lost time" in the waiting room of a health clinic, the health care setting conveys a degree of legitimacy to families. Monitoring interventions delivered within institutions that are perceived as being supportive of families and of healthy youth development are likely to be received positively by a wide range of families.

In sum, we recommend that monitoring interventions take advantage of real-world opportunities and behaviors that are naturally associated with family life. Monitoring interventions need to be brief and accessible for families. Intervention developers should partner with institutions that families find both familiar and trustworthy. In addition to health clinics, other novel contexts for delivering a monitoring intervention include community neighborhood associations and tenant's associations of large housing projects. Both institutions are familiar to families and lend themselves to reaching large numbers of parents. In addition, schools, parent employment settings, religious institutions, and community-based organizations all are potential venues through which to reach large numbers of parents.

Social scientists often stress the importance of contexts as determinants of adolescent risk behavior. These include such contexts as the peer context, the school context, the family context, the neighborhood context, the work context, the health care provider context, the religious context, the state government context, and the media context, to name a few. We propose that each of these contexts can be viewed as a potential source of outreach to parents for purposes of administering a monitoring intervention. By carefully analyzing possible outreach opportunities within each of these contexts, it should be possible to identify a range of strategies for reaching parents. Practitioners and researchers alike are urged to think critically about family life for their context of interest and directly ask parents about ideal times and settings through which to reach them in those contexts. From an applied perspective, it is critical to explore the delivery options that are most appropriate for your target parents and family contexts.

Parenting styles versus parenting behaviors. A final issue addresses the distinction between parenting styles and parenting behaviors. Parents can invoke numerous strategies to monitor and parent their adolescent children. Some of these behaviors were discussed by Belle and Phillips in chapter 3 and by Turrisi and colleagues in chapter 5. These behaviors are often reflective of an underlying parenting style. Parenting style encompasses a number of different parenting behaviors and typically reflects the values, beliefs, and cultural norms of parents. In contrast, parenting behaviors are discrete strategies that a given parent invokes to influence the adolescent child. This distinction is critical because intervention developers must decide which they are going to target, with discrete strategies probably being easier to change than the more broad-based parenting styles. This is not to say that parental values, beliefs, and cultural norms regarding child rearing cannot be influenced. However, changing the parenting style of a parent requires intensive efforts that often are outside of the scope of family-based interventions. By contrast, a clearly defined parenting behavior may be more amenable to being targeted as part of a time-limited intervention. In this context, the goal may be to extinguish a specific parenting behavior or to encourage a parent to adopt a specific monitoring behavior that supports the overall goal of the parent-based intervention.

Consider the case of a parent-based intervention to prevent adolescent sexual behavior. A large body of research indicates that the age discrepancy between the members of an adolescent couple is a predictor of sexual activity: There is a greater likelihood of sexual behavior when one member of an adolescent couple is two or more years older than the partner. Most often, we think of cases where an adolescent boy is older than his female partner. This is because adolescent girls often develop faster than their male counterparts, and tend not to feel romantically attracted to their underdeveloped, same-aged male peers. As a result, an "age-discrepant dyad" forms consisting of a younger girl (i.e., a 9th grade adolescent female) and an older male (i.e., an 11th grade adolescent male), which lends to a greater likelihood of sexual activity.

Parents are likely to have differing opinions and perspectives about adolescent romantic relationships. Whereas some parents may not allow their adolescent daughter to date an older boy, other parents won't allow their daughter to date at all, while still others may allow dating when a certain age is reached, at which point in time they may not have a specific parental rule about the age of their daughter's partner. In general, parents' rules and opinions about their daughter dating are likely to reflect different values, beliefs, and cultural norms which, in their entirety, may not be amenable to intervention. However, the extant literature is clear that sexual intercourse is more likely to occur when a partner is approximately two years older. Thus, this is a specific parenting behavior to target in a monitoring intervention, namely, parents' behavioral expectations or rules about the age of their adolescent's romantic partner and how parents can monitor if this expectation is adhered to. In an intervention context, parents can be given evidence-based perspectives on how age discrepancies in adolescent romantic relationships are related to sexual behavior and can be encouraged to adopt specific monitoring behaviors that discourage their adolescent child from dating an older partner.

In sum, we have highlighted three core issues in developing a parent-based monitoring intervention: (a) the importance of using a strong theory, (b) the importance of developing an intervention that can be easily integrated into the lives of families, and (c) the importance of targeting specific parenting behaviors versus a more global parenting style. In the next section, we present an adaptation of an intervention we developed, *The Linking Lives Health Education Program*, to illustrate how each of these issues was addressed when designing a parent-based intervention to prevent adolescent risk behavior. Parental monitoring was a small component of this larger intervention. We emphasize here how to incorporate the monitoring constructs and theories described in part I of this book to design an intervention focused on improving parental monitoring as opposed to other components of the *Linking Lives Health Education Program*.

Designing an Intervention to Address Parental Monitoring Constructs

In 2001 the Centers for Disease Control and Prevention's Division of Adolescent and School Health (DASH) funded the development and implementation of the *Linking Lives Health Education Program*, a parent-based sexual and tobacco risk-reduction intervention for early adolescents. The editors of this volume are the primary architects of the *Linking Lives* program.

THE STRUCTURE OF THE PROGRAM

One of the first issues that we addressed focused on designing a practical and sustainable program for our target population, which was African American and Latino middle school–aged adolescents and their mothers residing in inner-city, resource-poor communities in the boroughs of New York City. The CDC was interested in supporting a program that focused on at-risk youth and could be disseminated and maintained independent of research funds to develop and evaluate the intervention. As a result, *Linking Lives* was expressly designed to reach a large number of families and to do so in a cost-effective manner.

We first conducted qualitative research on a representative sample of the target population, asking parents about their preferences regarding the form and delivery of a parenting program. Our data suggested that parents would not attend numerous workshop sessions. Mothers described obligations and life commitments that made it difficult to attend numerous face-to-face sessions. As a result, the *Linking Lives* intervention was designed to have just two face-to-face sessions. Some face-to-face contact was necessary because parents needed structured time to meet with program staff and for behavioral practice of parental monitoring strategies. The two intervention sessions provided parents with the opportunity to review intervention materials and to practice the skills and activities they were being asked to implement with their adolescent child. Additionally, parents felt that two sessions were reasonable and would not place an undue burden on their time. We fully recognized that not all parents would attend both sessions.

Our qualitative research with parents also suggested that it was important to recruit families through well-known and respected community-based institutions, such as their adolescent's school. As a result, the *Linking Lives* program was advertised to parents and adolescents as a program that was being offered to families at their son's or daughter's school as a way to support adolescent health and well-being. Program staff visited each participating school to meet with administrators, teachers, student organizations, and parent organizations to discuss the purpose of the program and to ensure each group that they would be part of program development. We secured from the schools a small office, over which was placed a colorful "*Linking Lives*" banner. The project established a telephone number for families to call with questions or concerns about problems with their school children more generally. The intervention sessions were to be held at schools in the evening and weekend hours. Taken together, these activities ensured that the program was partnered with a known and respected institution in the community and that families could access the program at convenient times and locations.

CONSIDERING PROGRAM SUSTAINABILITY DURING THE DESIGN PHASE OF THE INTERVENTION

The intervention form that evolved from this initial research required resources that are beyond the capacities of many inner-city schools. One such requirement is the staffing of the project office with a trained social worker who could help serve the needs of students and parents more generally and who would build community credibility for the program as a whole. In addition, there is need for a volunteer workforce that will personally contact the mothers of students to inform them of the intervention sessions and to encourage their participation. Such personal contact, our research showed, is important. A third requirement is the need to provide child care options to parents who, without a place to care for their younger or older children, may not be able to attend sessions. Finally, there is the need for trained program staff to administer the intervention sessions.

We suggest that these demands can be addressed by building partnerships between schools, colleges/universities, and school-based parent organizations. The first step in the partnership process is to build a relationship between the target school and either a School of Social Work, School of Public Health, or some other university/college department that places student interns into communities as part of an accredited bachelor's or master's degree program. For example, students obtaining a social work degree are required by the Council on Social Work Education to complete 400 hours of field instruction for a BSW and 900 hours for an MSW. Similarly, the Council for the Education of Public Health requires a field practicum for MPH students, which typically range from 200 to 600 hours, depending on the program/school. As a result, Social Work and Public Health schools/programs are generally in need of internship placements for students and will welcome the opportunity to place students in school-based settings where they can reach large numbers of students and families. These are natural translation-support structures (National Center for Chronic Disease Prevention and Health Promotion 2008a, 2008b) that have been underused in attempts to bridge the gap between research and practice. The interns can be used to staff the project office and to serve as trained interventionists. School administrators will be grateful to receive in-kind assistance of MSW and MPH interns. We do not describe in detail here the steps involved in building such partnerships, but they are straightforward.

One of the first tasks of the interns should be to strengthen the parent organization within the school. Our experience with inner-city schools is that most have small parent organizations consisting of five to ten parents. The interns will mobilize these parents to take an active part in helping the school on the important topic at hand (e.g., addressing sexual behavior, tobacco use, or some other health behavior) and ask them to recruit two friends who are parents of students in the school to join the effort of other parents in the organization. Token remuneration can be provided for all parents who participate. The parents, in conjunction with the student interns, become the voluntary workforce that calls and outreaches to parents for the intervention and who can provide child care services at the intervention sessions. By building partnerships between universities, schools, and parents, the intervention becomes feasible and sustainable. In addition, the strategy places "ownership" of the program in three different sources (the School of Social Work or School of Public Health for purposes of placing interns, the school administration, and the parent organization), thereby increasing its likely sustainability.

MAXIMIZING PARENTAL PARTICIPATION

Most parent-based interventions consist of multiple sessions. Unfortunately, dropouts after the first session or failure to complete all sessions is common. We believe that many efficacious parent-based programs are unrealistic in the number of sessions they ask parents to attend and ultimately will prove to be of little utility when applied in practice. As previously mentioned, we sought in the *Linking Lives* program to have two sessions, separated by a week.

It is important that interventionists explicitly consider strategies to maximize participation in the initial sessions and to address as part of the intervention those strategies for encouraging return to the future session(s). We conceptualize parent participation as a hierarchy of strategies involving three primary components. The first component focuses on initial re-cruitment into the program. The second component focuses on support-ing parental involvement and the extent to which parents participate in the different aspects of adolescent health promotion programs. The third com-ponent focuses on parents applying what was learned in the intervention to their family after the intervention is complete.

The recruitment component. The overall purpose of the recruitment component is to develop a set of evidence-based strategies that can success-fully recruit large numbers of parents. Based on extant translational re-search, the recruitment component must address at least three barriers to parental recruitment: (a) the use of inflexible or limited recruitment strate-gies, (b) the presence of schedule conflicts in the lives of parents, and (c) the use of overly general and decontextualized recruitment protocols. To over-come these barriers, one should seek to developed a recruitment protocol that is (a) flexible for the needs of diverse types of families, (b) contextual-ized for the target population and community, (c) designed to address com-mon barriers, and (d) low-cost and easy to implement with minimal re-sources. Whereas traditional parent-based programs may outreach to parents via a single mechanism (e.g., a flyer sent home with the child from school), we suggest using a multimodal and individualized recruitment strategy. This can include outreaching to parents via telephone, and send-ing a personalized letter to the family that contains important community endorsements, e.g., from principals. Studies have shown that recruitment methods are successful when they are contextualized for the target popula-tion, provide parents with initial factual and science-based information, and highlight the benefits of parental participation for adolescents, par-ents, and the broader community. These elements should be a part of any recruitment protocol. In *Linking Lives*, for example, we stress how the pro-gram is specifically designed to support the health needs of adolescents and families in the target community, i.e., Latino and African American families in the Bronx. The recruiter also discusses how parental participa-tion in the program benefits both adolescents and parents.

Major barriers to participation in the initial session are schedule con-flicts, which include transportation barriers, lack of child care, and incon-venient timing of program events. To overcome these barriers, we suggest interventionists consider scheduling multiple program options in the afternoons, evenings, and on the weekends. In addition, child care services should be provided at all program events. In the *Linking Lives* program, we have found that maintaining such flexible scheduled options is crucial for parent recruitment.

The participation component. The overall purpose of the participation component is to encourage continued parental participation in the program once parents have attended the initial session. Like the recruitment component, the participation component is maximized if it is flexible and the intervention is meeting the needs of the families. Flexible scheduling of subsequent sessions and provision of child care are, again, important strategies for this component. Families also should be called in advance of the event to remind them of the event and to offer opportunities to reschedule should a conflict arise. Some research has found that providing social support can retain parents and that parents are motivated by opportunities to interact with other parents in their community (McKay et al. 2007). Program designers should consider appealing to social support mechanisms during the initial session when encouraging parents to participate in future sessions, and during the reminder calls. At the conclusion of the initial intervention session, parents should be provided with a meaningful opportunity to provide feedback on the intervention session and to provide recommendations for how to improve the next session. Finally, program designers might consider conducting qualitative research to determine the most effective nature and content of formal appeals to encourage parents to return to the next session.

The application component. Application of the intervention materials and principles is, in part, a function of how useful parents find the material covered in the sessions. This component should include structuring interactions between program staff and parents so that staff can determine how useful and practical parents find the program materials. If there are reservations in this respect, they need to be addressed. Interactions also should be structured to allow staff to determine from parents what parents see as the obstacles to implementation and application of the principles learned. Booster calls after the intervention sessions to discuss obstacles to implementation also are advised.

THE STRUCTURE AND CONTENT OF THE SESSIONS

The next set of issues considered in the development of *Linking Lives* focused on the intervention materials and content. Because the intervention was limited to two face-to-face sessions, parents needed to have additional materials and activities that could be easily used at home. The decision was made to use written materials over a video because our formative research with parents in our target population indicated that many families did not have regular, ongoing access to a VCR or a DVD player. However, both parents and adolescents were receptive to written materials and liked the idea of activities that would provide them with structured opportunities to interact with each other. To address variations in literacy, the written materials were geared to a fourth-grade reading level and were available in English and Spanish, with families choosing their language preference. Interactive assignments between parents and adolescents were also available in a bilingual format, so that parents who read Spanish only but had adolescents who read only in English could participate in activities together.

The content for the face-to-face sessions and intervention materials can be structured using the theoretical perspectives described in this text. We relied heavily on the framework articulated by Jaccard and colleagues in chapter 7. Thus, the face-to-face sessions and the supporting written materials both drew upon a strong theoretical model of parental monitoring. Intervention facilitators were trained on the key theoretical points and explained the importance of parental monitoring to parents in an evidence-based but straightforward manner. For example, during the face-to-face sessions for the sexual risk-reduction intervention, facilitators discussed the importance of setting clear behavioral expectations, explaining to adolescents the purpose of behavioral rules and the importance of using appropriate consequences when adolescents transgressed parents' rules. This message was then highlighted in the written intervention materials, which consisted of a parent workbook, a family activity workbook, an adolescent workbook, and a set of structured activities that fostered communication and the transmission of parental expectations and values to their adolescent children. In addition, the structured activities allowed adolescents to offer their perspectives to parents through an open communication process.

The sessions themselves should use principles of active rather than passive learning. Instead of telling parents information about monitoring in a passive way, formal activities should be structured so that they "learn by doing." For example, one intervention task might be to coordinate with a literature or health class in school and, as part of the homework for that class, give students a short, three- to four-page story to read. Then, as homework, students are asked to take the story home, have their mothers read it, and then interview the mother about her reactions to the story. The story actually is written by the interventionists, and it highlights crucial points and is designed to create an opportunity for discussion between parent and child about those points. One of the session activities for parents might be to forewarn them that their children will be given this assignment and then to review with them what the story covers and the opportunities it creates for conversation. Specific points the parent can make with the child as a result of the story can be discussed with parents in a group context and then parents can practice by role-playing the child-parent interview. The underlying principle is to invoke active learning for those points that are essential to intervention success.

As noted, we provided parents with materials to take home and use as reference. We make a point of going through these materials with parents during the face-to-face sessions and providing them with specific strategies for using the materials. Thus, by the time they leave the face-to-face sessions, they are very familiar with the materials they are taking home and how to use those materials. We then structure booster calls to ensure they are using the materials and engaging in the home activities we recommend.

The theoretical framework we use for monitoring is (a) to ensure that parents clearly convey their behavioral expectations to their children, (b) to teach parents strategies to monitor their children to ensure the children adhere to those expectations, and (c) to teach parents effective discipline strategies when their child transgresses so as to minimize future transgressions. In addition, we provide parents with specific behavioral strategies that will encourage their child to respect parental behavioral expectations and be less likely to transgress (for elaboration of this framework, see chapter 7).

As an example, a construct that research has shown to be important for monitoring related activities is adolescent satisfaction with the maternal relationship. Adolescents who are satisfied with their relationships with their mothers are more likely than adolescents who are dissatisfied with their relationships to self-disclose to their mothers, to be motivated to please their mothers and thereby act in accord with their mothers' expectations, to accept monitoring as a legitimate parenting activity on the part of their mothers, and to keep their mothers informed of their activities. What specific strategies can mothers be told about to foster adolescent relationship satisfaction? Here is an excerpt from the larger *Linking Lives* component on this topic:

There are many things you can do to help improve the relationship between you and your teen. We give you below a list of things to consider. Maybe not all are right for you. But think about them and try out ones you are comfortable with.

Keep in Touch. Touch base with your teen regularly. It is easy not to talk to your teen when everything is going smoothly. Make it a point to take time and share your thoughts. Let your teen know what's going on in your life and find out what he or she is up to. Keeping in touch with your teen is one of the most important things you can do as a parent.

Show Courtesy. Show simple, basic courtesy. Small courtesies like saying "please" and "thanks" and helping out in small ways all show that you care. Amazingly, people often show more courtesy to strangers than to members of their own family. Simple good manners convey sensitivity and respect. And if you give respect, you will get respect.

Be Thoughtful. Remember special days. Show your teen that he or she is remembered. It doesn't have to be with an expensive gift or activity: Just remember and let your teen know. Provide your teen with "little surprises" where you do something small but special for no particular reason.

Recognize Special Efforts. Don't take your teen for granted. Praise his or her special efforts.

Show Caring. Say you care. Tell your teen that you care about him or her. Do it regularly.

Be Supportive. When your teen has a bad day, give a shoulder to lean on. Even though your teen wants to be grown-up, he or she still needs your support.

Avoid Hurtful Teasing. Sometimes we tease in a way that puts a person down in front of others. Avoid this.

Eliminate Irritating Habits. Think if there are little things that you do that get under the skin of your teen. Make an extra effort not to do them.

Use Humor. Lighten up. Use humor once in a while with your teen. Joking around encourages a positive relationship.

Don't Treat Your Teen Like a Small Child. Although your teen is not an adult, he or she is no longer a small child and should not be treated as one. Don't talk down to your teen. Be straight with him or her when possible. Statements like "You're not old enough to know about this" suggest disrespect.

Don't Nag Your Teen. No one likes constant nagging and it accomplishes little. Try to cut back on the nagging.

Don't Compare Your Teen with Other Family Members. Accept your teen for who he or she is. Statements like, "Why can't you be more like your older brother?" or "Your sister never gave me this much trouble" don't help. Every person has their own special strengths. Recognize and acknowledge the positive qualities of your teen instead of focusing on what he or she appears to be lacking.

The general philosophy is to provide parents with a menu of specific strategies that they can consider using in their interactions with their adolescent children that will help to foster adolescent relationship satisfaction. The focus is on parenting behaviors rather than general parenting styles. Each strategy can be discussed with parents, asking them to identify specific exemplars of each strategy and to elaborate implementation issues. Again, the emphasis should be on active as opposed to passive learning, where possible.

As another example, here is intervention content aimed at the construct of power sharing and reasoned discipline when establishing, maintaining, and enforcing parents' behavioral rules and expectations:

Parents and teens often make agreements only to have the teen break them. A teen may agree to be home at 11 p.m., but then not show up. Why does this happen? It usually is because the "agreement" that was reached was not a true agreement. Instead, the parent simply laid down the law and the teen had no choice.

How can you make an agreement that your teen will honor? The key is power-sharing. When setting a curfew, for example, ask your teen for his or her opinion. Take it seriously. Say you and your daughter differ by only an hour on when she should come home from a party. She wants a midnight curfew. You want her home by 11 p.m. Is there a "middle ground" that you can agree on? How about 11:30 p.m.? Or, perhaps you can make an exception for a special occasion. The important thing is to make your teen feel he or she has some say in the agreement.

If your teen breaks an agreement, talk about it. Make your disappointment clear. Some parents ask teens what they think a fair punishment is for breaking a rule.

Other parents decide this on their own. Some parents do not punish their teen the first time a rule is broken. But they make it clear for the next time that punishment will follow. You need to be the judge of what is best in your case.

Some parents prefer to avoid conflict and not raise the issue if their teen breaks an agreement. Reducing conflict with your teen is a good idea, but there are times when you must talk directly, even if conflict occurs. If your teen breaks rules and agreements, you need to talk about it. You do not want it to happen again. Your teen needs to understand why the rules are important.

Parents who discuss the logic of rules help their teens to think logically. Even if your teen argues with your reasons, he or she will think about them later.

Our family workbooks address parenting behaviors that are deemed important for monitoring based on extant theory. Formative research with adolescents can be as rich a source for monitoring intervention strategies as research with parents. For example, in our formative research on adolescent cigarette smoking, youth disclosed that one effective strategy for reducing their access to cigarettes would be for parents who smoke to count their own cigarettes each day and to convey these counts to their adolescent children. Adolescents said this would make it more difficult to take cigarettes from their parents without the parent knowing about it and, in turn, it would reduce the likelihood of them smoking. This simple parental monitoring strategy was incorporated into the intervention and again highlights a core issue of targeting specific monitoring behaviors versus a parent's global parenting style.

BOOSTER SESSIONS

Finally, we believe it is important for interventions to consider brief booster sessions that can monitor progress, address problems with implementation of program principles and activities, and that can serve as a "cue to action" to keep the intervention message salient to parents. In *Linking Lives*, the booster session took the form of a brief telephone call made to participating parents to (a) reinforce intervention content, (b) support the likelihood that the family would complete the activities in the family workbook, and (c) offer additional support to parents as they attempted to effectively monitor their adolescent. In our early research, the vast majority of parents reported having access to a home telephone or to a cellular telephone, which made phone calls an ideal medium to deliver the booster sessions. In addition, families were able to call our office if they had any questions about the intervention. Although similar booster sessions may not be feasible for all practice settings, we encourage researchers and practitioners to work with parents to identify feasible ways to support parents' ongoing efforts to monitor their children in ways that are likely to reduce adolescent risk behavior.

Conclusion

The development of effective parent-based monitoring interventions holds promise for reducing and/or preventing adolescent involvement in a range of problem behaviors. Effective monitoring interventions should be (a) based on strong theories of parental monitoring, (b) feasible and acceptable for the everyday lives of diverse families, and (c) target specific parental monitoring behaviors that are connected with adolescent risk behavior. Applied researchers and practitioners need to consider all of these issues as they seek to develop parental monitoring interventions. Interventions that are atheoretical, require numerous sessions, and attempt to change a parent's global approach to parenting are not sustainable, effective, or feasible for most families. Such practices will almost certainly result in low family participation and retention rates. In the *Linking Lives Health Education Program*, we sought to address each of these issues via the delivery of a brief, theory-based intervention that was tailored to meet the needs of participating families. It also is critical that interventions be developmentally appropriate. Behavioral strategies for middle school–aged children will not work for older, high school–aged children. We encourage researchers and practitioners to think critically about how to design applied monitoring interventions for the populations and behaviors that are of most importance to them. Attention to these issues, as well as to the other themes highlighted in this volume, is likely to increase the efficacy of parental monitoring interventions and to support our overall efforts to help parents keep their adolescents safe from harm.

References

Bandura, A. (1975). *Social learning theory*. Englewood Cliffs, NJ: Prentice-Hall.

Barnes, G. M. (1990). Impact of the family on adolescent drinking patterns. In R. L. Collins, K. E. Leonard, & J. S. Searles (Eds.), *Alcohol and the family: Research and clinical perspectives* (pp. 137–161). New York: Guilford.

Bronstein, P., Duncan, P., Clauson, J., Abrams, C. C., Yannett, N., Ginsburg, G., & Milne, M. (1998). Preventing middle school adjustment problems for children from lower income families: A program for aware parenting. *Journal of Applied Developmental Psychology, 19*, 129–152.

Dishion, T. J., Bullock, B. M., & Kiesner, J. (2008). Vicissitudes of parenting adolescents: Daily variations in parental monitoring and the early emergence of drug use. In M. Kerr, H. Stattin, & R. C. M. E. Engels (Eds.), *What can parents do? New insights into the role of parents in adolescent problem behavior* (pp. 113–133). Chichester, England: Wiley.

Dishion, T. J., Burraston, B., & Li, F. (2002). Family management practices: Research design and measurement issues. In W. Bukoski & Z. Amsel (Eds.), *Handbook for drug abuse prevention theory, science, and practice* (pp. 587–607). New York: Plenum.

Dishion, T. J., & Kavanagh, K. (2003). *Intervening in adolescent problem behavior: A family-centered approach*. New York: Guilford.

Dishion, T. J., & McMahon, R. J. (1998). Parental monitoring and the prevention of child and adolescent problem behavior: A conceptual and empirical formulation. *Clinical Child and Family Psychology Review, 1*, 61–75.

Dishion, T. J., Nelson, S. E., & Bullock, B. M. (2004). Premature adolescent autonomy: Parent disengagement and deviant peer process in the amplification of problem behavior. *Journal of Adolescence, 27*, 515—530.

Dishion, T. J., Nelson, S. E., & Kavanagh, K. (2003). The family check-up with high-risk adolescents: Motivating parenting monitoring and reducing problem behavior. In J. E. Lochman & R. Salekin (Eds.), Behavior oriented interventions for children with aggressive behavior and/or conduct problems [Special Issue]. *Behavior Therapy, 34*, 553–571.

Dishion, T. J., & Stormshak, E. (2007). *Intervening in children's lives: An ecological, family-centered approach to mental health care*. Washington, D.C.: American Psychological Association.

Dumka, L. E., Garza, C. A., Roosa, M. W., & Stoerzinger, D. H. (1997). Recruitment and retention of high-risk families into a preventive parent training intervention. *Journal of Primary Prevention, 18*, 25–39.

Fishbein, M.. & Azjen, I. (1975). *Belief, attitude, intention, and behavior: An introduction to theory and research.* Reading, MA: Addison-Wesley.

Guilamo-Ramos, V., Jaccard, J., & Dittus, P. (2003). *The Linking Lives/Uniendo Vidas Health Education Program.* Authors.

Guilamo-Ramos, V., Jaccard, J., Dittus, P., & Bouris, A. (2006). Parental expertise, trustworthiness, and accessibility: Parent-adolescent communication and adolescent risk behavior. *Journal of Marriage and Family, 68*, 1229–1246.

Hawkins, J. D., Catalano, R. F., & Miller, J. Y. (1992). Risk and protective factors for alcohol and other drug problems in adolescence and early adulthood: Implications for substance abuse prevention. *Psychological Bulletin, 112*, 64–105.

Hayes, L., Hudson, A., & Matthews, J. (2003). Parental monitoring: A process model of parent-adolescent interaction. *Behavior Change, 20*, 13–24.

Kiesner, J., Dishion, T. J., Poulin, F., & Pastore, M. (Under review). Reconstructing parent monitoring: Concurrent and longitudinal analyses of parenting and adolescent problem behavior. *Child Development.*

Larson, R., & Richards, M. H. (1994). *Divergent realities: The emotional lives of mothers, fathers, and adolescents.* New York: Basic Books.

McKay, M., Pinto, R., Bannon, W. M., & Guilamo-Ramos, V. (2007). Understanding motivators and challenges to involving urban parents as collaborators in HIV prevention research efforts. *Social Work in Mental Health, 5*, 165–181.

National Center for Chronic Disease Prevention and Health Promotion (NCCDPHP) Translation Schematic, Centers for Disease Control and Prevention, NCCDPHP Work Group on Translation, July 2, 2008a. Adapted from K. M. Wilson, F. Fridinger, & the National Center for Chronic Disease Prevention and Health Promotion work Group on Translation. (2008). Focusing on public health: A different look at translating research into practice. *Journal of Women's Health, 17*, 173–179.

National Center for Chronic Disease Prevention and Health Promotion (NCCDPHP) Translation Schematic, Centers for Disease Control and Prevention, NCCDPHP Work Group on Translation, May 2008b, Glossary. Adapted from K. M. Wilson, F. Fridinger, & the National Center for Chronic Disease Prevention and Health Promotion work Group on Translation. (2008). Focusing on public health: A different look at translating research into practice. *Journal of Women's Health, 17*, 173–179.

Stacey, J. (1991). *Brave new families: Stories of domestic upheaval in late twentieth century America.* New York: Basic Books.

Stanton, B., Cole, M., Galbraith, J., Li, X., Pendleton, S., Cottrel, L., et al. (2004). A randomized trial of a parent intervention: Parents can make a difference in long-term adolescent risk behaviors, perceptions, and knowledge. *Archives of Pediatrics and Adolescent Medicine, 158,* 947–955.

Stoolmiller, M. (1994). Antisocial behavior, delinquent peer association, and un-supervised wandering for boys: Growth and change from childhood to early adolescence. *Multivariate Behavioral Research, 29,* 263–288.

Whiting, B. B., & Edwards, C. P. (1988). *Children of different worlds: The formation of social behavior.* Cambridge: Harvard University Press.

Wilson, H. (1980). Parental supervision: A neglected aspect of delinquency. *British Journal of Criminology, 20,* 203–235.

Wood, M. D., Read, J. P, Mitchell, R. E., & Brand, N. H. (2004). Do parents still matter? Parent and peer influences on alcohol involvement among recent high school graduates. *Psychology of Addictive Behaviors, 18,* 19–30.

List of Contributors

Caitlin Abar is a doctoral student in human development and family studies at Pennsylvania State University. She received her master's degree in human development and family studies from Pennsylvania State University and her bachelor's degree in psychology and sociology from the State University of New York College at Genesco. Caitlin's interests lie in the developmental period of adolescence and the transition to adulthood, and include the etiology and prevention of health risk behaviors focusing on substance use and risky sexual behavior.

Deborah Belle, Ed.D., is a professor of psychology at Boston University. She received her doctoral degree in human development from the Harvard Graduate School of Education. Her research focuses on social networks and social support and on the stresses that arise at the intersection of paid employment and family life.

Alida Bouris, Ph.D., is an assistant professor in the University of Chicago's School of Social Service Administration. Professor Bouris was a postdoctoral research scientist at the Columbia University School of Social Work. She received her Ph.D., M.Phil., and M.S.W. from the Columbia University School of Social Work, and her B.A. in women's studies from the University of California at Berkeley. Her primary research areas are in the identification of parental influences on adolescent and young adult sexual behavior and health.

Thomas J. Dishion, Ph.D., is the founder and co-director of the Child and Family Center at the University of Oregon. He received his doctoral degree in clinical psychology from the University of Oregon. His research interests include understanding the development of antisocial behavior and substance abuse in children and adolescents, as well as designing effective interventions and prevention programs.

Patricia Dittus, Ph.D., a Health Scientist in the Division of Adolescent and School Health at the Centers for Disease Control and Prevention (CDC) in Atlanta, Georgia, at the time this book was written, is currently a Behavioral Scientist in the Division of STD Prevention at CDC. Her research focuses on parent-adolescent communication about sex, adolescent sexual risk behavior, and the development of parenting and multilevel interventions to prevent or delay adolescent sexual risk behaviors.

Jennifer S. Galbraith, Ph.D., is a member of the Operational Research Team-Prevention Research Branch in the Division of HIV/AIDS Prevention at the Centers for Disease Control and Prevention in Atlanta, Georgia.

Vincent Guilamo-Ramos, Ph.D., is a Professor of Social Work and Global Public Health at the New York University of Social Work. Dr. Guilamo-Ramos received his doctoral degree from the State University of New York at Albany, School of Social Welfare. His principal focus of investigation is the role of parents in the prevention of adolescent health risk behaviors. Other research interests include alcohol, tobacco, and other drug use and sexual risk behavior among Latino and African American youth, parent-adolescent communication, and intervention research. He has conducted research primarily in urban, resource-poor settings, most recently in the South Bronx, Harlem, and Lower East Side communities of New York City. In addition, Dr. Guilamo-Ramos has conducted research in international contexts, specifically the Dominican Republic and India.

James Jaccard, Ph.D., is a professor of psychology at Florida International University. His research has focused extensively on parent-adolescent communication about sex and birth control. His research also has examined alcohol use among adolescents and young adults. He was on the core research team of the National Longitudinal Study of Adolescent Health (Add Health), one of the largest health surveys of adolescents ever undertaken in the United States.

Margaret Kerr, Ed.D., is a professor at the University of Pittsburgh where she holds joint appointments in the Departments of Administrative and Policy Studies, Psychology in Education, and Child Psychiatry. She received her doctoral degree from American University. Also licensed as a superintendent, Dr. Kerr has worked in urban school districts throughout her academic career. Her focus has been the improvement of services for students with emotional and behavioral problems.

Jeff Kiesner, Ph.D., is a university researcher at the University of Padova. He received his B.A. in psychology, his M.A. in psychology, and his Ph.D. in school psychology from the University of Oregon. His research areas include affective and cognitive changes associated with the menstrual cycle, the associations between psychological and physical symptoms of the menstrual cycle and the development of, and reciprocal relations among, peer relations, antisocial behavior, depression, and ethnic prejudice.

Robert D. Laird, Ph.D., is an associate professor of Psychology at the University of New Orleans. He received his doctoral degree in human development and family studies from Auburn University. Dr. Laird's research interests center on the contexts in which children develop social and behavioral competencies with an emphasis on parent-child and peer relationships.

Matthew M. Marrero, M.S., is a doctoral student at the University of New Orleans and served as project manager for the Baton Rouge Families and Teens Project. He received his B.S. in psychology from the University of New Orleans and his M.S. in human ecology from Louisiana State University. Matthew's research interests include parental influences on child development as well as child influences on parenting.

Brenda Caldwell Phillips, Ph.D., is a postdoctoral fellow at Vanderbilt University. She completed her Ph.D. in developmental psychology at Boston University. She also holds a clinical psychology degree from Saint Michael's College in Vermont. Brenda studies the cognitive, social, and cultural factors that impact how children acquire knowledge from others in formal and informal learning contexts.

François Poulin, Ph.D., is a professor in the Department of Psychology at Université du Québec à Montréal and a member of the Research Unit on Children's Psychosocial Maladjustment. He earned his doctorate in developmental psychology from Université Laval in 1996. He subsequently completed a postdoctoral fellowship at the Oregon Social Learning Center and the University of Oregon.

Anne E. Ray is a doctoral candidate in the Department of Biobehavioral Health at Penn State University. She received her bachelor's degree in psychology from Penn State University in 2004. Her research interests include studying peer and parental influences on college students' alcohol use to develop health promotion and intervention programs to reduce alcohol use among this population. She is also interested in models that predict why students engage in risky and protective behaviors when drinking and studying how this information can improve existing prevention and intervention programs.

Jennifer K. Sherwood is the Coordinator of Student Services at Louisiana State University.

Bonita Stanton, M.D., is Schotanus Professor and chair of the Department of Pediatrics and Pediatrician-in-Chief at Children's Hospital of Michigan Center. Dr. Stanton received her B.A. from Wellesley College and her M.D. from Yale University School of Medicine. Her research interests include prevention in adolescents and adolescent risk reduction, HIV in low-income adolescents and community health. She has been funded by the National Institutes of Health for more than fifteen years and has consulted with numerous national and international groups.

Håkan Stattin, Ph.D., earned his doctoral degree at Uppsala University, Sweden. He is a past president of the European Association of Research on Adolescence (EARA). Dr. Stattin is best known for his studies on the development of antisocial behavior and the role of pubertal maturation in development. More recently, he has entered into prevention and intervention research.

Lauree Tilton-Weaver, Ph.D., is a lifespan developmental psychologist, trained at the University of Victoria, British Columbia. Her training focused on cognitive, emotional, and social development across the lifespan with a particular emphasis on the development of adolescents. Her research focuses broadly on psychosocial development during adolescence and early adulthood. More specifically, she has studied the context and correlates of problem or risky behavior in adolescents.

Rob Turrisi, Ph.D., is currently a professor at Penn State University with a joint appointment in the Department of Biobehavioral Health and the Prevention Research Center. He received his doctoral degree in social psychology from the University at Albany, State University of New York. His research focus is on the application of behavioral decision-making to prevent underage drinking, drunk driving, and heavy binge-type drinking. Dr. Turrisi served as Director of the Prevention of Adolescent Drinking Program at SUNY Albany and was formerly a professor at Boise State University.

Sonia Venkatraman, Ph.D., received her masters and doctoral degrees in clinical psychology from the University of Oregon. Her research interests include studying the preventative effects of parental behaviors and general family management on adolescent behavior, particularly in the areas of adolescent substance use, health, and chronic illness.

Index

Protect Your Child from AIDS (cont.)
problems, 169–70; summary,
170–71; target audience problems,
169. *See also* ImPACT (Informed
Parents and Children Together
—remaking: adding narration, 163;
condom demonstration, 164; core
elements, 160–64; with credible
professionals, 163; emphasizing key
messages, 161–62; increasing
entertainment value, 162–63; with
real people (not actors), 160
Proximal Mediators, 128–29
PRS (Prevention Research Synthesis),
154, 157
pubertal maturation, and parental
knowledge variability, 46
punishing the parent, noncompliance
to rules, 227

Quebec, Canada families. *See*
cross-cultural analysis

reasoned discipline in interventions,
260–61
relationship qualities: behavior
problems, effects of, 54–56; effects
on perceived knowledge, 57; and
monitoring processes, 56; and
perceived knowledge, 57. *See also*
parent-child relationship
REP (Replicating Effective Programs),
157
reports: from spouses, source of
monitoring knowledge, 30, 182. *See
also* youth disclosure
—by parents and youth: cross-cultural
analysis, 100; discrepancies
between, 212–13, 215–16, 217;
measuring monitoring, 214

research. *See* studies
risk analysis, alcohol misuse among
college students, 126
risky behaviors: drug use, correlation
with parental knowledge, 40;
influence on monitoring, 221;
motivation toward, monitoring, 217.
See also specific behaviors
risky behaviors, influence of
monitoring: high-risk drinking,
232; measurement issues, 231–32;
moderators, 232; parent-child
relationship, 231; as a protective
factor, 231–32
—expert opinions: Belle, Deborah,
230–31; Dishion, Thomas, 231;
Laird, Robert, 231–32; Stanton,
Bonita, 232; Stattin, Håkan, 232;
Turrisi, Rob, 232
risky behaviors, sexual: correlation
with parental knowledge, 40; future
research needs, 196; from middle
school to high school, 177–78;
sexually transmitted infections,
178; unwanted pregnancies, 178
—monitoring: adolescent gender
differences, 184; effects of, 178–79;
moderators of, 184; process for (*see*
three-process monitoring system)
—predictors of: family income, 178;
family process variables, 178–79;
family structural variables, 178–79;
initial level of problem activity, 184;
maternal attitudes about adolescent
sexuality, 178; maternal marital
status, 178; maternal monitoring, 178;
maternal work status, 184; mother-
adolescent communication, 178;
parental education, 178; perception
of parental disapproval, 181